THIRD EDITION

CONSUMER BEHAVIOR

Buying, Having, and Being

Michael R. Solomon

Auburn University

Prentice Hall, Englewood Cliffs, New Jersey 07632

Library of Congress Cataloging-in-Publication Data
Solomon, Michael R.
Consumer behavior : buying, having, and being / Michael R. Solomon. — 3d ed.
p . cm.
Includes bibliographical references and index.
ISBN 0-13-365768-X.—ISBN 0-13-367939-X (pbk.)
1. Consumer behavior. I. Title.
HF5415.32.S6 1995
658.8'342—dc20

94-47068
CIP

••

To Gail, Amanda, Zachary, and Alexandra—Still My Favorite Consumers!

••

Acquisitions Editor: David Borkowsky
Production Management, Composition, and Prepress: GTS Graphics, Inc.
Illustration: Alexander Teshin Associates
In-house Liaison: Edith Pullman
Design Director: Patricia H. Wosczyk
Interior/Cover Design: Suzanne Behnke
Photo Research: Image Quest
Permissions Editor: Lisa Black
Buyer: Vincent Scelta
Associate Editor: Melissa Steffens
Editorial Assistant: Theresa Festa
Cover Art: Tom Herzberg © 2 Peace

© 1996, 1994, 1992 by Prentice Hall, Inc.
A Simon & Schuster Company
Englewood Cliffs, New Jersey 07632

Printed in the United States of America.
10 9 8 7 6 5 4 3 2 1

ISBN: 0-13-365768-X

Prentice-Hall International (UK) Limited, *London*
Prentice-Hall of Australia Pty. Limited, *Sydney*
Prentice-Hall Canada Inc., *Toronto*
Prentice-Hall Hispanoamericana, S.A., *Mexico City*
Prentice-Hall of India Private Limited, *New Delhi*
Prentice-Hall of Japan, Inc., *Tokyo*
Simon & Schuster Asia Pte. Ltd., *Singapore*
Editora Prentice-Hall do Brasil, Ltda., *Rio de Janeiro*

Chapter Opening Photo Credits

Chapter 1, p. 4, Courtesy of Tony Freeman/PhotoEdit; Chapter 2, p. 54, Oliverio Toscani for BENETTON; Chapter 3, p. 88, Courtesy of Brooks Kroft, Sygma; Chapter 4, p. 125, Copyright © 1992 by Dingo Women's National Consumer Magazine Ad/Acme Boot Company; Chapter 5, p. 157, Courtesy of General Motors do Brazil Ltda.; Chapter 6, p. 190, Courtesy of PETA; Chapter 7, p. 225, Reproduced by Special Permission of *Playboy* magazine. Copyright © 1994 by Playboy; Chapter 8, p. 266, Courtesy of CNA Insurance Companies; Chapter 9, p. 302, Courtesy of Michael Newman/PhotoEdit; Chapter 10, p. 338, Courtesy of Harley-Davidson Motor Company; Chapter 11, p. 380, Courtesy of Heublein, Inc.; Chapter 12, p. 424, Courtesy of Jaguar Cars, Inc.; Chapter 13, p. 462, Courtesy of Felicia Martinez/PhotoEdit; Chapter 14, p. 500, Copyright © 1991 by General Media, Inc.; Chapter 15, p. 536, Universal Shooting Star. © All rights reserved; Chapter 16, p. 576, © Laima Druska/Stock Boston; Chapter 17, p. 617, © Greg Davis/Sygma.

Michael R. Solomon is Human Sciences Professor of Consumer Behavior in The Department of Consumer Affairs at Auburn University. Before joining Auburn in 1995, Professor Solomon was Chairman of the Department of Marketing in the School of Business at Rutgers University, New Brunswick, New Jersey. Prior to that appointment, he was a member of the faculty of the Graduate School of Business Administration at New York University. Professor Solomon earned B.A. degrees in Psychology and Sociology at Brandeis University and an M.A. and a Ph.D. in Social Psychology at The University of North Carolina at Chapel Hill.

Professor Solomon's primary research interests include consumer behavior and lifestyle issues, the symbolic aspects of products, the psychology of fashion and image, and services marketing. He has published many articles on these and related topics in academic journals. He is an Editorial Board Member of the *Journal of Consumer Research,* the *Journal of Retailing,* and *Psychology & Marketing.*

Professor Solomon received the first Cutty Sark Men's Fashion Award in 1981 for his research on the psychological aspects of clothing. He is the editor of *The Psychology of Fashion* and coeditor of *The Service Encounter: Managing Employee/Customer Interaction in Services Businesses,* both published in 1985 by Lexington Books.

Professor Solomon is also a frequent contributor to mass media. His feature articles have appeared in *Psychology Today, Gentleman's Quarterly,* and *Savvy.* He has been quoted in numerous national magazines and newspapers, including *Allure, Elle, Glamour, Mademoiselle, Mirabella, Newsweek, The New York Times Magazine, Self, USA Today,* and *The Wall Street Journal.* He has been a guest on "The Today Show," "Good Morning America," CNBC, Whittle Communications' Channel One, "Newsweek on the Air," "Inside Edition," and National Public Radio.

Professor Solomon has provided input to a variety of organizations on issues related to consumer behavior. He has been a consultant to such companies as the Celanese Corporation, Levi Strauss & Company, Johnson & Johnson, Kayser-Roth, United Airlines, and Hakuhodo Advertising (Tokyo). He is also in demand as a speaker to many business groups on consumer behavior and marketing topics. He lives with his wife, Gail; their three children, Amanda, Zachary, and Alexandra; and Chloe, their golden retriever, in Auburn, Alabama.

Brief Contents

Contents

Preface

I wrote this book because I'm fascinated by the everyday activities of people. The field of consumer behavior is, to me, the study of how our world is influenced by the action of marketers. Since I'm a consumer myself, I have a selfish interest in learning more about how this process works—and so do you.

In many courses, students are merely passive observers, learning about topics that affect them only indirectly, if at all. Not everyone is a plasma physicist, a medieval French scholar, or even an industrial marketer. We are, however, all consumers. As a result, many of the topics dealt with in this book are of both professional and personal relevance to the reader, whether he or she is a student, professor, or marketing practitioner. Nearly everyone can relate to the trials and tribulations associated with last-minute shopping, primping for a big night out, agonizing over an expensive purchase decision, fantasizing about a week in the Caribbean, celebrating a holiday, or commemorating a landmark event, such as a graduation, getting a driver's license, or (dreaming about) winning the lottery.

BEYOND CANNED PEAS: BUYING, HAVING, AND BEING

As the book's subtitle suggests, my version of this field goes beyond looking at the act of buying to having and being as well. Consumer behavior is more than *buying* things, such as a can of peas; it also embraces the study of how *having* (or not having) things affects our lives and how our possessions influence the way we feel about ourselves and about each other—our state of *being*.

In addition to understanding why people buy things, we also try to appreciate how products, services, and consumption activities contribute to the broader social world we experience. Whether shopping, cooking, cleaning, playing basketball, hanging out at the beach, or even looking at ourselves in the mirror, our lives are touched by the marketing system. And, as if these experiences were not complex enough, the task of understanding the consumer multiplies geometrically when a multicultural perspective is taken. This book not only probes the psyche of the American consumer, but also attempts wherever possible to consider the many other consumers around the world whose diverse experiences with buying, having, and being are equally valid and vital to understand. In addition to the numerous examples of marketing and consumer practices relating to consumers and companies outside the United States that appear throughout the book, chapters contain boxes called "Multicultural Dimensions" that highlight cultural differences in consumer behavior. I developed the models of consumer behavior that appear at the beginning of text sections to underscore the complex—and often inseparable—interrelationships between the individual consumer and his or her social realities.

THE RELEVANCE OF CONSUMER RESEARCH

The field of consumer behavior is young, dynamic, and in flux. It is constantly being cross-fertilized by perspectives from many different disciplines. I have tried to express the field's staggering diversity in these pages. Consumer researchers represent virtually every social science discipline, plus a few represent the physical sciences and the arts for good measure. From this melting pot has come a healthy "stew" of research perspectives, viewpoints regarding appropriate research methods, and even deeply held beliefs about what are and what are not appropriate issues for consumer researchers to study in the first place.

Several unique features in the book will help you to experience the potential of consumer research. The ABC News Connection at the end of each chapter provides a visual, real-world tie-in to relevant topics currently reported in the news. Related video segments showing the ABC news stories are also available. These have been selected to complement what you read in the text. In addition, the exercises featured in the Simmons Connection features (and contained on the Simmons Data Disk made available to your instructor) will allow you to "play with" real data from the Simmons Market Research Bureau, a process that can illuminate some of the consumption activities described in the text. These data are the same findings used by many actual marketing organizations to develop their consumer targeting and communications strategies, so you'll be "reading from the same page" as many of the important decision makers in the field of marketing. Finally, I hope this course will inspire you to consider the field of consumer research as a career. If that's the case, you'll find the career information presented in Appendix I helpful. Appendix II, Careers in Consumer Research, provides an overview of possible career paths, and it also includes some suggested references for further exploration.

CONSUMERS AND MARKETING STRATEGY

The book also emphasizes the importance of understanding consumers in formulating marketing strategy. Many (if not most) of the fundamental concepts in marketing are based on the practitioner's ability to know people. After all, if we don't understand why people behave as they do, how can we identify their needs? If we can't identify their needs, how can we satisfy those needs? If we can't satisfy people's needs, we don't have a marketing concept, so we might as well fold our tents and go home! To illustrate the potential of consumer research to inform marketing strategy, the text contains numerous examples of specific applications of consumer behavior concepts by marketing practitioners as well as of windows of opportunity where such concepts could be used (perhaps by alert strategists after taking this course!). Many of these possibilities are highlighted in special features called "Marketing Opportunities."

THE GOOD, THE BAD, AND THE UGLY

This strategic focus is, however, tempered by an important qualification: Unlike some contemporary treatments of consumer behavior, this book does not assume that *everything* marketers do is in the best interests of consumers or of their environment. Likewise, as consumers, we do many things that are not positive either. People are plagued by addictions, status envy, ethnocentrism, racism, sexism, and other "isms," and, regrettably, there are times when marketing activities—deliberately or not—encourage or exploit these human flaws. This book deals with the totality of consumer behavior, warts and all. Marketing mistakes or ethically suspect activities are also highlighted in special features labeled "Marketing Pitfalls."

On the other hand, marketers have helped to create many wonderful (or at least unusual) things, such as holidays, comic books, the music industry, "pet rocks," and the many stylistic options available to us in the domains of clothing, home design, the arts, cuisine, and so on. I have also taken pains to acknowledge the sizable impact of marketing on popular culture. Indeed, the final section of this book reflects very recent work in the field that scrutinizes, criticizes, and sometimes celebrates consumers in their everyday worlds. I hope you will enjoy reading about such wonderful things as much as I enjoyed writing about them.

ACKNOWLEDGMENTS

I am grateful for the many helpful comments on how to improve the third edition that were provided by my peer reviewers. Special thanks go to the following people: Ottilia Voegtli, University of Missouri–St. Louis; Vaughan Judd, Auburn University at Montgomery; Gail Tom, California State University, Sacramento; Ron Goldsmith, Florida State University; Bill Rodgers, St. Cloud State University; James W. Cagley, University of Tulsa; Michael Lynn, University of Houston; Elaine Notarantonio, Bryant College; Sevgin Eroglu; Kathy Lacher, Auburn University; Shelly Tapp, Saint Louis University; Dana Lascu, University of Richmond; and Fredric Kropp, University of Oregon.

Many colleagues made significant contributions to this edition. I would like to thank, in particular, the following people who made constructive suggestions and/or who provided me with a "sneak peek" at their research materials and manuscripts now in press or under review:

Jennifer Aaker, Stanford University
Aaron Ahuvia, University of Michigan
Linda Alwitt, DePaul University
Eric Arnould, University of South Florida
Soren Askegaard, Odense University (Denmark)
Siva Balasubramanian, Southern Illinois University
Gary Bamossy, Vrije Universiteit (Netherlands)
Sharon Beatty, University of Alabama
Russell Belk, University of Utah
Ida Berger, Queen's University
James Bettman, Duke University
Elizabeth Blair, Ohio University
Claus Buhl, Denmark
Leslie Burns, Oregon State University
Jeffrey Burroughs, Brigham Young University, Hawaii
Dipankar Chakravarti, University of Arizona

Amitava Chattopadhyay, University of British Columbia
Cindy Clark, C.D. Clark, Inc.
Larry Compeau, Clarkson University
Janeen Costa, University of Utah
Robin Higie Coulter, University of Connecticut
Pratibha Dabholkar, University of Tennessee
John Deighton, Harvard University
Jeffrey Durgee, Rensselaer Polytechnic Institute
Fuat Firat, Arizona State University West
Eileen Fischer, York University
Susan Fournier, Harvard University
Ellen Foxman, Bentley College
Mary Gilly, University of California, Irvine
Robert Gilmore, Long Island University—C.W. Post
Cathy Goodwin, University of Manitoba
Roberto Grandi, University of Bologna (Italy)
Stephen Grove, Clemson University
Ron Groves, Edith Cowan University (Australia)
Audrey Guskey, Duquesne University
Ron Hill, Villanova University
Morris Holbrook, Columbia University
Doug Holt, Pennsylvania State University
Deborah Roedder John, University of Minnesota
Annamma Joy, Concordia University
Frank Kardes, University of Cincinnati
Hal Kassarjian, University of California, Los Angeles
James Kellaris, University of Cincinnati
Arthur Kover, Fordham University
Carole Macklin, University of Cincinnati
Mary Ann McGrath, Loyola University
Tom O'Guinn, University of Illinois
Anna Olofsson, University of Umeå (Sweden)
Cele Otnes, University of Illinois
Julie Ozanne, Virginia Polytechnic Institute and State University
Connie Pechmann, University of California, Irvine
Lisa Peñaloza, University of Illinois
Greta Pennell, Rutgers University, New Brunswick
Rick Pollay, University of British Columbia
Marsha Richins, University of Missouri
Scott Roberts, Old Dominion University
Robert Schindler, Rutgers University, Camden
John Schouten, University of Portland
Linda Scott, University of Illinois
John Sherry, Northwestern University
Terry Shimp, University of South Carolina
L.J. Shrum, Rutgers University, New Brunswick
Itamar Simonson, Stanford University
Craig Smith, Georgetown University
Ruth Ann Smith, Virginia Polytechnic Institute and State University
Hiroshi Tanaka, Dentsu Advertising (Japan)

Craig Thompson, University of Wisconsin
Bruce Vanden Bergh, Michigan State University
Alladi Venkatesh, University of California, Irvine
Janet Wagner, University of Maryland
Melanie Wallendorf, University of Arizona
Cynthia Webster, Mississippi State University
Bill Wells, University of Minnesota
Judy Zaichkowsky, Simon Fraser University
Jerry Zaltman, Harvard University

Extra special thanks are also due to the preparers of the supplements: Richard Shaw from Rockhurst College for preparation of the *Instructor's Manual;* M. Frances Estep of Pace University for completely revising the *Test Bank;* and Lewis Hershey for the transparency masters. Additional thanks go to Basil Englis of Rutgers University for preparation of the Simmons Connection database exercises and their accompanying student and instructor materials.

I would also like to thank the good people at Prentice Hall who have done yeoman service on this edition. In particular I am indebted to my tenacious editor, Dave Borkowsky, for helping me to navigate the sometimes treacherous waters of publishing. Thanks also go to Theresa Festa, Melissa Steffens, Edie Pullman, and Lisa Black for their assistance during production.

My friends and colleagues have been fantastic since this project began. Without their support and tolerance, I would never have been able to sustain the "illusion" that I was still an active department chairman and researcher during the two years I worked on this edition. Special thanks go to Carol Gibson for her assistance throughout. I am also particularly indebted to Basil Englis for his intellectual and emotional support—he personifies my image of what a good colleague and friend should be.

Also, I am grateful to my students, who have been a prime source of inspiration, examples, and feedback. The satisfaction I have garnered from teaching them about consumer behavior motivated me to write a book I felt they would like to read.

Last but not least, I would like to thank my family and friends for sticking by me during this revision. They know who they are, since their names pop up in chapter vignettes throughout the book. My apologies for "distorting" their characters in the name of poetic license! My gratitude and love go out to my parents, Jackie and Henry, and my in-laws, Marilyn and Phil. A special note of thanks goes to Dave Greenberg, who gave me my start. My super children, Amanda, Zachary, and Alexandra, always made the sun shine on gray days. Finally, thanks above all to Gail, my wonderful wife, friend, and occasional research assistant: I still do it all for you.

ANCILLARY MATERIALS AVAILABLE FOR INSTRUCTORS

The following supplements are available with this text:
Instructor's Manual with Transparency Masters and Video Guide.
ISBN# 0-13-367269-7

Completely revised and expanded, the Instructor's Manual provides instructors with the resources for a more interactive and innovative classroom. Key features include Summary Bullets, Lecture/Discussion Ideas, Field Project Ideas, Consumer Behavior Challenges, Video Guide, Simmons Connection User Guide, and Transparency Masters.

Test Item File

ISBN# 0-13-367277-8

The Test Item File includes a large number of multiple-choice, true/false, short answer, and essay questions. Several questions per chapter are based on the chapter-opening vignette, the chapter-closing ABC News Connection, and (where applicable) the Simmons Connection.

3.5" IBM Test Manager

ISBN# 0-13-367319-7

This powerful computerized testing package, available for DOS-based computers, allows instructors to create their own personalized exams using questions from the Test Item File. It offers full mouse support, complete question editing, random test generation, graphics, and printing capabilities.

ABC News/Prentice Hall Video Library

ISBN# 0-13-367293-X

Our ABC News/Prentice Hall Video Library contains timely and relevant video segments from acclaimed ABC News programs, such as Nightline, World News Tonight, and Business World, available for the college market exclusively through Prentice Hall. Designed specifically to complement the text, this library is an excellent tool for bringing students into contact with the world outside the classroom.

Color Transparencies

ISBN# 0-13-367285-9

50 full-color transparencies highlight key concepts for presentation and offer additional advertisements for class discussion and analysis. Each transparency is accompanied by a full page of teaching notes that includes relevant key terms and discussion points from the chapters as well as additional material from supplementary sources.

Electronic Transparencies

All acetates and lecture notes are available on Powerpoint 4.0. The disk is designed to allow you to present the transparencies to your class electronically.

Simmons Data Disk

Contains real market data from the Simmons Study of Media & Markets, a widely used syndicated data service.

Presentation Manager

An applicaton of the popular Authorware software program, Presentation Manager allows you to easily prearrange your multimedia classroom lecture by accessing any of our available media materials on laserdisk, VHS tape, CD-ROM, and 3.5" disk. Choose the order of the materials you would like to present in class for a list that appears on-screen, and Presentation Manager for Marketing will do the rest.

New York Times/Prentice Hall "Themes of the Times" Program for Marketing

Prentice Hall and *The New York Times,* one of the world's top news publications, join to expand your students' knowledge beyond the walls of the classroom. Upon adoption, professors and students receive a specialized "mini-newspaper" containing a broad spectrum of carefully chosen articles that focus on events and issues in the world of marketing as well as on some of the news-making marketing professionals of the 1990s. To ensure complete timeliness, this supplement is updated twice a year.

SIMMONS CONNECTION EXERCISES: STUDENT INTRODUCTION AND INSTRUCTIONS

Several practical data-oriented exercises have been designed for selected chapters in the text. These exercises are designed to give students some hands-on experience with the sort of data that marketers use better to understand the behavior of consumers. Each exercise is keyed to examples and concepts covered in the chapter in which it appears. There is also a computer disk that contains real market data. In order to "solve" the various problems posed in these exercises, students will need to access the data contained on the disk. The exercises are user-friendly and will increase your involvement in the learning process. Most of the exercises relate directly to the opening vignettes of the chapters in which they are assigned. Students may wish to reread the vignette before they begin working on an exercise. The only thing you will need to run the exercises is a standard spreadsheet program and access to either a DOS or Macintosh computer.

The data come from a widely used, syndicated data service—the Simmons Study of Media & Markets. This very extensive study includes data on over 800 product and service categories. The data provided on the Simmons disk are taken from the 1994 study, which interviewed a total of 22,051 adult Americans (11,063 men and 10,988 women). The real value of this database is that it allows marketers to look at patterns of buying behavior as a function of a wide array of consumer characteristics, including demographics (age, education, income, race, and so on) and psychographics (attitudes, self-concept, buying style, and so on).

The Simmons Study of Media & Markets is conducted annually, and the results are tabulated into 34 separate volumes that are offered as Simmons products. Additional tabulations are prepared on a custom basis for individual clients. Simmons also conducts studies of special groups; for example, CompPro is its study of computer professionals, STARS focuses on teens between 12 and 19 years old, and KIDS focuses on children younger than 12. For the exercises in your text, we have extracted portions of the 1994 database and provided summary data in the form of spreadsheets containing the critical information needed to work on each exercise.

Although Simmons provides a great deal of information *at the brand level,* for many of the exercises the data have been aggregated to the product category level.

To use the data from the Simmons disk, you will need access either to a DOS or Macintosh computer *and* a standard spreadsheet such as Lotus, Excel, Quattro, or another comparable program. The files are saved on the disk in what is called a "WKS" format, which is a generic format for spreadsheets. This means that any standard program should have no problem reading the information from the disk.

Since the disk itself is already a DOS disk, DOS users can access the files with no prior translation. If you are using your own computer *and* the computer has a hard disk, then you should first copy all of the files from the floppy disk onto the computer's hard drive.

If you are using a Macintosh computer and some version of System 7, you should be able to insert the Simmons disk and get an immediate translation to Macintosh format. For users of earlier versions of the Macintosh operating system, you will need to run a utility program such as Apple File Exchange. All users of System 6 should have received this program. If you do not have it, you can obtain it either through your local Macintosh Users Group or directly through Apple. The following instructions apply whether you are copying the files onto another floppy in Macintosh format or onto a hard drive (only the destination changes). To translate the files using Apple File Exchange, first open the Apple File Exchange icon. Then insert the Simmons disk into your floppy drive. The dialog box will show the Simmons files on the right-hand portion of the screen. Select all of the Simmons data files and click on the "Translate" button. The next dialog box will ask how you want the files translated. Just select the format that matches your spreadsheet program.

Fourteen files are on the disk. Ten files are titled *Chap#.* These are keyed to the chapters in which you will find the Simmons exercises. The other four files are labeled *Self, Style, Media1,* and *Media2.* These general reference files may come in

MAGAZINES		BASE= ALL ADULTS	ALL ADULTS EDUCATION GRADUATED	ALL ADULTS EDUCATION GRADUATED
ROW	CELL	TOTAL	HIGH SCHOOL	COLLEGE
TOTAL	(000)	187747	73139	37353
TOTAL	Resps	22051	8179	5832
TOTAL	Index	100	100	100
ARCHITECTURAL DIGEST	(000)	2939	591	1414
ARCHITECTURAL DIGEST	Resps	883	151	488
ARCHITECTURAL DIGEST	Index	100	52	242
HUNTING	(000)	3410	1642	292
HUNTING	Resps	636	323	83
HUNTING	Index	100	124	43
MADEMOISELLE	(000)	4237	1775	854
MADEMOISELLE	Resps	1027	392	253
MADEMOISELLE	Index	100	108	101

handy for several of the exercises. The following is an example of what you will find in the spreadsheets.

Hint: It is much easier to browse through spreadsheets if you learn how to have the spreadsheet program keep the row and column titles visible on the screen. Although the method varies from program to program, most have this capability.

Each file contains a cross-tabulation of data—columns by rows. For example, consider the sample table shown above for three magazines broken down by the gender of the reader. You should open several of the files and browse through them to familiarize yourself with the kinds of information they contain.

For each cell in the spreadsheet (a cell is defined as the intersection of a row and column), there are three pieces of information. The first number is identified by a ROW label of (000), which is a projection based on the raw count for each cell and the total U.S. population. This lets marketers immediately project the Simmons sample values onto the total U.S. population and thereby estimate total potential market size. In the example above, if the Simmons panel were projected onto all U.S. consumers, there would be 2,939,000 readers of *Architectural Digest,* 3,410,000 readers of *Hunting,* and 4,237,000 readers of *Mademoiselle* magazines.

The population projections are not a simple matter of multiplying the raw cell count by a constant. Instead, each respondent is assigned a weight that reflects his or her "representativeness" in the U.S. population as a whole (this relates to the probability of their selection in the first place). This weighting is a complex and proprietary procedure designed to provide the best possible population estimates. It is important to remember that because individual cases receive unique weights, two cells with the same raw count may have different population projection figures.

The second number listed is the actual number of respondents (out of a total of 22,051) that fit the characteristics defined by the column and row labels. In the sample above, the intersection of *Architectural Digest* and TOTAL shows a value of 883. This means that of the entire sample, 883 people reported that they are readers of *Architectural Digest.*

The last number—INDEX—is extremely valuable for marketers because it tells them whether a particular consumer group is more or less likely than all members of a particular "universe" of consumers to consume a particular product (or product category). For example, if we are interested in magazine preferences we would consider all adult magazine readers as our universe. Each Simmons file identifies the universe of consumers that form the basis for these index values. The top-left-most cell containing numerical information identifies the population base used in computing the index values in that spreadsheet (or portion of a spreadsheet when multiple bases are used).

For any breakdown defined by row labels—say, education of reader—a value of 100 would mean that a particular group of consumers would be no more or less likely to be a reader of, for example, *Architectural Digest* than the total universe (all adults). If you look at the intersection of Graduated College and *Architectural Digest,* you will see an index value of 242. This means that college graduates are 142 percent *more likely* (242−100) to be readers of *Architectural Digest* than are all adult readers of the magazine. Similarly, high school graduates are 48 percent *less likely* to be readers of *Architectural Digest* than are all adult readers of the magazine.

The index values are always computed using the projected population values according to the following formula: The percentage value of each cell against the category listed in the column is computed. The index is arrived at by dividing the cell percentage by the row-total percentage and multiplying the result by 100. For example, 3.8 percent of college graduates read *Architectural Digest* ([1414/37353] × 100 = 3.786). Readers of *Architectural Digest* represent 1.6 percent of the total population ([2939/187747] × 100 = 1.565). Dividing these values yields the cell index of 242 ([3.786/1.565] × 100 = 241.9).

Because the index values are a direct comparison of a market segment's behavior with that of a relevant universe of consumers, they provide extremely useful information for marketers. The index values are a particularly useful tool in defining market segments whose tastes, preferences, and past consumption behavior are particularly well suited for a particular product or product category.

Of course, there are numerous other measures that can be derived from the data. Percentages and averages across the appropriate categories will be useful for many of the exercises. It is a good idea to learn how to insert formulas into the cells of your spreadsheets and how to identify the appropriate cells for each computation that you want to make. In general, if you compute your own indexes, you should use the population projections because these are the more reliable indicators of the total size of the groups with which you are working.

TABLE P ▼ Simmons Data Files

FILE NAME	COLUMNS	ROWS
Chap1	*Subset of Magazines* Seventeen Mademoiselle Harper's Bazaar Ladies' Home Journal Vogue Elle	*Subset of Demographics* Age Education Occupation Sex
Chap3	*Credit Cards Used* Last 12 months Last 30 days Number of times used	*Subset of Buying Style* Ad believer Cautious Economy minded Experimenter Impulsive Planner
Chap5	*Environmental Issues* 17 issues Willingness to pay more taxes	*Subset of Demographics* Age Education Occupation *Buying Style* Ecologist
Chap6	*Single Products* Disposable diapers Disposable plates Tobacco (all) Veal Weed killer Fur jackets/coats—real Fur jackets/coats—synthetic	*Environmental Issues (all)* *Buying Style* Ecologist *Demographics* Age
Chap8	*Shopping Influence—Male* Automobiles Household furnishings Food shopping	*Demographics* Size of household Number of employed adults Education Age *Psychographics* Broad-minded Creative Dominating Efficient
Chap9	*Health Care Products* Contact lenses Diet control Doctor's visits (general checkups) Hearing aids *Travel* Health or resort spa	*Self-Concept (all)*
Chap11	*Motorcycles* Most recent bought (new/used) Make Engine size—less than 399 cc, 400–1000 cc, more than 1000 cc *Sports, Leisure* Motorcycling	*Demographics* Age (18- to 34-year-olds only) Income (HH) Education—less than HS, HS grad, less than college grad, college grad Marital status

*The three general reference files all use the same set of demographic variables: age, sex, HHI, education, race, and marital status.

FILE NAME	COLUMNS	ROWS

Chap12	*Malt Beverages & Wines*
	  Wine by the case
	Distilled Spirits
	  Spirits by the case
	Travel
	  Passports
	  Theme parks
	Coffee, Tea
	  Espresso/Cappuccino
	  International flavored instant
		Demographics
		  Index of Social Position
		  HHI— > $40,000
		  Occupation

Chap13	*Distilled Spirits*
	  Jack Daniels
	  Absolut Vodka
	  The Glenlivet Single-Malt Scotch
	Malt Beverages & Wines
	  Champagne (aggregated, all brands)
	  Malt liquor
	New Autos
	  BMWs (aggregated, all models)
	  Trans Ams/Camaros
	  Minivans (aggregated, all brands)
		Demographics
		  Occupation
		  Income
		  Index of Social Position

Chap14	*Tobacco*
	  Cigarettes
	  Cigars
	Malt Beverages & Wine
	  Malt liquor
	  Dry beer
	General Foods
	  Rice/rice dishes
	Pets
	  Cat/dog ownership
		Race
		  African-American, White,
		  Asian, Latino
		Demographics
		  Locality type
		  Geographic region

Chap17	*Travel*
	  Theme parks
	Books, Discs, etc.
	  Digital audio tape
	  Surround-sound decoder
	  Cellular, car, or
	    portable phone
	  Laser disc player
	  Interactive computer services
	Banking
	  Home banking by computer
		Buying Style (all)
		Self-Concept (all)

Media	*Magazines* A random set of magazines	*Demographics**
Style	*Buying Style* (all)	*Demographics**
Self	*Self-Concept* (all)	*Demographics**

I

CONSUMERS IN THE MARKETPLACE

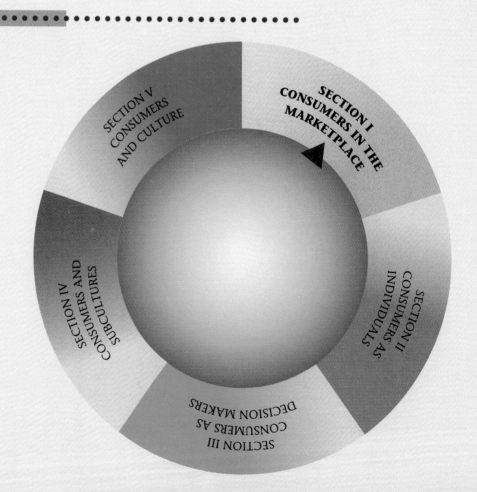

SECTION V
CONSUMERS
AND CULTURE

SECTION I
CONSUMERS IN THE
MARKETPLACE

SECTION IV
CONSUMERS AND
CONSUMERS
SUBCULTURES

SECTION II
CONSUMERS AS
INDIVIDUALS

SECTION III
CONSUMERS AS
DECISION MAKERS

This introductory section provides an overview of the field of consumer behavior. Chapter 1 looks at how the field of marketing is influenced by the actions of consumers and also at how we as consumers are influenced by marketers. It describes the discipline of consumer behavior and some of the different approaches to understanding what makes consumers tick. The chapter also provides a bit of a "refresher course" on marketing research as it briefly summarizes some of the many and varied techniques that are available to scientists who study consumers in the marketplace, in their homes, and in the laboratory.

Gail is killing time before class by browsing in the college bookstore. While studying for exams, she hasn't looked at a magazine in weeks. Now it's time for some *really* educational reading.

The magazine section is filled with dozens of selections, from *Motor Trend* to *Mother Jones*. Gail is a dedicated *Seventeen* reader, but as she scans the racks, she is struck by the glamorous models on the covers of other women's magazines. She thinks it's time to expand her horizons, listen to her sorority sisters, and remake her innocent image. She considers *Vogue*, but it seems a bit too old and stodgy. *Cosmopolitan* features slightly older working women in revealing dresses, and *Allure* and *McCall's* look like magazines her mother would read. She sees *Family Circle* and *Ladies' Home Journal* when she visits her Aunt Ellen in the suburbs—as if she cared about endless diets and home decorating ideas.

Finally, Gail is intrigued by a new magazine, *Marie Claire*. The cover model has a new, short hairstyle that she's been wanting to try. *Marie Claire* publishes in 22 countries and is now trying to make it in America.[1] As Gail scans the pages, her attention is caught by the many clothes ads and a whiff of the new perfume her friend Lisa just bought. This magazine is just what she needs to help create the New Gail. Lisa and the other sisters will be proud of her. . . .

TABLE 1–3 ▼ Sampler of Federal Legislation Intended to Enhance Consumers' Welfare

YEAR	ACT	PURPOSE
1951	Fur Products Labeling Act	Regulates the branding, advertising, and shipment of fur products.
1953	Flammable Fabrics Act	Prohibits the transportation of flammable fabrics across state lines.
1958	National Traffic and Safety Act	Creates safety standards for cars and tires.
1958	Automobile Information Disclosure Act	Requires automobile manufacturers to post suggested retail prices on new cars.
1966	Fair Packaging and Labeling Act	Regulates packaging and labeling of consumer products. (Manufacturers must provide information about package contents and origin.)
1966	Child Protection Act	Prohibits sale of dangerous toys and other items.
1967	Federal Cigarette Labeling and Advertising Act	Requires cigarette packages to carry a warning label from the Surgeon General.
1968	Truth-in-Lending Act	Requires lenders to divulge the true costs of a credit transaction.
1969	National Environmental Policy Act	Established a national environmental policy and created the Council on Environmental Quality to monitor the effects of products on the environment.
1972	Consumer Product Safety Act	Established the Consumer Product Safety Commission to identify unsafe products, establish safety standards, recall defective products, and ban dangerous products.
1975	Consumer Goods Pricing Act	Bans the use of price maintenance agreements among manufacturers and resellers.
1975	Magnuson-Moss Warranty-Improvement Act	Creates disclosure standards for consumer product warranties and allows the Federal Trade Commission to set policy regarding unfair or deceptive practices.
1990	The Nutrition Labeling and Education Act	Reaffirms the legal basis for the Food and Drug Administration's new rules on food labeling and establishes a timetable for the implementation of those rules. Regulations covering health claims became effective May 8, 1993. Those pertaining to nutrition labeling and nutrient content claims went into effect May 8, 1994.

are not exploited by program-length toy commercials masquerading as television shows.

Of course, to a large degree consumers are dependent on their governments to regulate and police safety and environmental standards. The extent of supervision may depend on such factors as the political climate in a country (e.g., regulation activity by the Federal Trade Commission and other U.S. bodies was fairly low during the laissez-faire Reagan years, and it started to become more active—or meddlesome, depending upon your point of view!— in the Clinton administration).

In addition, a country's traditions and beliefs may make it more sympathetic to the needs of consumers or producers. In Japan, for example, there is a tendency to subvert the needs of consumers to those of manufacturers, and taking legal action against companies is extremely rare. Thus, it is not surprising that no health warnings appear on alcoholic beverages and that Japanese cigarettes carry watered-down

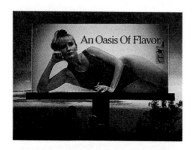

This antismoking television commercial, prepared on behalf of the Minnesota Department of Health, illustrates the activist role played by some government agencies on health-related issues. The commercial criticizes cigarette companies for targeting women in their ads. The model on a cigarette billboard is shown putting out her cigarette on the head of one of the tobacco company executives who is admiring the ad. Courtesy of Minnesota Department of Health and Martin & Williams Advertising.

warning labels, such as, "Because there is a danger of damaging your health, be careful not to smoke too much."[32]

CONSUMER BEHAVIOR AS A FIELD OF STUDY

Although people have certainly been consumers for a long time, it is only recently that consumption per se has been the object of formal study. In fact, while many business schools now require that marketing majors take a Consumer Behavior course, most colleges did not even offer such a course until the 1970s. Much of the impetus for the attention now being given to consumer behavior was the realization by many business people that the consumer really *is* the boss.

Interdisciplinary Influences on the Study of Consumer Behavior

Consumer behavior is a very young field, and, as it grows, it is being influenced by many different perspectives. Indeed, it is hard to think of a field that is more interdisciplinary. People with training in a very wide range of fields—from psychophysiology to literature—can now be found doing consumer research. Consumer researchers are employed by universities, manufacturers, museums, advertising agencies, and governments. Several professional groups, such as the Association for

Consumer Research, have been formed since the mid-1970s. A summary of career opportunities in consumer behavior can be found in Appendix II.

To gain an idea of the diversity of interests of people who do consumer research, consider the list of professional associations that sponsor the field's major journal, the *Journal of Consumer Research*. They are the American Home Economics Association, the American Statistical Association, the Association for Consumer Research, the Society for Consumer Psychology, the International Communication Association, the American Sociological Association, the Institute of Management Sciences, the American Anthropological Association, the American Marketing Association, the Society for Personality and Social Psychology, the American Association for Public Opinion Research, and the American Economic Association.

These diverse researchers approach consumer issues from different perspectives. You might remember a children's story about the blind men and the elephant. The gist of the story is that each man touched a different part of the animal, and, as a result, the descriptions each gave of the elephant were quite different. This analogy applies to consumer research as well. A similar consumer phenomenon can be studied in different ways and at different levels, depending on the training and interests of the researchers studying it.

Figure 1–2 provides a glimpse at some of the disciplines working in the field and the level at which each approaches research issues. These diverse disciplines can be roughly characterized in terms of their focus on micro versus macro consumer

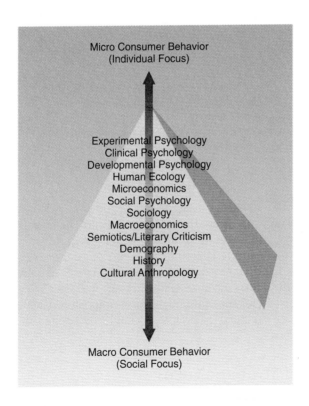

FIGURE 1–2 ▼ **The Pyramid of Consumer Behavior**

TABLE 1–4 ▼ Interdisciplinary Research Issues in Consumer Behavior

DISCIPLINARY FOCUS	MAGAZINE USAGE SAMPLE RESEARCH ISSUES
Experimental Psychology: product role in perception, learning, and memory processes	How specific aspects of magazines, such as their design or layout, are recognized and interpreted; which parts of a magazine are most likely to be read
Clinical Psychology: product role in psychological adjustment	How magazines affect readers' body images (e.g., do thin models make the average woman feel overweight?)
Microeconomics/Human Ecology: product role in allocation of individual or family resources	Factors influencing the amount of money spent on magazines in a household
Social Psychology: product role in the behavior of individuals as members of social groups	Ways that ads in a magazine affect readers' attitudes toward the products depicted; how peer pressure influences a person's readership decisions
Sociology: product role in social institutions and group relationships	Pattern by which magazine preferences spread through a social group (e.g., a sorority)
Macroeconomics: product role in consumers' relations with the marketplace	Effects of the price of fashion magazines and expense of items advertised during periods of high unemployment
Semiotics/Literary Criticism: product role in the verbal and visual communication of meaning	Ways in which underlying messages communicated by models and ads in a magazine are interpreted
Demography: product role in the measurable characteristics of a population	Effects of age, income, and marital status of a magazine's readers
History: product role in societal changes over time	Ways in which our culture's depictions of "femininity" in magazines have changed over time
Cultural Anthropology: product role in a society's beliefs and practices	Ways in which fashions and models in a magazine affect readers' definitions of masculine versus feminine behavior (e.g., the role of working women, sexual taboos)

behavior topics. The fields closer to the top of the pyramid concentrate upon the individual consumer (micro issues), while those toward the base are more interested in the aggregate activities that occur among larger groups of people (macro issues), such as consumption patterns shared by members of a culture or subculture.

To demonstrate that the same marketing issue can be explored at different levels, we return to the choice faced by Gail when she was selecting a magazine to buy. Table 1–4 lists research issues that might be of interest to each contributing discipline and provides examples of how these might be applied in the marketing of women's magazines.

The Issue of Strategic Focus

Many people regard the field of consumer behavior as an applied social science. Accordingly, the value of the knowledge generated should be evaluated in terms of its ability to improve the effectiveness of marketing practice. Recently, though, some researchers have argued that consumer behavior should not have a strategic focus at all; that is, the field should not be a "handmaiden to business." It should instead focus on the understanding of consumption for its own sake, rather than because the knowledge can be applied by marketers.[33] This rather extreme view is probably not held by most consumer researchers, but it has encouraged many to expand the scope of their work beyond the field's traditional focus on the purchase of consumer goods such as food, appliances, cars, and so on. And, it has certainly led to some fiery debates among people working in the field!

This more critical view of consumer research has also led to the recognition that not all consumer behavior and/or marketing activity is necessarily beneficial to individuals or to society. As a result, current consumer research is likely to include attention to the "dark side" of consumer behavior, such as addiction, prostitution, homelessness, shoplifting, or environmental waste. This activity builds upon the earlier work of researchers who have studied consumer issues related to public policy, ethics, and consumerism. There is a growing movement in the field to develop knowledge about *social marketing*, which attempts to encourage such positive behaviors as increased literacy and to discourage negative activities, such as drunk driving.[34]

The Issue of Two Perspectives on Consumer Research

One general way to classify consumer research is in terms of the fundamental assumptions the researchers make about what they are studying and how to study it. This set of beliefs is known as a **paradigm.** Like other fields of study, consumer behavior is dominated by a paradigm, but some believe it is in the middle of a *paradigm shift,* which occurs when a competing paradigm challenges the dominant set of assumptions.

The basic set of assumptions underlying the dominant paradigm at this point in time is called **positivism** (or sometimes *modernism*). This perspective has significantly influenced Western art and science since the late 16th century. It emphasizes that human reason is supreme and that there is a single, objective truth that can be discovered by science. Positivism encourages us to stress the function of objects, to celebrate technology, and to regard the world as a rational, ordered place with a clearly defined past, present, and future.

The emerging paradigm of **interpretivism** (or *postmodernism*) questions these assumptions. Proponents of this perspective argue that there is too much emphasis on science and technology in our society and that this ordered, rational view of consumers denies the complex social and cultural world in which we live. Others feel that positivism puts too much emphasis on material well-being and that its logical outlook is dominated by an ideology that stresses the homogeneous views of a culture dominated by white males.

Interpretivists instead stress the importance of symbolic, subjective experience and the idea that meaning is in the mind of the person—that is, we each construct our own meanings based on our unique and shared cultural experiences, so there are no single right or wrong answers. In this view, the world in which we live is composed of a *pastiche,* or mixture of images.[35] The value placed on products because they help us to create order in our lives is replaced by an appreciation of consumption as a set

TABLE 1–5 ▼ Positivist Versus Interpretivist Approaches to Consumer Behavior

ASSUMPTIONS	POSITIVIST APPROACH	INTERPRETIVIST APPROACH
Nature of reality	Objective, tangible	Socially constructed
	Single	Multiple
Goal	Prediction	Understanding
Knowledge generated	Time free	Time bound
	Context independent	Context dependent
View of causality	Existence of real causes	Multiple, simultaneous shaping events
Research relationship	Separation between researcher and subject	Interactive, cooperative with researcher being part of phenomenon under study

Source: Adapted from Laurel A. Hudson and Julie L. Ozanne, "Alternative Ways of Seeking Knowledge in Consumer Research," *Journal of Consumer Research* 14 (March 1988): 508–21. Reprinted with the permission of The University of Chicago Press.

of diverse experiences. The major differences between these two perspectives on consumer research are summarized in Table 1–5.

AN OVERVIEW OF CONSUMER BEHAVIOR RESEARCH METHODS

There is no single right way or wrong way to conduct consumer behavior research. Because the field is composed of researchers from so many different disciplines, the researcher's "toolbox" is filled with a variety of approaches and techniques. The choice will depend both on the researcher's theoretical orientation and on the nature of the problem. For example, is the researcher's goal to *understand* current behavior for its own sake or to *predict* consumers' future behavior? Is the researcher interested in testing a hypothetical model or in looking for findings that can be incorporated into a marketing strategy?[36]

The first step in designing the research is defining the general problem to be addressed and specific objectives to be pursued. The problem may be to explore some consumer phenomenon that is of scientific or public policy interest, such as how consumers process nutritional information on product packages. In such a case, the objective might be identifying how consumers process packaging information rather than determining how these dynamics affect the fortunes of any one brand.

On the other hand, the research problem may be directly related to a marketing manager's desire to improve the performance of a particular brand in the marketplace. In this case, the researcher will address such issues as which version of three different packaging alternatives best communicates the desired image for the product or how packaging alternatives affect consumers' purchase behavior in the supermarket.

The researcher's next step is to identify the specific components of the research task. These include the characteristics of the consumer population of interest and the environmental context of the problem (e.g., a brand's performance relative to the prominence of nutritional information on the package or a brand's performance history when prior packaging changes were made). Depending on the researcher's theoretical foundation and assumptions of the problem, the same research components can be approached in radically different ways. One useful way to classify the approaches to consumer behavior research relies on the distinctions between exploratory and conclusive research.

Exploratory research is designed to provide insights into a problem where the phenomenon is not yet well defined. The research process is relatively flexible and unstructured and may involve the in-depth probing of relatively few consumers. Because of the emphasis on the subjective rather than objective nature of the research process, this book groups interpretive (or postpositivist) research methods under the rubric of exploratory research. This type of research is often used as a precursor to the design of problem-solving research.

Problem-solving research (or conclusive research) is designed to test specific hypotheses. The information needed is clearly defined, and the sample consumer population is intended to be representative of some larger group. The findings in this type of research are often used as input to decision making.

A summary of the methods and techniques used in these approaches to consumer behavior research is given in Figure 1–3. Although there are exceptions, many researchers equate qualitative methods with exploratory research and quantitative methods with conclusive research. In the next sections, we'll take a closer look at each type.

Exploratory Research

Exploratory research is performed to learn more about consumer behavior issues; to generate ideas for future, more rigorous studies; or to test a researcher's initial hunches about some phenomenon. It is not usually done to "explain" anything or to provide immediately actionable results to management, but rather to get a better sense of what further work needs to be done.

Since the researchers are not concerned that results will be generalizable to large groups of consumers, at this stage they usually have the luxury of being able to do more in-depth work with small numbers of consumers to really understand why these individuals feel or act the way they do. Exploratory research often consists of a "grab bag" of innovative methods that are used to understand the marketplace from the consumer's point of view. The researcher's experience and personal interpretation of the findings often are a crucial facet of the analysis.

In some cases, exploratory research can yield powerful insights simply by illustrating to marketers how consumers act in "natural" circumstances. One research firm helped convince French liqueur-marketer Pernot Ricard to use more aggressive techniques to sell its new cinnamon schnapps drink to young Americans. Researchers showed the client films of "typical" scenes in American bars on Saturday nights. The French were surprised to see that these settings actually resembled rambunctious fraternity parties; young revelers performed exotic acts with their drinks, including "waterfall shots" and "beer bongs."[37]

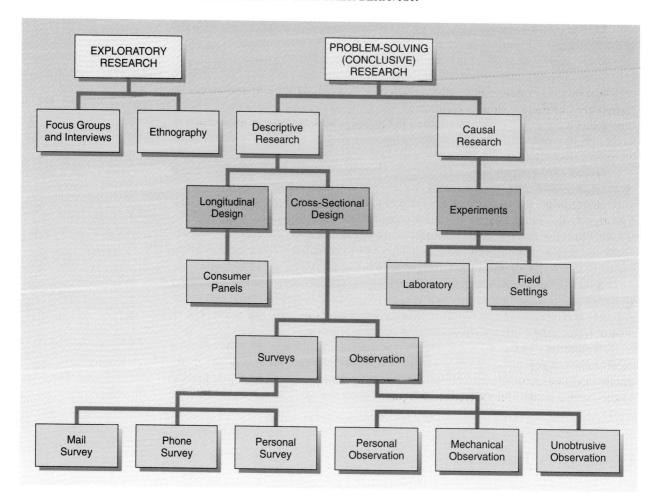

FIGURE 1–3 ▼ **Alternate Approaches to Consumer Behavior Research**

FOCUS GROUPS AND INTERVIEWS

Of all exploratory research techniques, **focus groups** are the most widely used.[38] Many thousands of focus groups are held by marketing researchers each year. This technique helps them to gather information from group interaction that is focused on a series of topics introduced by a discussion leader or moderator. Each participant is encouraged to express his or her views and to react to the views of others. The group typically consists of five to nine people who have been screened on some basis, often to represent demographic characteristics of the target market of interest.

Compared to an individual interview, the group setting may stimulate participants by allowing them to feed off of comments made by others. Group interplay makes meaningful comments more likely. It also allows the researcher access to useful data with little direct input.

In some situations the security of being in a group may also encourage more candor, especially if other group members share some important characteristic. For example, one project used groups of overweight women to explore their reactions to clothing and shopping. Amongst themselves, members had a tendency to bitterly refer to themselves as "fat ladies." They felt ignored by merchants and lost in a sea of thinner women. This insight allowed the client to develop a strategy that singled out this segment for special attention by providing products and messages that made them feel recognized and worthwhile.[39]

Another advantage of focus groups is that consumers representing specific, desired characteristics can be assembled. The client can obtain feedback from representatives of a distinct segment and can elicit responses from multiple segments. General Motors regularly conducts focus groups among both consumers and dealers to identify desirable car features possessed by competitors. These results led the company to model its air filter covers after Mazda's and to follow the example of Saab in putting fuses in the glove box.[40]

One drawback to focus groups is that, while they are easy to conduct, they are not often based in natural settings. As a result, there is always some uncertainty about the accuracy of responses.[41] Another problem is that individual decision-making processes are not always the same as group processes. For example, the degree to which people accept risk as members of a group tends to differ from when they make a decision alone. Group judgments tend to be polarized (i.e., more extreme) than individual judgments, and, under some circumstances, this factor leads to riskier decisions by groups. This increased tolerance of risk by groups is known as the *risky shift phenomenon.*

Projective Techniques. Techniques that involve the presentation of an ambiguous, unstructured object, activity, or person to which the consumer responds in some way are called **projective techniques.** The person may be asked to explain what the object is, tell a story about it, or perhaps draw a picture of it. Projectives are used when it is believed that a consumer will not or cannot respond meaningfully to direct questioning.

Projective techniques allow consumers to respond to neutral situations, where presumably their own feelings are not at issue and they are freer to respond openly. These techniques assume that a person's responses can then be inferred to reflect back to his or her own deep-seated feelings about an issue. Because there are no right or wrong answers, it is hoped that consumers will project their own unconscious feelings into their answers.

An early application of projective research illustrates the value of these procedures.[42] When Saran Wrap was introduced in the 1950s, consumers developed strong negative attitudes toward it because it was very difficult to handle. Depth interviews revealed that this product attribute per se was not responsible for the negative effect. At that time, women did not have an acceptable outlet to express their dislike of housekeeping. Their frustration with the product was a symbolic reflection of their frustration with the role of homemaker. This deep-seated feeling would not have been expressed in a straightforward interview. Acting on these findings, the product was made less clingy, and its nonkitchen uses were stressed in advertising.

Pictorial projectives can be used. Consumers enjoy working with pictures, and a number of projective techniques involve the use of pictorial stimuli. Some techniques are simply useful devices to stimulate associations by presenting a consumer in a situation and assessing reactions to it.

Bubble drawings depict a person in a commonplace situation (e.g., in a supermarket or driving a car) and require respondents to provide a caption. Alternatively, a consumer in the drawing might be shown confronting a new situation, such as a new product or a change in product packaging, and the respondent is asked to fill in

FIGURE 1–4 ▼ A Bubble Drawing Projective Instrument. The respondent is asked to supply the shopper's comments. Source: Wendy Gordon and Roy Langmaid, *Qualitative Market Research* (Hants, England: Gower, 1988), 104. By permission of Gower Publishing Group.

The advertising agency BBDO Worldwide uses a technique called "Photosort" where consumers express their feelings about a brand by associating it with pictures of different types of people whom they expect would use it. When the agency used the technique for General Electric, it found that respondents felt the brand was likely to be used by conservative, older people. To counteract that perception, GE developed its "Bring Good Things to Life" campaign. From Alfred S. Boote, "Psychographics: Mind Over Matter," American Demographics (April 1980). Photo courtesy of General Electric Co.

the consumer's comments in the bubble. In either case the responses are interpreted as the respondent's own feelings or doubts about the situation depicted. The bubble drawing in Figure 1–4 allows the respondent to voice concerns about trying a new product by imagining what the woman in the picture is saying.

One study employed a set of drawings specifically designed to assess underlying dimensions of grooming behaviors and rituals.[43] By responding to pictures of people engaged in various activities (e.g., applying makeup), respondents projected their own priorities and fantasies. Some of the resultant grooming themes included the magical and healing qualities attributed to cosmetics (e.g., restoration of youth), their linkage to sexual fortune, the use of grooming products to exhibit maturity and social capability, and the performance of "secret identities" (e.g., homosexual behavior).

Psychodrawing allows the respondent to express his or her perceptions of products or usage situations in a pictorial format. In Figure 1–5, a consumer has projected feelings before, during, and after toothbrushing. In a variation of this technique, an ad agency asked 50 consumers to sketch pictures of people who were likely to buy two brands of cake mixes. As seen in Figure 1–6, many subjects drew Pillsbury users as grandmotherly types, while Duncan Hines customers were younger and more dynamic.[44]

Autodriving uses visual and verbal recordings of consumers themselves as projectives. For example, a family might be photographed as it goes about preparing for dinner. These photographs are then shown to family members on a later occasion, and they are asked to talk about them. These interviews can shed light on underlying family dynamics (e.g., how are meal preparation tasks divided up among fam-

Cleaning Your Teeth: Before

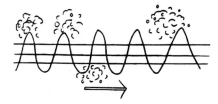

Cleaning Your Teeth: During

Cleaning Your Teeth: After

FIGURE 1–5 ▼ A Consumer's Psychodrawing of the Act of Toothbrushing. Source: Wendy Gordon and Roy Langmaid, *Qualitative Market Research* (Hants, England: Gower, 1988), 104. By permission of Gower Publishing Group.

Who Baked the Cake?

FIGURE 1–6 ▼ Consumers' Sketches of Typical Cake-Mix Users. Source: Annetta Miller and Dody Tsiantar, "Psyching Out Consumers," *Newsweek* (February 27, 1989): 46–47. By permission of McCann-Ericson (Research Department).

ily members?) or attitudes regarding the use of different food products or appliances. Here is how a full-time housewife who is in charge of meal preparation responded when she was "autodriven" by being shown a picture of her eight-year-old daughter removing stems from spinach. Note how her ambivalence about her housewife role starts to come to the surface in this narrative:

> I was Betty Crocker Homemaker of Tomorrow in high school, embarrassingly so. I think I'm a good cook and I enjoy it. . . . Sometimes I don't want to do it, but most of the time I do enjoy it. . . . I didn't like that image of myself. . . . Sometimes I wish I wasn't so domestic. But it's my nature and I'm real happy doing it. . . . Every so often I wonder if it would have suited me, I know it wouldn't have, but I sort of wish I had the personality where I could have stayed with my career and not chosen to stay home with the kids although I wouldn't have been happy doing that.[45]

Chilton Research Services, an American firm, goes a step farther: It gives consumers video cameras and asks them to tape scenes from their own lives to be used for later discussion. In order to help Bugle Boy, an apparel manufacturer, learn about how teens really live, the company had adolescents film themselves to give insights into their language, their school behavior, and the clothing they like to wear for specific occasions. These videos were then used to prompt discussion at focus groups held in unconventional locations like restaurants.[46]

Verbal projectives are also used. In addition to pictures, researchers rely on a variety of verbal exercises to allow subjects to project their feelings about products. With a sentence completion technique, for example, the respondent is given a sentence and is asked to fill in the missing word(s). In keeping with the intent of projection, the sentences are phrased in the third person. Sentence completion has the advantage of being focused and yielding concise answers. For this reason, it is especially useful in large groups, since it can be administered to more than one person at a time and responses across people can be easily compared. Commonly used examples include "The average person considers television _____." and "Most people feel that men who use cologne _____." Some versions supply a short story and ask people to describe how it ends.

One study employing this technique found that men and women view automobiles differently. When asked to complete the sentence "When you first get a car,

_____" women tended to supply responses like "you would go for a ride," while men responded "you check the engine," "you polish it," and so on. These results imply that women see a car as something to use, while for men it is an object to protect and be responsible for.

With a **stereotype technique,** respondents are given a description of a typical family or person and are asked to supply related information. For example, a description of a successful executive might be followed by the request to describe the contents of his wallet. By assessing which credit cards appear there, the researcher can determine some associations people have with this type of person.

In one of the classic demonstrations of this approach, women in the 1940s were asked to describe two housewives based on their shopping lists.[47] The only difference between the lists was that one included regular coffee, while the other instead specified instant coffee. The "instant coffee housewife" was described as lazy and a poor planner. This response revealed the concern of women (at that time) for buying time-saving products that would lead their husbands to think they were poor homemakers.

These findings were incorporated directly into marketing strategy. Advertisements for instant coffee were subsequently executed in family settings with the husband's approval clearly communicated. Obviously, this concern would not be present in today's society, where convenience is considered a virtue rather than a vice! Indeed, by 1970, researchers were unable to repeat these findings in a replication study.[48]

Interpretive Studies. Studies which attempt to generate a "thick description" of the experiences of one or a few people are called **interpretive studies.** The emphasis is on getting a lot of in-depth information from relatively few people to gain insights into deeper meanings of experiences or marketing communications. No attempt is made to generalize the experiences to others, although the interpretations of each informant can certainly be compared with and contrasted to others' explanations for the same event.

In interpretive studies, the researcher is considered a part of the interpretive process because his or her own beliefs and background influence what is being studied. Due to the interpretivist belief that consumer behavior cannot be studied apart from the natural context in which it occurs, researchers tend to prefer to travel to the site of consumption activities, rather than bring consumers into a laboratory setting. A consumer's responses in the laboratory cannot be compared to what he or she will reveal to friends or family.

An interpretive framework to understanding marketing communications can be illustrated by an analysis of one of the best-known and longest-running (1959–1978) advertising campaigns of all time—the work done by the advertising agency Doyle Dane Bernbach for the Volkswagen Beetle. This campaign, widely noted for its self-mocking wit, found many ways to turn the Beetle's homeliness, smallness, and lack of power into positive attributes at a time when most car ads were emphasizing just the opposite.

An interpretive analysis of these messages used concepts from literature, psychology, and anthropology to ground the appeal of this approach within a broader cultural context. The image created for the humble car was connected to other examples of what scholars of comedy call the "Little Man" pattern. This is a type of comedic character that is related to a clown or a trickster, a social outcast who is able to poke holes in the stuffiness and rigidity of bureaucracy and conformity. Other

Heard any Volkswagen jokes lately?

An interpretive analysis helps us to understand the long-running popularity of ads for the Volkswagen Beetle. In this typical ad, the car company shares in the fun of ridiculing the car by asking readers to send in Volkswagen jokes. From Bruce G. Vanden Bergh, "Volkswagen as 'Little Man,' " Journal of American Culture 15 (Winter 1992): 95–120, Fig. 9, p. 115. Photo courtesy of Volkswagen of America.

examples of the "Little Man" character include Hawkeye in the TV sitcom *M.A.S.H.,* the comedian Woody Allen, and Charlie Chaplin.[49] When one looks at the cultural meaning of marketing messages this way, it is perhaps not coincidence that IBM chose the Charlie Chaplin character some years later to help it "soften" its stuffy, intimidating image as it tried to convince consumers that its new personal computer products were user-friendly.

Although relatively new to consumer behavior research, interpretive studies are gaining popularity. They are being applied to topics ranging from the construction of shopping environments (e.g., the mixing of architectural styles, store types, and varieties of ethnic foods in a mall) to the rise of the "body culture" in our society, where consumers alter their bodies through dieting, exercise, and surgery to make unique statements about themselves. Some techniques for collecting data in interpretive studies have been around since the early days of consumer behavior, some are now being borrowed from other fields such as anthropology and literary criticism, and still others are under development.

Semiotics and Hermeneutics. Some analytical methods have been adapted from such fields as literature and linguistics to better understand what marketing messages mean. **Semiotics** focuses on the meanings in texts and pictures and how different elements of a message symbolize deeper meanings. The role played by semiotics in the understanding of how advertising communicates to consumers will be further explored in Chapter 2.

Hermeneutics is a method that stresses that perceivers evaluate messages (such as ads or music videos) by drawing on many preconceived notions and that focuses on how people's notions about themselves, about the world, and about the source of the message may be changed after being exposed to a message.[50] Using a hermeneutic analysis, for example, a researcher could explore how preconceptions taken for granted by a certain segment of the population might influence the meaning they attach to a particular celebrity's product endorsement.[51]

ETHNOGRAPHY

One increasingly popular method for studying consumers in their natural "habitats" is derived from techniques used by anthropologists when studying foreign cultures. This strategy involves *participant observation*, in which the researcher is immersed in the host culture. Although the researcher does not totally "go native," the aim is to try to understand people on their own terms. This in-depth study of a specific group's behaviors, social rules, and beliefs is called **ethnography.** Research is usually done in a natural setting and is reported in the form of a very detailed case study.[52]

The ethnographic approach has come to the forefront of consumer behavior research largely as the result of a project called the *Consumer Behavior Odyssey,* in which a team of marketing professors traveled across the United States in a recreational vehicle to interact with consumers in a wide variety of natural settings, ranging from swap meets and festivals to convents and museums.[53] The project yielded enormous quantities of field notes, still photos, and videotapes that documented interviews with many diverse types of consumers. The *Odyssey* was one of the first systematic attempts by consumer researchers to study consumers in their real environments rather than in controlled or laboratory settings. A recent "sequel" to the *Odyssey* project took place in Australia, where a team of researchers conducted an ethnography of aboriginal consumer culture.[54]

A major advertising agency also borrowed a page from anthropologists by going "undercover" in a typical American small town. The Chicago office of the Foote Cone & Belding agency decided to learn more about the increasing desire of consumers to return to a simpler life, so it chose a small Illinois town that it code-named "Laskerville" as the site of its project (the project is named after one of the agency's founders, Albert Lasker). On several occasions, agency researchers have visited the town, talking with local residents, reading local newspapers, and attending town functions (even funerals) to determine what issues are important to the consumers. No tape recorders or notes have been allowed, and the town's identity remains a closely guarded secret—even the agency's chief executive officer doesn't know its real name.[55]

Problem-Solving (Conclusive) Research

Problem-solving research is generally a goal-oriented process in which the researcher wants to make some definitive statements about relationships among variables. Since conclusive research aims to provide decision makers with actionable information, the emphasis is on descriptive information that is generalizable beyond the sample and quantifiable for comparison across individuals.

In obtaining generalizable data, this research perspective assumes that while there may be some individual variations or effects due to chance, the differences will "wash out" if enough different subjects are studied. In obtaining quantitative data, the aim is to maximize the reliability of the results and make it more likely that the same effect will be observed in future studies. The goal is not to predict the behavior of any one person, but rather to predict the typical or average responses of people who share certain characteristics.

The methods for collecting data require little interpretation on the part of the researcher, who is expected to remain an impartial observer. The responses elicited

···

${\mathcal{M}}$ARKETING PITFALL

The potential invasion of privacy by market researchers is an issue for researchers who go "underground" to study consumers in their natural environments. A California couple sued Nissan, charging that the company had planted a "spy" from Tokyo in their home. The researcher's assignment was to study the living and car purchasing patterns of U.S. consumers, and he allegedly rented a room in the couple's home while he observed the behavior of the plaintiffs and their neighbors. Although the suit was eventually dropped, the negative publicity from this incident certainly was not welcomed by Nissan.[56]

The growing use of sophisticated demographic databases also is not sitting well with many consumers, who are concerned about possible violations of privacy. After receiving 30,000 complaints, Lotus Development Corporation killed plans to sell its MarketPlace: Households software database, which contained demographic information on 80 million households. Around the same time, New England Telephone & Telegraph canceled plans to sell a list of 4.7 million of its customers.[57]

While the American Civil Liberties Union is pushing for a watchdog group to protect privacy rights, the direct marketing industry claims self-regulation is working. Executives point to the Direct Marketing Association's Mail Preference Service and Telephone Preference Service, which permit consumers to specify that their names be removed from mailing lists or that they not be called by telemarketers. Still, problems remain: Only about one-half of mailers participate in this service, and many consumers are unaware of its existence.[58]

from the studied consumers can be *physiological* (e.g., eye movements measured in eye-tracking studies to determine what parts of commercials capture the consumers' attention), *verbal* (e.g., responses to questions about commercials the consumers have seen), or *behavioral* (e.g., purchase volume after the consumers have been exposed to a special price promotion).

Problem-solving studies can be further divided into two types: descriptive and causal. The major goal of **descriptive research** is to describe something without necessarily explaining the reason for the phenomenon. **Causal research,** in contrast, is performed to obtain evidence of cause-and-effect relationships.

DESCRIPTIVE RESEARCH

Descriptive consumer research is usually done to identify the characteristics of a consumer segment or one or more products in the marketplace. For example, a brand manager for a soft drink might want to know the profile of the "heavy user" of her product as compared with people who drink her competitors' products. Or, this manager might want to track the public's consumption of diet versus regular soft drinks over time. In addition, she might want to know whether changes in promotional expenditures for the brand are associated with a change in the brand's sales.

A *longitudinal design* tracks the responses of the same sample of subjects over time. Market researchers often rely on *panel studies*, where a sample of respondents (usually drawn from consumer households) that is statistically representative of a larger market agrees to provide information about purchases on a regular basis. Participants respond to detailed questionnaires about their purchasing habits, media usage, and so on. One major survey of this type is the Simmons Survey of Media & Markets, which tracks the purchase of an American consumer sample composed of over 20,000 households. Actual data from this survey are used in the *Simmons Connection* exercises that accompany this text. A sample page from the Simmons survey is shown in Figure 1–7.

A *cross-sectional design* is the most widely used in marketing research. This format involves the collection of information from one or more groups of respondents at only one point in time. Specific types of surveys that are used in cross-sectional designs will be discussed at a later point.

CAUSAL RESEARCH

Causal research attempts to understand cause-and-effect relationships. Marketers often want to know what variables, called **independent variables,** cause a phenomenon and what variables, called **dependent variables,** are affected when the independent variables are changed. To be able to rule out alternative explanations, they must carefully design experiments that test prespecified relationships among variables.

For example, while a brand manager may find from descriptive research that sales tend to rise when the brand is promoted more heavily, he or she cannot be sure that the extra promotional effort is really the cause of the sales rise. Some third factor may be at work that is affecting sales at the same time. For example, people naturally buy more during the Christmas shopping season, so the product may sell more simply because people are out in the stores looking harder for things to buy.

Causal studies may be performed in laboratories or in carefully controlled field settings, such as stores, restaurants, or homes. In either case, the researcher must be able not only to manipulate the independent variables that are under study but to hold constant other factors. If a change in the dependent variable is observed after only the independent variable(s) has been manipulated, the researcher can be more confident in concluding that the independent variable(s) in fact exerts a causal (rather than merely correlational) relationship with the dependent variable(s).

For example, a manufacturer might want to assess whether a package change for one of its products (an independent variable) will increase sales (a dependent variable). With the cooperation of a store chain, it might select some outlets that are matched in terms of location, customer demographics, and so on. One set of stores might feature the product with the new package, while another set would continue to sell the product in its old package. Management could then compare sales of the brand between the two sets of stores. If sales rose significantly in stores carrying the new package, researchers could conclude with a reasonable degree of confidence that the new package did, in fact, exert a causal effect on sales.

Types of Data

The actual data collected by consumer researchers can be divided into two general categories: primary data and secondary data. Very simply, **primary data** comprise

PAGE P-3 — WOMEN'S TOILETRIES AND COSMETICS

NAIL POLISH

1a. Do you yourself use it?

Yes 43 ☐ 1 No ☐ 2

IF YOU DO

1b. Which brands do you use?

	Most Often	Others
Almay	44 ☐ 1	49 ☐ 1
Avon Color Last Plus	☐ 2	☐ 2
Avon Color Nail Solutions	☐ 3	☐ 3
Avon Color Single Stroke II	☐ 4	☐ 4
Other Avon Color	☐ 5	☐ 5
Clairol	☐ 6	☐ 6
Clarion	☐ 7	☐ 7
Clinique	☐ 8	☐ 8
Cover Girl Nail Slicks	☐ 9	☐ 9
Cover Girl Professional One Coat	☐ 0	☐ 0
Cover Girl Salon Solutions	☐ x	☐ x
Cutex Color Quick	☐ y	☐ y
Cutex Perfect Color	45 ☐ 1	50 ☐ 1
Cutex Shine-On	☐ 2	☐ 2
Cutex Strong Nail	☐ 3	☐ 3
Estee Lauder	☐ 4	☐ 4
Fashion Fair	☐ 5	☐ 5
Hazel Bishop	☐ 6	☐ 6
L'Oreal Colour Riche	☐ 7	☐ 7
L'Oreal Grow Strong	☐ 8	☐ 8
Max Factor Classic	☐ 9	☐ 9
Max Factor Diamond Hard	☐ 0	☐ 0
Max Factor Twice The Wear	☐ x	☐ x
Other Max Factor	☐ y	☐ y
Maybelline Long Wearing	46 ☐ 1	51 ☐ 1
Maybelline Revitalizing Nail Color	☐ 2	☐ 2
Maybelline Shades Of You	☐ 3	☐ 3
Nouvage	☐ 4	☐ 4
Revlon Creme/Crystalline Enamel	☐ 5	☐ 5
Revlon Instant Nail Color	☐ 6	☐ 6
Revlon Liquid Nail Wrap	☐ 7	☐ 7
Revlon Natural Wonder	☐ 8	☐ 8
Revlon Quick Drying	☐ 9	☐ 9
Revlon Super Lustrous	☐ 0	☐ 0
Revlon Super Nail	☐ x	☐ x
Revlon Polish	☐ y	☐ y
Sally Hansen Hard as Nails	47 ☐ 1	52 ☐ 1
Sally Hansen New Lengths	☐ 2	☐ 2
Wet 'n' Wild	☐ 3	☐ 3
Other Brands	☐ 4	☐ 4
	48Z	53Z

1c. About how many times did you use nail polish in the *last 30 days*?

10 or more	54 ☐ 1	3	☐ 5
7-9	☐ 2	2	☐ 6
5-6	☐ 3	1	☐ 7
4	☐ 4	NONE	☐ 0

COTTON BALLS OR SQUARES

2a. Do you yourself use them?

Yes 55 ☐ 1 No ☐ 2

IF YOU DO

2b. About how many times did you use cotton balls or squares in the *last 7 days*?

14 or more	56 ☐ 1	2-3	☐ 5
8-13	☐ 2	1	☐ 6
7	☐ 3	NONE	☐ 0
4-6	☐ 4		

MASCARA

3a. Do you yourself use it?

Yes 57 ☐ 1 No ☐ 2

IF YOU DO

3b. What kinds do you use?

	Most Often	Others
Waterproof	58 ☐ 1	59 ☐ 1
Water Resistant	☐ 2	☐ 2
Regular (Not Waterproof/Resistant)	☐ 3	☐ 3
Soap & Water Washable	☐ 4	☐ 4

3c. Which brands do you use?

	Most Often	Others
Almay One Coat	60 ☐ 1	66 ☐ 1
Avon Color Advanced Wear Waterproof	☐ 2	☐ 2
Avon Color Body Workout	☐ 3	☐ 3
Avon Color Lots O'Lash	☐ 4	☐ 4
Avon Color Model Perfect	☐ 5	☐ 5
Avon Color Pure Care	☐ 6	☐ 6
Avon Color Wash-Off Waterproof	☐ 7	☐ 7
Other Avon Color	☐ 8	☐ 8
Aziza Color & Care	☐ 9	☐ 9
Other Aziza	☐ 0	☐ 0
Clarion Aqua Lash	☐ x	☐ x
Clarion Infinite Lengths	☐ y	☐ y
Clarion Maximum Effects	61 ☐ 1	67 ☐ 1
Clarion Sudden Lash	☐ 2	☐ 2
Clinique	☐ 3	☐ 3
Cover Girl Anti-Smudge	☐ 4	☐ 4
Cover Girl Clean Lash	☐ 5	☐ 5
Cover Girl Extension	☐ 6	☐ 6
Cover Girl Extremely Gentle	☐ 7	☐ 7
Cover Girl Lasting Performance	☐ 8	☐ 8
Cover Girl Long'n Lush	☐ 9	☐ 9
Cover Girl Marathon	☐ 0	☐ 0
Cover Girl Natural Lash	☐ x	☐ x
Cover Girl Professional	☐ y	☐ y
Cover Girl Thick Lash 2	62 ☐ 1	68 ☐ 1
Other Cover Girl	☐ 2	☐ 2
Estee Lauder	☐ 3	☐ 3
Lancôme	☐ 4	☐ 4
L'Oreal Lash Out	☐ 5	☐ 5
L'Oreal Splash Out	☐ 6	☐ 6
L'Oreal Voluminous	☐ 7	☐ 7
Other L'Oreal	☐ 8	☐ 8
Mary Kay	☐ 9	☐ 9
Max Factor For Your Eyes Only	☐ 0	☐ 0
Max Factor Stretch	☐ x	☐ x
Max Factor Super Lashmaker	☐ y	☐ y
Max Factor Splish Splash Lash	63 ☐ 1	69 ☐ 1
Max Factor 2000 Calories	☐ 2	☐ 2
Other Max Factor	☐ 3	☐ 3
Maybelline Dial-a-Lash	☐ 4	☐ 4
Maybelline Fresh Lash	☐ 5	☐ 5
Maybelline Great Lash	☐ 6	☐ 6
Maybelline Illegal Lengths	☐ 7	☐ 7
Maybelline Magic Mascara	☐ 8	☐ 8
Maybelline No Problem	☐ 9	☐ 9
Maybelline Perfectly Natural	☐ 0	☐ 0
Maybelline Ultra Lash	☐ x	☐ x
Maybelline Ultra Thick Ultra Lash	☐ y	☐ y
Revlon Budget Line	64 ☐ 1	70 ☐ 1
Revlon Lashful	☐ 2	☐ 2
Revlon Premium Line	☐ 3	☐ 3
Wet 'n' Wild	☐ 4	☐ 4
Other Brands	☐ 5	☐ 5
	65Z	71Z

3d. About how many times did you use mascara in the *last 7 days*?

14 or more	72 ☐ 1	2-3	☐ 5
8-13	☐ 2	1	☐ 6
7	☐ 3	NONE	☐ 0
4-6	☐ 4		

73-80Z

EYE SHADOW/EYE LINER/EYE BROW PENCIL 06-0 07-3

4a. Do you yourself use them?

	Eye Shadow	Eye Liner	Eye Brow Pencil
Yes	08 ☐ 1	17 ☐ 1	26 ☐ 1
No	☐ 2	☐ 2	☐ 2

IF YOU DO

4b. What kinds do you use?

	Eye Shadow	Eye Liner	Eye Brow Pencil
Cake	09 ☐ 1	18 ☐ 1	
Crayon	☐ 2	☐ 2	27 ☐ 2
Cream	☐ 3	☐ 3	
Liquid	☐ 4	☐ 4	
Pen	☐ 5	☐ 5	☐ 5
Pencil	☐ 6	☐ 6	☐ 6
Powder	☐ 7	☐ 7	
Other	☐ 8	☐ 8	☐ 8

4c. Which brands do you use?

	Eye Shadow	Eye Liner	Eye Brow Pencil
Almay	10 ☐ 1	19 ☐ 1	28 ☐ 1
Avon Color Glimmersticks Brow	☐ 2	☐ 2	☐ 2
Avon Color Glimmersticks Eye	☐ 3	☐ 3	☐ 3
Avon Color Luxury Eye	☐ 4	☐ 4	☐ 4
Avon Color Silk Finish	☐ 5	☐ 5	☐ 5
Other Avon Color	☐ 6	☐ 6	☐ 6
Aziza Color & Care	☐ 7	☐ 7	☐ 7
Aziza Contact Lens	☐ 8	☐ 8	☐ 8
Aziza Eye Glider	☐ 9	☐ 9	☐ 9
Other Aziza	☐ 0	☐ 0	☐ 0
Clarion Captive Color	☐ x	☐ x	☐ x
Clarion Pen Silks	☐ y	☐ y	☐ y
Clarion Silk Palette	11 ☐ 1	20 ☐ 1	29 ☐ 1
Other Clarion	☐ 2	☐ 2	☐ 2
Clinique	☐ 3	☐ 3	☐ 3
Cover Girl Extremely Gentle Soft Liner	☐ 4	☐ 4	☐ 4
Cover Girl Liquid Pencil	☐ 5	☐ 5	☐ 5
Cover Girl Perfect Blend	☐ 6	☐ 6	☐ 6
Cover Girl Perfect Point	☐ 7	☐ 7	☐ 7
Cover Girl Pro-Color One-Kit	☐ 8	☐ 8	☐ 8
Cover Girl Professional Brow Enhancer	☐ 9	☐ 9	☐ 9
Cover Girl Professional Color Match	☐ 0	☐ 0	☐ 0
Cover Girl Soft Radiants	☐ x	☐ x	☐ x
Other Cover Girl	☐ y	☐ y	☐ y
Elizabeth Arden	12 ☐ 1	21 ☐ 1	30 ☐ 1
Estee Lauder	☐ 2	☐ 2	☐ 2
Lancôme	☐ 3	☐ 3	☐ 3
L'Oreal	☐ 4	☐ 4	☐ 4
Mary Kay	☐ 5	☐ 5	☐ 5
Max Factor Shadow Sweep	☐ 6	☐ 6	☐ 6
Max Factor Visual Eyes	☐ 7	☐ 7	☐ 7
Other Max Factor	☐ 8	☐ 8	☐ 8
Maybelline Blooming Colors	☐ 9	☐ 9	☐ 9
Maybelline Expert Eyes	☐ 0	☐ 0	☐ 0
Maybelline Lineworks	☐ x	☐ x	☐ x
Maybelline Natural Accents	☐ y	☐ y	☐ y
Maybelline Performing Color	13 ☐ 1	22 ☐ 1	31 ☐ 1
Maybelline Revitalizing Shadow	☐ 2	☐ 2	☐ 2
Maybelline Shadow Slims	☐ 3	☐ 3	☐ 3
Maybelline Ultra Liner	☐ 4	☐ 4	☐ 4
Other Maybelline	☐ 5	☐ 5	☐ 5
Merle Norman	☐ 6	☐ 6	☐ 6
Revlon Custom Eyes	☐ 7	☐ 7	☐ 7
Revlon Day Into Night Stick	☐ 8	☐ 8	☐ 8
Revlon Overtime Shadows	☐ 9	☐ 9	☐ 9
Revlon Ultima II	☐ 0	☐ 0	☐ 0
Other Revlon	14 ☐ 1	23 ☐ 1	32 ☐ 1
Wet 'n' Wild	☐ 2	☐ 2	☐ 2
Other Brands	☐ 3	☐ 3	☐ 3
	15Z	24Z	33Z

4d. About how many times did you use eye shadow, eye liner, or eye brow pencil in the *last 7 days*?

	Eye Shadow	Eye Liner	Eye Brow Pencil
14 or more	16 ☐ 1	25 ☐ 1	34 ☐ 1
8-13	☐ 2	☐ 2	☐ 2
7	☐ 3	☐ 3	☐ 3
4-6	☐ 4	☐ 4	☐ 4
2-3	☐ 5	☐ 5	☐ 5
1	☐ 6	☐ 6	☐ 6
NONE	☐ 0	☐ 0	☐ 0

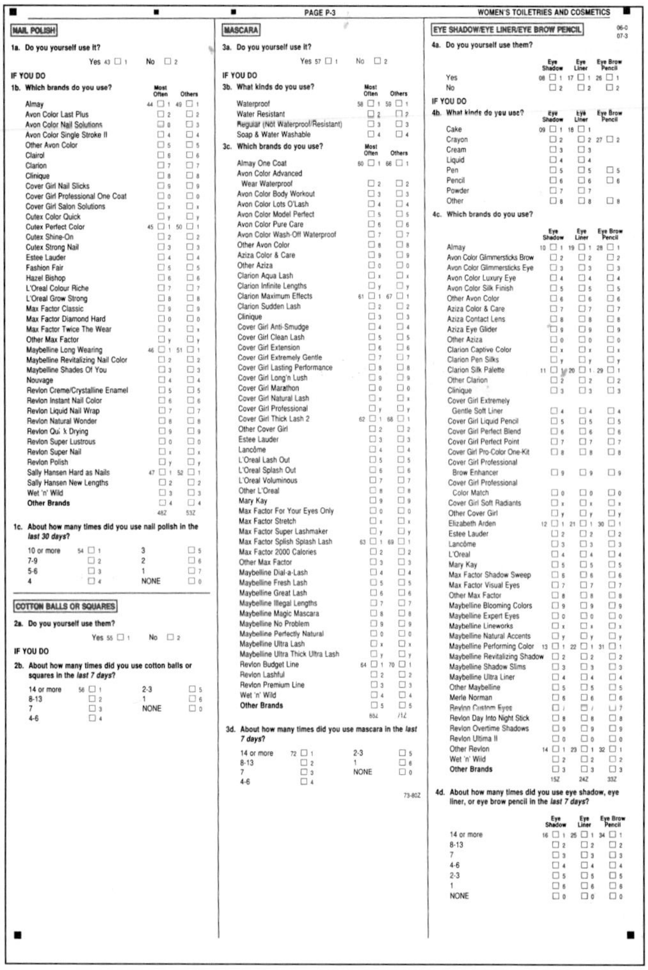

FIGURE 1–7 ▼ A Page from a Typical Survey Form. This page, which is part of the Simmons Survey of Media & Markets questionnaire, illustrates the detailed information syndicated services collect from consumer panelists regarding their purchase patterns. Note: Responses to the items in this survey are used in the Simmons Connection Boxes that appear throughout this text.

information that is collected specifically for the purposes of the present study. **Secondary data,** on the other hand, include information that already exists in some form; that is, it has been originally collected for another purpose but may be very useful to the present research.

PRIMARY DATA

Primary data, which are collected by the researcher, can take many forms. Exploratory research designs often rely upon qualitative methods like those already discussed. Problem-solving research designs involve either experimentation (in the laboratory or field), surveys, or observational techniques. *

Types of Survey Questions.   Most surveys consist of some type of questionnaire, where a respondent is presented with a set of statements and is asked to respond to them. These questionnaires can take many forms, but the most widely used is a *Likert scale*. The respondent simply checks or circles a number that indicates how much he or she agrees or disagrees with a statement:

Sears is a fun place to shop.

Disagree   1   2   3   4   5   Agree

A *semantic-differential scale* is also popular. This consists of a series of bipolar adjectives (e.g., good/bad, pretty/ugly) that anchor either end of a set of numbers; the respondent evaluates a concept along the various dimensions.

The atmosphere at Sears is

Cold   1   2   3   4   5   Warm

Another measuring device is a *rank-order scale*, where the respondent is asked to rank products or stores in order of preference according to some criterion.

In terms of stores that are fun places to shop, please rank the following from 1 to 4.

_____ JCPenney

_____ Kmart

_____ Sears

_____ Wal-Mart

Modes of Survey Data Collection.   Essentially, a researcher who wants to administer a survey to a large number of consumers has three choices: Use the telephone, use the mail, or interview people in person.

● Mail surveys usually consist of a one-shot questionnaire that is sent to a sample of consumers, often with some incentive to return the survey (the incentive may be a dollar bill attached to the survey or the promise to donate money to the respondent's favorite charity). Alternatively, a consumer may belong to a panel like those described earlier and receive a packet of materials in the mail on a regular basis. Mail surveys are relatively easy to administer and offer a high degree of anonymity to respondents. On the down side, the researcher has little flexibility in the types of questions asked and little control over the circumstances under which the questionnaire is answered (or, for that matter, who actually answers it).

● Telephone surveys usually consist of a short phone conversation where an interviewer reads a series of brief questions. Technological developments have made computer-assisted telephone interviewing much more common; the interviewer reads questions from a CRT screen, and the respondent's answers are recorded directly into the computer. While telephone interviewing can

*This section will very briefly review some survey and observational methods; experimental designs are beyond the scope of this book. Any good Marketing Research text will provide this information.

yield data from large numbers of consumers very quickly, researchers are limited in that the respondent can't be asked to react to any visual stimuli. Furthermore, the proliferation of telemarketing, where business solicitations are made over the phone, has eroded the willingness of many consumers to participate in phone surveys.

● Personal interviews can be conducted in the respondent's home, although this practice has declined markedly in recent years due to escalating costs and security concerns. More typically, the researcher conducts a "mall-intercept" study, where participants are recruited in shopping malls or other public areas and asked to respond to a survey. The advantage of being able to tailor the interview based on the responses obtained (e.g., the researcher can probe, or ask further questions, to follow up on what a person has said) may not materialize because respondents are often reluctant to answer questions of a personal nature in a face-to-face context.

Obtaining Observational Research Data. Observational research situations are those in which the researcher wishes to record some aspect of consumer behavior without actually intervening in any way or manipulating the situation. Observational research data can be very useful as a way to corroborate respondents' own reports of what they do.

For example, when mothers were interviewed in focus groups, they claimed they bought a fruit snack made by General Mills because of its "wholesomeness." When researchers hung around supermarkets and observed mothers shopping with their children, however, a different story emerged: Children tended to beg their mothers for different food items, and mothers did not appear to care which brand they bought. In other words, the desire to buy wholesome food was relevant to the category of fruit snacks but did not translate into the motivation to buy a specific brand.[59]

● When *personal observation* is employed, the behavior of people is simply recorded. For example, a researcher might observe customers in a store, noting what questions they ask of salespeople and how they handle the product.

● *Mechanical observation* relies on devices to record behavior. Turnstiles in stores are used to track how many people have visited the establishment over a certain period. The widespread use of the Universal Product Code (UPC) on products has fostered the growth of *scanning technology*, where consumers' purchases can be recorded to track buying patterns. In another use of this technology, marketers can tailor their promotions to the specific needs of consumers (e.g., by issuing diaper coupons to consumers who have purchased baby food). Another widespread application of mechanical observation is the meter method used by A. C. Nielsen to record consumers' television watching. The data obtained from metering devices are used to determine who is watching which shows; these television ratings are how the networks determine how much they will charge advertisers for commercials (and which shows eventually get canceled or renewed).

● **Unobtrusive measures** are methods of data collection that do not require direct human responses. These techniques are sometimes called *trace analysis* because they rely on the physical traces, or evidence, of past behavior. They are often used when the researcher suspects that people will probably distort their responses, either because they may not be able to accurately recall their behavior or perhaps they want to portray themselves in a more favorable light. For example, instead of asking a person to report on the products that are currently in his or her home, the researcher might actually go to the house and perform a "pantry check," recording the products that are actually on the person's shelves. One innovative research method, called *garbology,* involves sifting through people's garbage (after it has been anonymously collected and labeled) to determine product usage. This unobtrusive technique is especially useful when the individual might be reluctant to report his or her usage truthfully, as for such sensitive products as liquor or contraceptives.[60]

SECONDARY DATA

Secondary data are not directly collected by the researcher. Sources of secondary data can range from a company's sales history (internal data are generated by the organization itself) to such government sources as the U.S. Census Bureau (external data are information obtained from a source other than the organization). Secondary data are often helpful in understanding a problem (and interpreting primary data) by placing it in a broader context. Many general business sources of secondary data are available (usually for a fee). These range from business directories and computerized databases to syndicated services such as VALS, Simmons, and the Yankelovich Monitor that track the purchases, attitudes, and lifestyles of different consumer segments. A list of sources of secondary data is provided in Appendix I.

LEARNING ABOUT CONSUMER BEHAVIOR

This book covers many facets of consumer behavior, and many of the research perspectives briefly described in this chapter will be highlighted in later chapters. The plan of the book is simple: It goes from micro to macro. Think of the book as a sort of photograph album of consumer behavior: Each chapter provides a "snapshot" of consumers, but the lens used to take each picture gets successively wider.

The book begins with issues related to the individual consumer and expands its focus until it eventually considers the behaviors of large groups of people in their social settings. The topics to be covered correspond to the wheel of consumer behavior presented in Figure 1–8.

Section II, "Consumers as Individuals," considers the consumer at his or her most micro level. It examines how the individual receives information from his or her immediate environment and how this material is learned, stored in memory, and used to form and modify individual attitudes—both about products and about oneself. Section III, "Consumers as Decision Makers," explores the ways in which consumers use the information they have acquired to make decisions about consumption activities, both as individuals and as group members. Section IV, "Consumers and Subcultures," further expands the focus by considering how the consumer functions as a part of a larger social structure. This structure includes the influence of different social groups with which the consumer belongs and/or identifies, including social class, ethnic groups, and age groups. Finally, Section V, "Consumers and Culture," completes the picture as it examines marketing's impact on mass cul-

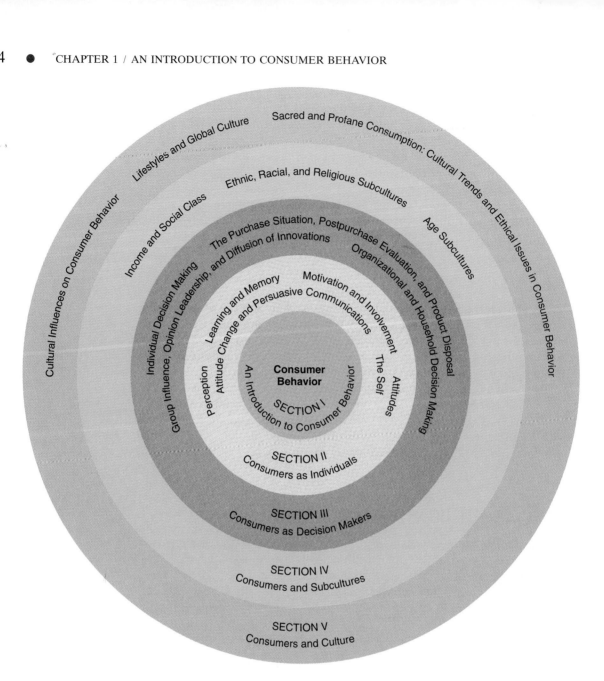

FIGURE 1–8 ▼ The Wheel of Consumer Behavior

ture. These effects include the relationship of marketing to the expression of cultural values and lifestyles, how products and services are related to rituals and cultural myths, and the interface between marketing efforts and the creation of art, music, and other forms of popular culture that are so much a part of our daily lives.

CHAPTER
SUMMARY

- Consumer behavior is the study of the processes involved when individuals or groups select, purchase, use, or dispose of products, services, ideas, or experiences to satisfy needs and desires.

- A consumer may purchase, use, and/or dispose of a product, but these functions may be performed by different people. In addition, consumers may be thought of as role players who need different products to help them play their various parts.

- Market segmentation is an important aspect of consumer behavior. Consumers can be segmented along many dimensions, including product usage, demographics (the objective aspects of a population, such as age and sex), and psychographics (psychological and lifestyle characteristics). Emerging developments, such as the new emphasis on relationship marketing and the practice of database marketing, mean that marketers are much more attuned to the wants and needs of different consumer groups.

- Marketing activities exert an enormous impact on individuals. Consumer behavior is relevant to our understanding of both public policy issues (e.g., ethical marketing practices) and the dynamics of popular culture.

- The field of consumer behavior is interdisciplinary; it is composed of researchers from many different fields who share an interest in how people interact with the marketplace. These disciplines can be categorized by the degree to which their focus is micro (the individual consumer) versus macro (the consumer as a member of groups or of the larger society).

- There are many perspectives on consumer behavior, but research orientations can roughly be divided into two approaches. The positivist perspective, which currently dominates the field, emphasizes the objectivity of science and the consumer as a rational decision maker. The interpretivist perspective, in contrast, stresses the subjective meaning of the consumer's individual experience and the idea that any behavior is subject to multiple interpretations rather than one single explanation.

- Consumer research can be either exploratory or problem solving. Exploratory research is designed to learn more about the nature of a problem or phenomenon, while problem-solving research is designed to obtain actionable information or to test predictions (hypotheses) based on prior knowledge or models of behavior. Exploratory methods include the use of focus groups, depth interviews, and ethnography. Problem-solving methods include the use of controlled experiments, surveys, consumer panels, and observational techniques ranging from scanning technology to garbology.

- Primary data refers to information that is collected for the purposes of a specific observational or experimental research study, while secondary data refers to existing information that may be adapted to the current study. Secondary data sources include computerized databases, the U.S. Census, and many syndicated studies conducted by companies and made available to clients for a fee.

Q. CAN YOU FIND THE HIDDEN PLEASURE IN REFRESHING SEAGRAM'S GIN?

A. If you think this is just a bubble, look again.

This Seagram's ad pokes fun at the belief that advertisers frequently embed pleasurable images in the ice cubes in pictures of drinks. Courtesy of The House of Seagram.

Low-level auditory stimulation has also been used. One auditory technique, known as *psycho-acoustic persuasion,* actually does appear to work. Subtle acoustical messages such as "I am honest. I won't steal. Stealing is dishonest." are broadcast in more than 1,000 stores in the United States to prevent shoplifting. Unlike subliminal perception, though, these messages are played at a (barely) audible level, using a technique known as threshold messaging.[41] After a nine-month test period, theft losses in one six-store chain declined almost 40 percent, saving the company $600,000.

Some evidence indicates, however, that these messages are effective only on individuals whose value systems make them predisposed to suggestion. For example, someone who might be thinking about taking something on a dare but who feels guilty about it might be susceptible to these messages, but they will not sway a professional thief or a kleptomaniac (someone who feels a compulsion to steal for psychological reasons).[42]

Does It Work? Evaluating the Evidence

Some research by clinical psychologists suggests that people can be influenced by subliminal messages under very specific conditions, though it is doubtful that these techniques would be of much use in most marketing contexts. While the possibility that subliminal persuasion can cause a consumer to choose one brand over another is quite low, the possibility that this technique could be used to stimulate basic needs has not been completely ruled out. Still, to be effective, messages must be very specifically tailored to individuals, rather than to a mass audience as required by advertising.[43] These messages should also be as close to the liminal threshold as possible. Other discouraging factors include the following issues.

1. **There are wide individual differences in threshold levels.** In order for a message to avoid conscious detection by consumers who have a low threshold, it would have to be so weak that it would not reach those who have a high threshold.

2. **Advertisers lack control over consumers' distance and position from a screen.** In a movie theater, for example, only a small portion of the audience would be in exactly the right seats to be exposed to the subliminal message.

3. **The consumer must be paying absolute attention to the stimulus.** People watching a television program or a movie typically shift their attention periodically and might not even be looking when the stimulus is presented.

4. **Even if the desired effect is induced, it operates only at a very general level.** For example, a message might increase a person's thirst, but not necessarily for a specific drink. Because basic drives are affected, marketers could find that after all the bother and expense of creating a subliminal message, demand for competitors' products increases as well!

PERCEPTUAL SELECTION

Although we live in an "information society," we can have too much of a good thing. Consumers are often in a state of sensory overload, i.e., exposed to far more information than they are capable or willing to process. People who have been in the middle of a noisy, crowded bar or who have partied for several hours might feel the need to step outside periodically to take a break. A consumer can experience a similar feeling of being overwhelmed after being forced to sift through the claims made by hundreds of competing brands. Further, the competition for our attention is increasing steadily. In 1971 about 2,600 television commercials ran each week; now cable and network stations carry more than 6,000 during the same time period.[44]

*M*ARKETING PITFALL

Consumers and marketers alike are getting madder and madder about advertising clutter. Advertising professionals feel that the proliferation of ads in both traditional media and nontraditional locations, such as movie theaters and TV monitors in doctors' offices, is threatening the quality of their work. They fear that consumers will be so bombarded by competing stimuli that they won't be in a receptive frame of mind when *their* messages are transmitted.

In a survey of advertising professionals and consumers by the Roper Organization and the trade paper *Advertising Age,* 31 percent of consumers said they found ads shown in movie theaters before movies begin annoying, as compared to 65 percent of the professionals! The pros were also about twice as likely to be annoyed by the use of TV monitors in high school classrooms and at messages inserted on rental videotapes.[45]

Because the brain's capacity to process information is limited, consumers are very selective about what they pay attention to. The process of **perceptual selectivity** means that people attend to only a small portion of the stimuli to which they are exposed. Consumers practice a form of psychic economy, picking and choosing among stimuli, to avoid being overwhelmed by *advertising clutter*. This overabundance of advertising stimuli highlights two important aspects of perceptual selectivity as they relate to consumer behavior: exposure and attention.

Exposure

Exposure is the degree to which people notice a stimulus that is within range of their sensory receptors. Consumers concentrate on some stimuli, are unaware of others, and even go out of their way to ignore some messages. An experiment by a Minneapolis bank illustrates consumers' tendencies to miss or ignore information in which they are not interested. After a state law was passed that required banks to explain details about money transfer in electronic banking, the Northwestern National Bank distributed a pamphlet to 120,000 of its customers at considerable cost to provide the required information, which was hardly exciting bedtime reading. In 100 of the mailings, a section in the middle of the pamphlet offered readers $10 just for finding that paragraph. Not a single person claimed the reward.[46]

SELECTIVE EXPOSURE

Experience, which is the result of acquiring stimulation, is one factor that determines how much exposure to a particular stimulus a person accepts. *Perceptual filters* based on consumers' past experiences influence what they decide to process.

Perceptual vigilance is a factor in selective exposure. Consumers are more likely to be aware of stimuli that relate to their current needs. These needs may be conscious or unconscious. A consumer who rarely notices car ads will become very much aware of them when he or she is in the market for a new car. A newspaper ad

The photograph in this ad for Pensions & Investment Age *illustrates how visual stimuli can cause advertising clutter, the sensory overload to which consumers are exposed in the marketplace.* Courtesy of Pensions & Investment Age. *Concept: W. Bisson; Copy: W. Bisson; Design: J. Hunt, Donna Klein.*

for a fast-food restaurant that would otherwise go unnoticed becomes significant when one glances at the paper in the middle of a five o'clock class.

The advent of the VCR has allowed consumers armed with remote control fast-forward buttons to be much more selective about which television messages they are exposed to. By "zipping," viewers fast-forward through commercials while playing recorded tapes of their favorite programs. A VCR marketed by Mitsubishi in Japan even removes the need for zipping. It distinguishes between the different types of TV signals used to broadcast programs and commercials and automatically pauses during ads.[47]

How big an issue is zipping for marketers? The jury is still out on this question. In one survey, 69 percent of VCR owners said that they had increased their television viewing time, so overall exposure to commercials might actually increase as people continue to purchase VCRs.[48]

Zipping has enhanced the need for advertising creativity. Interesting commercials do not get zipped as frequently. Evidence indicates that viewers are willing to stop fast-forwarding to watch an enticing or novel commercial. In addition, longer commercials and those that keep a static figure on the screen (such as a brand name or a logo) appear to counteract the effects of zipping; these executions are not as affected by a speed increase, since the figure remains in place longer.[49]

ADAPTATION

Another factor affecting exposure is **adaptation,** that is, the degree to which consumers continue to notice a stimulus over time. The process of adaptation occurs when consumers no longer pay attention to a stimulus because it is so familiar. Almost like drug addiction, a consumer can become "habituated" and require increasingly stronger "doses" of a stimulus for it to continue to be noticed. For example, a consumer en route to work might read a billboard message when it is first installed, but after a few days, it becomes part of the passing scenery.

Generally, several factors can lead to adaptation.

- *Intensity.* Less intense stimuli (e.g., soft sounds or dim colors) habituate because they have less of a sensory impact.
- *Duration.* Stimuli that require relatively lengthy exposure in order to be processed tend to habituate because they require a long attention span.
- *Discrimination.* Simple stimuli tend to habituate because they do not require attention to detail.
- *Exposure.* Frequently encountered stimuli tend to habituate as the rate of exposure increases.
- *Relevance.* Stimuli that are irrelevant or unimportant will habituate because they fail to attract attention.

Attention

Attention is the degree to which consumers focus on stimuli within their range of exposure. Because consumers are being exposed to so many advertising stimuli, marketers are becoming increasingly creative in their attempts to gain attention for their products.

A dynamic package is one way to gain this attention. Recall that Gary was attracted by a distinctive black bottle, and the package essentially sold the product to him. Some consulting firms have established elaborate procedures to measure package effectiveness, using such instruments as an *angle meter,* that measures package visibility as a shopper moves down the aisle and views the package from different angles.

Data from *eye-tracking tests,* in which consumers' eye movements as they look at packages and ads are followed and measured, can result in subtle but powerful changes that influence the impact of packages and ads. For example, eye-tracking tests on an ad for Bombay gin showed that virtually no consumers were reading the message (in relatively small type) below the visual portion and that the Bombay bottle (also relatively small) positioned to the right of the visual portion was not seen by nine out of ten readers. The result was low recall scores for the ad. In a revised ad, the bottle's size was increased, and the message was emphasized. Recall scores for this version were almost 100 percent higher than for the original.[50]

COUNTERING ADVERTISING CLUTTER

Many marketers are making specific attempts to counter the sensory overload caused by advertising clutter in order to call attention to their products. One expensive strategy involves buying large blocks of advertising space in a medium in order to dominate consumers' attention. Designer Ralph Lauren filled 15 consecutive, full pages in a single issue of *Vanity Fair* for this purpose.

Other companies are using "bookend ads," where a commercial for one product is split into parts that are separated by commercials for other products. The first part creates conflict, and the second resolves it. This technique motivates the viewer to keep watching in order to get the rest of the story. For example, an ad for Excedrin depicts a woman taking two tablets for her headache. She then reappears after a few other commercials have aired to announce that the headache is gone.[51]

Another solution has been to put ads in unconventional places, where there will be less competition for attention. These places include the backs of shopping carts, tunnels, sports stadiums, and even movies.[52] An executive at Campbell's Soup, commenting on the company's decision to place ads in such locations as church bulletins, noted, "We have to shake consumers up these days in order to make them take notice. . . . Television alone won't do that. Now we have to hit them with our ads where they shop and play and on their way to work."[53]

Marketers continue to come up with new tricks to get and keep consumers' attention. For example, the NBC network has gone so far as to move directly from one show to another without inserting the usual set of commercials. By creating "value-added entertainment moments" that compress the show credits into one-third of the screen and adding brief final scenes and trivia questions about other NBC shows, the network hopes to keep viewers from doing something else during station breaks.[54]

CREATING CONTRAST

When many stimuli are competing to be noticed, one will receive attention to the extent that it differs from those around it. Stimuli that fall into unpredictable patterns often command a lot of attention.

Size and color differences are also powerful ways to achieve contrast. A black-and-white object in a color ad is quite noticeable, as is a block of printed type surrounded by large amounts of white space. The size of the stimulus itself in contrast to the competition is also important. Readership of a magazine ad has been shown to increase in proportion to the size of the ad.[56]

INTERPRETATION: DECIDING WHAT THINGS MEAN

Interpretation refers to the meaning that people assign to sensory stimuli. Just as people differ in terms of the stimuli that they perceive, the eventual assignment of meanings to these stimuli varies, as well. Two people can see or hear the same event, but their interpretations of it can be like night and day.

In a classic experiment, students at Princeton and Dartmouth viewed a movie of a particularly rough football game between the two schools. Although everyone was exposed to the same stimulus, the degree to which students saw infractions, and the blame they assigned for those they did see, was quite different depending on which college they attended.[57] The assignment of meaning can be colored by what one expects or hopes to see.[58]

Consumers assign meaning to stimuli based on the schema, or set of beliefs, to which the stimulus is assigned. Certain properties of a stimulus will more likely evoke a schema than others. (This process is known as **priming**.) As evidenced by Gary's cologne selection, a brand name can communicate expectations about prod-

This ad for a phone book is a vivid reminder of the power of contrast in drawing attention to a marketer's message. Courtesy of Bell Atlantic.

uct attributes and can color consumers' perceptions of product performance by activating a schema. When Toro introduced a lightweight snow thrower, it was named the "Snow Pup." Sales were disappointing because the word pup called up a schema that grouped things which are small and cuddly—not the desirable attributes for a snow thrower—together. When the product was renamed the "Snow Master," sales went up markedly.[59]

Stimulus ambiguity occurs when a stimulus is not clearly perceived or when it conveys a number of meanings. In such cases, consumers tend to project their own wishes and desires to assign meaning. Although ambiguity in product advertisements is usually undesirable to marketers, it can be used creatively to generate controversy or interest. For example, a popular ad for Benson & Hedges cigarettes featured a group of people sitting around a dinner table, while a man wearing only pajama bottoms stands in the background. This ambiguous character yielded valuable publicity for the company as people competed to explain the meaning of the mysterious "pajama man."

Stimulus Organization

People do not perceive a single stimulus in isolation. They tend to view it in terms of relationships with other events, sensations, or images. A number of perceptual principles describe how stimuli are perceived and organized.

These principles are based on work in **Gestalt psychology,** a school of thought maintaining that people derive meaning from the *totality* of a set of stimuli, rather than from any individual stimulus. The German word *gestalt* roughly means whole, pattern, or configuration, and this perspective is best summarized by the saying "the whole is greater than the sum of its parts." The importance of a gestalt is underscored when consumers' interpretations of stimuli are affected by aesthetic, symbolic, or sensory qualities. Set in a context that is painfully familiar to most students, the Colombian coffee ad shown here demonstrates the formation of a meaningful image

This J&B ad illustrates use of the principle of closure, in which people participate in the ad by mentally filling in the gaps. Reprinted with permission by The Paddington Corporation ©.

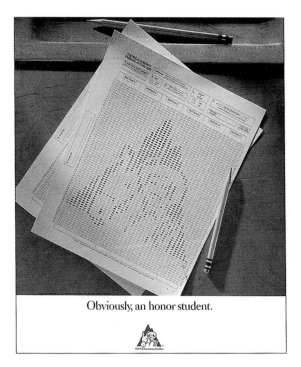

Obviously, an honor student.

This ad for Colombian coffee illustrates Gestalt principles of perception, in which the individual parts (the colored circles) are seen as a whole (the familiar symbol used to promote Colombian coffee). Courtesy of the National Federation of Coffee Growers of Colombia.

from the individual colored circles on a Scantron sheet when viewed in totality. A piecemeal perspective that analyzes each component of the stimulus separately will be unable to capture the total effect. For instance, a "punk" black leather jacket and "preppie" khaki pants might look good separately, but the gestalt created when they are worn together would not be "right." The gestalt perspective provides several principles relating to the way stimuli are organized. Three of these principles, or perceptual tendencies, are illustrated in Figure 2–4.

The gestalt **principle of closure** implies that consumers tend to perceive an incomplete picture as complete. That is, we tend to fill in the blanks based on our prior experience. This principle explains why most of us have no trouble reading a neon sign even if one or two of its letters are burned out or filling in the blanks in an incomplete message. The principle of closure is also at work when we hear only part of a jingle or theme. Utilization of the principle of closure in marketing strategies encourages audience participation, which increases the chance that people will attend to the message.

FIGURE 2–4 ▼
Principles of Stimulus Organization Derived from Gestalt Psychology

PRINCIPLE OF CLOSURE   PRINCIPLE OF SIMILARITY   PRINCIPLE OF FIGURE-GROUND

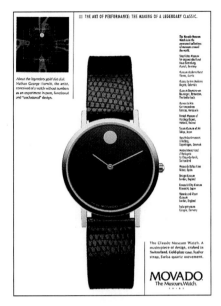

This advertisement for Movado watches illustrates the figure-ground principle. The eye is immediately drawn to the oversized watch—that is, the figure that dominates the copy, or ground. Courtesy of Movado Watch Company.

The **principle of similarity** tells us that consumers tend to group together objects that share similar physical characteristics; that is, they group like items into sets to form an integrated whole. Green Giant relied upon this principle when the company redesigned the packaging for its line of frozen vegetables. It created a "sea-of-green" look to unify all of its different offerings.

Another important gestalt concept is the **figure-ground principle,** in which one part of a stimulus will dominate (the *figure*) while other parts recede into the background. This concept is easy to understand if one thinks literally of a photograph with a clear and sharply focused object (the *figure*) in the center. The figure is dominant, and the eye goes straight to it. The parts of the configuration that will be perceived as figure or ground can vary depending on the individual consumer as well as other factors. Similarly, in marketing messages that use the figure-ground principle, a stimulus can be made the focal point of the message or merely the context that surrounds the focus.

The Role of Symbolism in Interpretation

When we try to "make sense" of a marketing stimulus, whether a distinctive package, an elaborately staged television commercial, or perhaps a model on the cover of a magazine, we do so by interpreting its meaning in light of associations we have with these images. For this reason, much of the meaning we take away is influenced by what we make of the symbolism we perceive. After all, on the surface many marketing images have virtually no literal connection to actual products. What does a cowboy have to do with a bit of tobacco rolled into a paper tube? How can a celebrity like basketball star Michael Jordan enhance the image of a soft drink or a fast-food restaurant?

For assistance in understanding how consumers interpret the meanings of symbols, some marketers are turning to a field of study known as **semiotics,** which examines the correspondence between signs and symbols and their role in the assignment of meaning.[60] Semiotics is important to the understanding of consumer behavior since consumers use products to express their social identities. Products have learned meanings, and we rely on advertising to help us figure out what those meanings are. As one set of researchers put it, ". . . advertising serves as a kind of culture/consumption dictionary; its entries are products, and their definitions are cultural meanings."[61]

From a semiotic perspective, every marketing message has three basic components: an object, a sign or symbol, and an interpretant. The **object** is the product that is the focus of the message (e.g., Marlboro cigarettes). The **sign** is the sensory imagery that represents the intended meanings of the object (e.g., the Marlboro cowboy). The **interpretant** is the meaning derived (e.g., rugged, individualistic, American). This relationship is diagrammed in Figure 2–5.

According to semiotician Charles Sanders Peirce, signs are related to objects in one of three ways. They can resemble objects, be connected to them, or be conventionally tied to them.[62] An *icon* is a sign that resembles the product in some way (e.g., Bell Telephone uses an image of a bell to represent itself). An *index* is a sign that is connected to a product because they share some property (e.g., the pine tree on some of Procter & Gamble's Spic and Span cleanser products conveys the shared property of fresh scent). A *symbol* is a sign that is related to a product through either conventional or agreed-upon associations (e.g., the lion in Dreyfus Fund ads provides the conventional association with fearlessness that is carried over to the company's approach to investments).

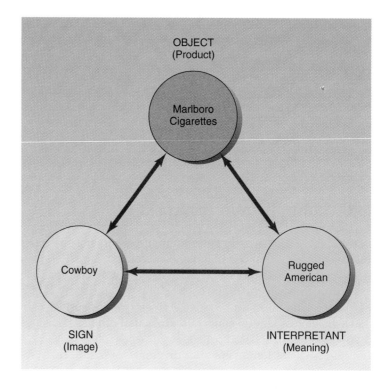

FIGURE 2–5 ▼ Relationships of Components in Semiotic Analysis of Meaning

This Cognac Hennessy ad illustrates some of the subtle semiotic processes that convey meaning in advertising. The product, cognac, is an upscale alcoholic beverage associated with a soft, smooth taste; luxurious surroundings; and a large price tag. The label is an icon—that is, it literally represents the product. Silk, because it is smooth and also associated with luxury, is used as an index that shares properties with the cognac. The woman wrapped in a silk gown is a symbol—a symbol that stands for sex appeal, smoothness, and luxury. The creators of the ad hope that these properties will transfer to people's perceptions of the product. Reprinted with permission by Schieffelin & Somerset Co.

The use of symbols provides a powerful means for marketers to convey product attributes to consumers. For example, expensive cars, designer fashions, and diamond jewelry—all widely recognized symbols of success—frequently appear in ads to associate products with affluence or sophistication.

One of the hallmarks of modern advertising is that it creates a condition that has been termed **hyperreality.** Hyperreality refers to the becoming real of what is initially simulation or "hype." Advertisers create new relationships between objects and interpretants by inventing new connections between products and benefits, such as equating Marlboro cigarettes with the American frontier spirit.[63] To a large extent, over time the true relationship between the symbol and reality is no longer possible to discern, and the "artificial" associations between product symbols and the real world may take on lives of their own.

For example, Tasters' Choice coffee presents an ongoing series of "soap opera" commercials where a romantic relationship is slowly cultivated between two actors. The pink Energizer Bunny™ who began life in regular Eveready Battery commercials now goes gaily marching through fake commercials for totally unrelated

The popular pink Energizer Bunny™, gaily marching through fake commercials, creates a condition of hyperreality in which product symbols take on a life of their own. Courtesy of the Eveready Battery Company, Inc.

products such as "Alarm" bath and shower soap—a commercial where the Bunny is appropriately dressed in rain gear. As illustrated by the film clips shown here, the Bunny's antics take the actors in these simulated commercials by surprise and usually the viewers as well.

....

CHAPTER SUMMARY

- Perception is the process by which physical sensations, such as sights, sounds, and smells, are selected, organized, and interpreted. The eventual interpretation of a stimulus allows it to be assigned meaning. A perceptual map is a widely used marketing tool that evaluates the relative standing of competing brands along relevant dimensions.

- Marketing stimuli have important sensory qualities. We rely on colors, odors, sounds, tastes, and even the "feel" of products when forming evaluations of them.

- Not all sensations successfully make their way through the perceptual process. Many stimuli compete for our attention, and the majority are not noticed or accurately comprehended.

- People have different thresholds of perception. A stimulus must be presented at a certain level of intensity before it can be detected by an individual's sensory receptors. In addition, a consumer's ability to detect whether two stimuli are different (the differential threshold) is an important issue in many marketing contexts, such as changing a package design, altering the size of a product, or reducing its price.

- A lot of controversy has been sparked by so-called subliminal persuasion and related techniques, by which people are exposed to visual and audio messages below the threshold. Although evidence that subliminal persuasion is effective is virtually nonexistent, many consumers continue to believe that advertisers use this technique.

- Some of the factors that determine which stimuli (above the threshold level) do get perceived are the amount of exposure to the stimulus, how much attention it generates, and how it is interpreted. In an increasingly crowded stimulus environment, advertising clutter occurs when too many marketing-related messages compete for attention.

- A stimulus that is attended to is not perceived in isolation. It is classified and organized according to principles of perceptual organization. These principles are guided by a gestalt, or overall pattern. Specific grouping principles include closure, similarity, and figure-ground relationships.

- The final step in the process of perception is interpretation. Symbols help us to make sense of the world by providing us with an interpretation of a stimulus that is often shared by others. The degree to which the symbolism is consistent with our previous experience affects the meaning we assign to related objects. Every marketing message contains a relationship between the product, the sign or symbol, and the interpretation of meaning. A semiotic analysis involves the correspondence between stimuli and the meaning of signs.

- Signs function on several levels. The intended meaning may be literal (e.g., an icon, such as a street sign with a picture of children playing). The meaning may be indexical; it may rely on shared characteristics (e.g., the red in a stop sign means danger). Finally, meaning may be conveyed by a symbol, in which an image is given meaning by convention or by agreement among members of a society (e.g., stop signs are octagonal, while yield signs are triangular).

CONSUMER BEHAVIOR CHALLENGE

1. Many studies have shown that our sensory detection abilities decline as we grow older. Discuss the implications of the absolute threshold for marketers attempting to appeal to the elderly.

2. Interview 3–5 male and 3–5 female friends regarding their perceptions of both men's and women's fragrances. Construct a perceptual map for each set of products. Based on your map of perfumes, do you see any areas that are not adequately served by current offerings? What (if any) gender differences did you obtain regarding both the relevant dimensions used by raters and the placement of specific brands along these dimensions?

3. Assuming that some forms of subliminal persuasion may have the desired effect of influencing consumers, do you think the use of these techniques is ethical? Explain your answer.

4. Assume that you are a consultant for a marketer who wants to design a package for a new premium chocolate bar targeted to an affluent market. What recommendations would you provide in terms of such package elements as color, symbolism, and graphic design? Give the reasons for your suggestions.

5. Do you believe that marketers have the right to use any or all public spaces to deliver product messages? Where would you draw the line in terms of places and products that should be restricted?

6. Find one ad that is rich in symbolism and perform a semiotic analysis of it. Identify each type of sign used in the ad and the product qualities being communicated by each. Comment on the effectiveness of the signs that are used to communicate the intended message.

7. Using magazines archived in the library, track the packaging of a specific brand over time. Find an example of gradual changes in package design that may have been below the JND.

8. Collect a set of current ads for one type of product (e.g., personal computers, perfumes, laundry detergents, or athletic shoes) from magazines, and analyze the colors employed. Describe the images conveyed by different colors, and try to identify any consistency across brands in terms of the colors used in product packaging or other aspects of the ads.

9. Look through a current magazine and select one ad that captures your attention over the others. Give the reasons why.

10. Find ads that utilize the techniques of contrast and novelty. Give your opinion of the effectiveness of each ad and whether the technique is likely to be appropriate for the consumers targeted by the ad.

ABC NEWS CONNECTION

Hidden Messages

For the last forty years, consumers have fretted about the possibility that their thoughts and feelings are being manipulated by hidden messages embedded in television programming and sound recordings. In a controversial and ultimately unsuccessful court case, for example, the parents of two teenagers who had died in a suicide pact sued CBS Records and the heavy metal band Judas Priest for allegedly encouraging the teens' deaths by embedding the messages "Do it" and "Let's be dead" in the album *Stained Glass*.[1]

Nowadays, though, the supposed power of auditory messages broadcast at a subliminal level is being harnessed for positive reasons—or is it? Many people are spending large sums on self-help tapes that supposedly contain subliminal messages designed to help them stop smoking, lose weight, or even improve their chances of getting a date on Saturday night.

As noted in the chapter, there is limited evidence that most forms of subliminal persuasion work at all outside of very limited, controlled situations where the message is carefully tailored to the precise needs of specific individuals.[2] In any case, this discouraging evidence has done little to diminish the sales of self-help tapes.

Even the most faithful potential buyers should be aware of the results of one study that examined the effectiveness of auditory subliminal messages using sophisticated audiological equipment: The researchers were unable to find any evidence that the messages on the tapes they studied had any effect. To add insult to injury, they also discovered that many of the commercially available tapes they examined did not even have subliminal messages on them to begin with![3] So, as the old expression goes, *caveat emptor* ("let the buyer beware")!

---

[1] See "Blaming Deaths Hidden Messages," *Newsweek* (July 30, 1990): 58.

[2] See L. H. Silverman, "Psychoanalytic Theory: The Reports of My Death Are Greatly Exaggerated," *American Psychologist* 31 (September 1976): 62–137; Joel Saegert, "Why Marketing Should Quit Giving Subliminal Advertising the Benefit of the Doubt," *Psychology & Marketing* 4 (Summer 1987): 107–20.

[3] See Philip M. Merikle, "Subliminal Auditory Messages: An Evaluation," *Psychology & Marketing* 5 (1988): 355–72.

SIMMONS CONNECTION

Personal Fragrances

For many consumers, a personal fragrance in the form of aftershave, cologne, or perfume is essential. These people would not dream of leaving the house without first putting on their favorite scent. As noted in the chapter opening, Gary is concerned about making a good impression on Janeen. And, he thinks that using the "right" scent will help him to do this.

The Simmons datafile for this chapter contains information about the purchase of several different brands of men's and women's fragrances. It also provides some demographic information.

Gary has selected Drakkar Noir as the scent he will purchase. Assuming that Gary is a typical purchaser of this scent, what is your best estimate of his age? What other demographic characteristic(s) can be used to describe Gary?

Most likely Janeen will also wear a scent. If she falls into the same demographic category as Gary, then what scent(s) is she most likely to be wearing? (*Hint:* Try using percentages in answering this part.)

Gary is concerned about the image he wants to cultivate for Janeen. He assumes that his scent will convey something about himself as a person. The Simmons datafile contains a few items taken from the Simmons inventory of personal views. Using a cutoff of 25%, generate a personal views profile of Drakkar Noir users. Which of the women's perfumes that you selected for Janeen best matches the profile for Drakkar Noir?

NOTES

1. Kim Foltz, "Campaign on Harmony Backfires for Benetton," *New York Times* (November 20, 1989): D8.

2. Jerome S. Bruner, "On Perceptual Readiness," *Psychological Review* 64 (March 1957): 123–52.

3. Joseph Pereira and Barbara Carton, "Toys 'R' Us to Banish Some 'Realistic' Toy Guns," *Wall Street Journal* (October 14, 1994): B1 (2 pp.).

4. Elizabeth C. Hirschman and Morris B. Holbrook, "Hedonic Consumption: Emerging Concepts, Methods, and Propositions," *Journal of Marketing* 46 (summer 1982): 92–101.

5. Kevin Goldman, "More Advertisers Listen to Sign Language," *Wall Street Journal* (November 10, 1993): B8.

6. Joseph Bellizzi and Robert E. Hite, "Environmental Color, Consumer Feelings, and Purchase Likelihood," *Psychology & Marketing* 9 (1992): 347–63; Ayn E. Crowley, "The Two-Dimensional Impact of Color on Shopping," *Marketing Letters* (in press); Gerald J. Gorn, Amitava Chattopadhyay, and Tracey Yi, "Effects of Color as an Executional Cue in an Ad: It's in the Shade" (unpublished manuscript, University of British Columbia, 1994).

7. Wendy Bounds, "Mood Is Indigo for Many Food Marketers," *Wall Street Journal* (September 23, 1993): B2.

8. Mark G. Frank and Thomas Gilovich, "The Dark Side of Self- and Social Perception: Black Uniforms and Aggression in Professional Sports," *Journal of Personality and Social Psychology* 54, 1 (1988): 74–85.

9. Glenn Collins, "Owens-Corning's Blurred Identity," *New York Times* (August 19, 1994): D4.

10. "Crystal Clear Persuasion," *Tufts University Diet & Nutrition Letter* (January 1993): 1.

11. Dianne Solis, "Cost No Object for Mexico's Makeup Junkies," *Wall Street Journal* (June 7, 1994): B1.

12. Ronald Alsop, "Color Grows More Important in Catching Consumers' Eyes," *Wall Street Journal* (November 29, 1984): 37; Meg Rosen and Frank Alpert, "Protecting Your Business Image: The Supreme Court Rules on Trade Dress," *Journal of Consumer Marketing* 11, 1 (1994): 50–5.

13. "Court Refuses Trademark for Package Color," *Marketing News* (May 27, 1991): 25.

14. Anthony Ramirez, "Lessons in the Cracker Market: Nabisco Saved New Graham Snack," *New York Times* (July 5, 1990): D1.

15. Helen Mundell, "How the Color Mafia Chooses Your Clothes," *American Demographics* (November 1993): 21 (2 pp.).

16. Deborah L. Jacobs, "The Titans of Tint Make Their Picks," *New York Times* (May 29, 1994): F7.

17. Quoted in Cynthia Morris, "The Mystery of Fragrance," *Essence* 71, 3 (May 1988): 71.

18. Deborah Toth, "To Relax or Stay Alert: New Mood-Altering Scents," *New York Times* (September 24, 1989): F15.

19. Suein L. Hwang, "Seeking Scents that No One Has Smelled," *Wall Street Journal* (August 10, 1994): B1" (2 pp.).

20. "How to Smell Like the Gang," *Newsweek* (September 26, 1994): 59.

21. James LaRossa, Jr., "Home Fragrances Bloom in Wide-Open Field," *Home Textiles* 54 (May 8, 1989): 4.

22. Eben Shapiro, "When It Rains, It Removes Odors," *New York Times* (October 6, 1992): D5.

23. Gail Tom, "Marketing with Music," *Journal of Consumer Marketing* 7 (spring 1990): 49–53; J. Vail, "Music as a Marketing Tool," *Advertising Age* (November 4, 1985): 24. For empirical work on the effects of music on consumer behavior, see James J. Kellaris and Robert J. Kent, "An Exploratory Investigation of Responses Elicited by Music Varying in Tempo, Tonality, and Texture," *Journal of Consumer Psychology* 2, 4 (1994): 381–401; James J. Kellaris, Anthony D. Cox, and Dena Cox, "The Effect of Background Music on Ad Processing: A Contingency Explanation," *Journal of Marketing* 57, 4 (October 1993): 114–25.

24. Joan E. Rigdon, "Hallmark Cards Can Send a Message That's a Real Earful for a Loved One," *Wall Street Journal* (November 5, 1993): A5I.

25. Otto Friedrich, "Trapped in a Musical Elevator," *Time* 110 (December 10, 1984): 3.

26. James MacLachlan and Michael H. Siegel, "Reducing the Costs of Television Commercials by Use of Time Compression," *Journal of Marketing Research* 17 (February 1980): 52–7.

27. James MacLachlan, "Listener Perception of Time Compressed Spokespersons," *Journal of Advertising Research* 2 (April/May 1982): 47–51.

28. Danny L. Moore, Douglas Hausknecht, and Kanchana Thamodaran, "Time Compression, Response Opportunity, and Persuasion," *Journal of Consumer Research* 13 (June 1986): 85–99.

29. See Leslie Davis Burns and Sharron J. Lennon, "The Look and the Feel: Methods for Measuring Aesthetic Perceptions of Textiles and Apparel," in M. R. DeLong and A. M. Fiore, *Aesthetics of Textiles and Clothing: Advancing Multi-Disciplinary Perspectives* (Monument, CO: International Textile and Apparel Association, 1994): 120–30.

30. Jacob Hornik, "Tactile Stimulation and Consumer Response," *Journal of Consumer Research* 19 (December 1992).

31. Eben Shapiro, "The People Who Are Putting Taste Back on the Table," *New York Times* (July 22, 1990): F5.

32. Judann Dagnoli, "Cookie Tasters Chip in for Nabisco," *Advertising Age* (August 21, 1989): 58.

33. See Tim Davis, "Taste Tests: Are the Blind Leading the Blind?" *Beverage World* (April 1987): 43.

34. Quoted in Davis, "Taste Tests," 44.

35. Stuart Elliott, "Another Remarkable Story of the Brand-Name Lexicon," *New York Times* (August 13, 1992): D9. IBM is the world's ninth most popular brand.

36. Michael Lev, "No Hidden Meaning Here: Survey Sees Subliminal Ads," *New York Times* (May 3, 1991): D7.

37. *New Yorker* (September 21, 1957): 33.

38. Erv Wolk, "Can Subliminal Ads Work for You?" *Modern Floor Coverings* (June 1986): 23.

39. Philip M. Merikle, "Subliminal Auditory Messages: An Evaluation," *Psychology & Marketing* 5, 4 (1988): 355–72.

40. Timothy E. Moore, "The Case Against Subliminal Manipulation," *Psychology & Marketing* 5 (winter 1988): 297–316.

41. Sid C. Dudley, "Subliminal Advertising: What Is the Controversy About?" *Akron Business and Economic Review* 18 (summer 1987): 6–18; "Subliminal Messages: Subtle Crime Stoppers," *Chain Store Age Executive* 2 (July 1987): 85; "Mind Benders," *Money* (September 1978): 24.

42. Moore, "The Case Against Subliminal Manipulation."

43. Joel Saegert, "Why Marketing Should Quit Giving Subliminal Advertising the Benefit of the Doubt," *Psychology & Marketing* 4 (summer 1987): 107–20. See also Dennis L. Rosen and Surendra N. Singh, "An Investigation of Subliminal Embed Effect on Multiple Measures of Advertising Effectiveness," *Psychology & Marketing* 9 (March/April 1992): 157–73. For a more recent review, see Kathryn T. Theus, "Subliminal Advertising and the Psychology of Processing Unconscious Stimuli: A Review of Research," *Psychology & Marketing* (May/June 1994): 271–90.

44. Kim Foltz, *New York Times* (October 23, 1989).

45. Adrienne Ward Fawcett, "Even Ad Pros Hate Ad Clutter," *Advertising Age* (February 8, 1993): 33.

46. "$10 Sure Thing," *Time* (August 4, 1980): 51.

47. David Kilburn, "Japanese VCR Edits Out the Ads," *Advertising Age* (August 20, 1990): 16.

48. Kate Lewin, "Getting Around Commercial Avoidance," *Marketing and Media Decisions* (December 1988): 116.

49. Craig Reiss, "Fast-Forward Ads Deliver," *Advertising Age* (October 27, 1986): 3; Steve Sternberg, "VCRs: Impact and Implications," *Marketing and Media Decisions* 22, 5 (December 1987): 100.

50. Elliot Young, "Overcoming the Zapping Problem in Magazines: New Learning from Eye Tracking

Research" (paper presented at Copy Research Workshop, Advertising Research Federation, New York, May 3, 1988).

51. Quoted in Kim Foltz, "Ads Popping Up All Over," *Newsweek* (August 12, l985): 50.

52. "Traffic Now Tuned to Boston's Tunnel Radio," *New York Times* (August 1, 1982); Alison Fahey, "In the Lobby," *Advertising Age* (September 18, 1989); Kim Foltz, "Ads Popping Up All Over," *Newsweek* (August 12, 1985): 50.

53. Kim Foltz, *New York Times* (October 23, 1989): D11.

54. Bill Carter, "NBC Cancels the Pause Between Shows," *New York Times* (October 3, 1994): D6.

55. Michael Lev, "Music Industry Broadens Its Campaigns," *New York Times* (January 17, 1992): D15.

56. Roger Barton, *Advertising Media* (New York: McGraw-Hill, 1964).

57. Albert H. Hastorf and Hadley Cantril, "They Saw a Game: A Case Study," *Journal of Abnormal and Social Psychology* 49 (1954): 129–34.

58. Roberto Friedmann and Mary R. Zimmer, "The Role of Psychological Meaning in Advertising," *Journal of Advertising* 17, 1 (1988): 31–40.

59. Gail Tom, Teresa Barnett, William Lew, and Jodean Selmants, "Cueing the Consumer: The Role of Salient Cues in Consumer Perception," *Journal of Consumer Marketing* 4, 2 (1987): 23–7.

60. See David Mick, "Consumer Research and Semiotics: Exploring the Morphology of Signs, Symbols, and Significance," *Journal of Consumer Research* 13 (September 1986): 196–213.

61. Teresa J. Domzal and Jerome B. Kernan, "Reading Advertising: The What and How of Product Meaning," *Journal of Consumer Marketing* 9 (summer 1992): 48–64.

62. Arthur Asa Berger, *Signs in Contemporary Culture: An Introduction to Semiotics* (New York: Longman, 1984); Mick, "Consumer Research and Semiotics"; Charles Sanders Peirce, in *Collected Papers,* eds. Charles Hartshorne, Paul Weiss, and Arthur W. Burks (Cambridge, MA: Harvard University Press, 1931–1958).

63. Jean Baudrillard, *Simulations* (New York: Semiotext(e), 1983); A. Fuat Firat and Alladi Venkatesh, "The Making of Postmodern Consumption," in *Consumption and Marketing: Macro Dimensions,* eds. Russell Belk and Nikhilesh Dholakia (Boston: PWS-Kent, 1993); A. Fuat Firat, "The Consumer in Postmodernity," in *Advances in Consumer Research* 18, eds. Rebecca H. Holman and Michael R. Solomon (Provo, UT: Association for Consumer Research, 1991): 70–6.

As soon as Joe saw the ads for Woodstock '94, he knew he had to be there, hype or no hype. What memories that name brought back! When he piled into Ron's psychedelic Volkswagen van in 1969 to head to a concert in upstate New York, little did Joe know that Woodstock would become part of the memories of hundreds of thousands of people and that these memories would be intensively marketed 25 years later! And what memories they were—memories of half a million "love children" rolling in the mud and listening to Jimi Hendrix, Country Joe and the Fish, Richie Havens. . . .

Of course, Woodstock '94 turned out to be quite different. Unlike the original festival, this one featured product sponsorship by Pepsi, ATM machines, and even an official Woodstock '94 condom.[1] And, Joe's memory was sorely tested by some of the bands he heard, including Alice in Chains, Green Day, Nine Inch Nails, and the Spin Doctors. Of course, some things never change. Even in his "old age," Joe still enjoyed moshing in the mud. . . .

3

Learning and Memory

THE LEARNING PROCESS

Joe's memories from a quarter of a century ago still influence him today. The success of Woodstock '94 testifies to the power the original concert still exerts on many middle-aged people—as well as their sons and daughters, who were a primary target market for the second festival. In this chapter, we'll explore how learned associations among feelings, events, and products are important aspects of consumer behavior.

Learning refers to a relatively permanent change in behavior that is caused by experience. This experience does not have to directly affect the learner; we can learn *vicariously* by observing events that affect others.[2] We also learn even when we are not trying. Consumers, for example, recognize many brand names and can hum many product jingles, even those for product categories they themselves do not use. This casual, unintentional acquisition of knowledge is known as *incidental learning*. Like the concept of perception discussed in the last chapter, learning is a process. Our knowledge about the world is constantly being revised as we are exposed to new stimuli and receive ongoing feedback that allows us to modify behavior in other, similar situations. The concept of learning covers a lot of ground, ranging from a consumer's simple association between a stimulus such as a product logo (e.g., Coca-Cola) and a response (e.g., "refreshing soft drink") to a complex series of cognitive activities (e.g., writing an essay on learning for a Consumer Behavior exam). Psychologists who study learning have advanced several theories to explain the learning process. These theories range from those focusing on simple stimulus-response connections to perspectives that regard consumers as complex problem solvers who learn abstract rules and concepts by observing others.

Behavioral Learning Theories

Behavioral learning theories assume that learning takes place as the result of responses to external events. Psychologists who subscribe to this viewpoint do not focus on internal thought processes. Instead, they approach the mind as a "black box" and emphasize the observable aspects of behavior, as depicted in Figure 3–1. The observable aspects consist of things that go into the box (the *stimuli,* or events perceived from the outside world) and things that come out of the box (the *responses,* or reactions to these stimuli).

This view is represented by two major approaches to learning: classical conditioning and instrumental conditioning. People's experiences are shaped by the feedback they receive as they go through life. Similarly, consumers respond to brand names, scents, jingles, and other marketing stimuli based upon the learned connections they have formed over time. People also learn that actions they take result in rewards and punishments, and this feedback influences the way they will respond in similar situations in the future. Consumers who receive compliments on a product choice will be more likely to buy that brand again, while those who get food poisoning at a new restaurant will not be likely to patronize it in the future.

CLASSICAL CONDITIONING

Classical conditioning occurs when a stimulus that elicits a response is paired with another stimulus that initially does not elicit a response on its own. Over time, this second stimulus causes a similar response because it is associated with the first stimulus. This phenomenon was first demonstrated in dogs by Ivan Pavlov, a Russian physiologist doing research on digestion in animals.

Pavlov induced classically conditioned learning by pairing a neutral stimulus (a bell) with a stimulus known to cause a salivation response in dogs (he squirted dried meat powder into their mouths). The powder was an *unconditioned stimulus (UCS)* because it was naturally capable of causing the response. Over time, the bell

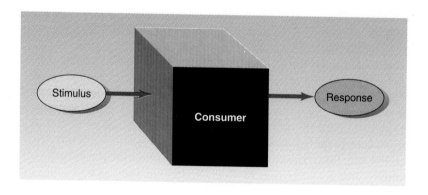

FIGURE 3–1 ▼ The Consumer As a "Black Box": A Behaviorist Perspective on Learning

How strong is the Chiquita name?
How many banana commercials can you sing?

Many classic advertising campaigns consist of product slogans that have been repeated so many times that they are etched in consumers' minds. The ad shown here brags about the high awareness of the Chiquita banana jingle ("I'm Chiquita banana, and I'm here to say. . . ." Used by permission of Chiquita Brands, Inc.

became a *conditioned stimulus (CS);* it did not initially cause salivation, but the dogs learned to associate the bell with the meat powder and began to salivate at the sound of the bell only. The drooling of these canine consumers over a sound, now linked to feeding time, was a *conditioned response (CR)*.

This basic form of classical conditioning demonstrated by Pavlov primarily applies to responses controlled by the autonomic (e.g., salivation) and nervous (e.g., eyeblink) systems. That is, it focuses on visual and olfactory cues that induce hunger, thirst, or sexual arousal. When these cues are consistently paired with conditioned stimuli, such as brand names, consumers may learn to feel hungry, thirsty, or aroused when later exposed to the brand cues.

Classical conditioning can have similar effects for more complex reactions, too. Even a credit card becomes a conditioned cue that triggers greater spending, especially since it is a stimulus that is present only in situations where consumers are spending money. People learn they can make larger purchases when using credit cards, and they also have been found to leave larger tips than they do when using cash.[3] Small wonder that American Express reminds us, "Don't leave home without it."

Conditioning effects are more likely to occur after the conditioned and unconditioned stimuli have been paired a number of times.[4] Repeated exposures increase the strength of stimulus-response associations and prevent the decay of these associations in memory.

Conditioning will not occur or will take longer if the CS is only occasionally presented with the UCS. One result of this lack of association may be **extinction,** which occurs when the effects of prior conditioning are reduced and finally disappear. This can occur, for example, when a product is *overexposed* in the marketplace so that its original allure is lost. The Lacoste polo shirt, with its distinctive crocodile crest, is a good example of this effect. When the once-exclusive crocodile started to appear on baby clothes and many other items, it lost its cachet and was soon replaced by other contenders, such as the Lauren polo player.[5]

Stimulus generalization refers to the tendency of stimuli similar to a CS to evoke similar, conditioned responses.[6] For example, Pavlov noticed in subsequent studies that his dogs would sometimes salivate when they heard noises that only resembled a bell (e.g., keys jangling). People react to other, similar stimuli in much the same way they responded to an original stimulus. A drug store's bottle of private brand mouthwash deliberately packaged to resemble Listerine mouthwash may evoke a similar response among consumers who assume that this "me-too" product shares other characteristics of the original.

Stimulus discrimination occurs when a stimulus similar to a CS is *not* followed by a UCS. In these situations, reactions are weakened and will soon disappear. Part of the learning process involves making a response to some stimuli but not to other, similar stimuli. Manufacturers of well-established brands commonly urge consumers not to buy "cheap imitations" because the results will not be what they expect.

OPERANT CONDITIONING

Operant conditioning, also known as *instrumental conditioning,* occurs as the individual learns to perform behaviors that produce positive outcomes and to avoid those that yield negative outcomes. This learning process is most closely associated with the psychologist B. F. Skinner, who demonstrated the effects of instrumental conditioning by teaching animals to dance, play ping-pong, and so on, by systematically rewarding them for desired behaviors.[7]

While responses in classical conditioning are involuntary and fairly simple, those in instrumental conditioning are made deliberately to obtain a goal and may be more complex. The desired behavior may be learned over a period of time, as intermediate actions are rewarded in a process called *shaping.* For example, the owner of a new store may award prizes to shoppers just for coming in, hoping that over time they will continue to drop in and eventually buy something.

Also, classical conditioning involves the close pairing of two stimuli. Instrumental learning occurs as a result of a reward received *following* the desired behavior and takes place over a period in which a variety of other behaviors are attempted and abandoned because they are not reinforced. A good way to remember the difference is to keep in mind that in instrumental learning, the response is performed because it is *instrumental* to gaining a reward or avoiding a punishment. Consumers over time come to associate with people that reward them and to choose products that make them feel good or satisfy some need.

Operant conditioning (instrumental learning) occurs in one of three ways. When the environment provides **positive reinforcement** in the form of a reward, the response is strengthened, and appropriate behavior is learned. For example, a woman who gets compliments after wearing Obsession perfume will learn that using this product has the desired effect, and she will be more likely to keep buying the product. **Negative reinforcement** also strengthens responses so that appropriate behavior is learned. A perfume company, for example, might run an ad showing a woman sitting home alone on a Saturday night because she did not use its fragrance. The message to be conveyed is that she could have *avoided* this negative outcome if she had only used the perfume. In contrast to situations wherein we learn to do certain things in order to avoid unpleasantness, **punishment** occurs when a response is followed by unpleasant events (such as being ridiculed by friends for wearing an offensive-smelling perfume). We learn not to repeat these behaviors.

When trying to understand the differences among these mechanisms, keep in mind that reactions from a person's environment to behavior can be either positive or negative and that these outcomes or anticipated outcomes can be applied or removed. That is, under conditions of both positive reinforcement and punishment, the person receives a reaction after doing something. In contrast, negative reinforcement occurs when a negative outcome is avoided; the removal of something negative is pleasurable and hence is rewarding. Finally, when a positive outcome is no longer received, extinction is likely to occur, and the learned stimulus-response connection will not be maintained (as when a woman no longer receives compliments on her perfume). Thus, positive and negative reinforcement *strengthen* the future linkage between a response and an outcome because of the pleasant experience. This tie is *weakened* under conditions of both punishment and extinction because of the unpleasant experience. The relationships among these four conditions are easier to understand by referring to Figure 3–2.

An important factor in operant conditioning is the set of rules by which appropriate reinforcements are given for a behavior. The issue of what is the most effective *reinforcement schedule* to use is important to marketers, because it relates to the amount of effort and resources they must devote to rewarding consumers in order to condition desired behaviors.

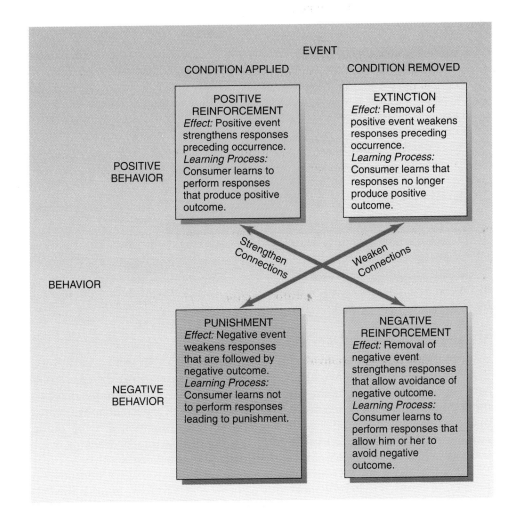

FIGURE 3–2 ▼ Four Types of Learning Outcomes

- *Fixed-interval reinforcement.*   After a specified time period has passed, the first response that is made brings the reward. Under such conditions, people tend to respond slowly right after being reinforced, but their responses speed up as the time for the next reinforcement looms. For example, consumers may crowd into a store for the last day of its seasonal sale and not reappear again until the next one.

- *Variable-interval reinforcement.*   The time that must pass before reinforcement is delivered varies around some average. Since the person does not know exactly when to expect the reinforcement, responses must be performed at a consistent rate. This logic is behind retailers' use of so-called secret shoppers—people who periodically test for service quality by posing as customers at unannounced times. Since store employees never know exactly when to expect a visit, high quality must be constantly maintained.

- *Fixed-ratio reinforcement.*   Reinforcement occurs only after a fixed number of responses. This schedule motivates people to continue performing the same behavior over and over. For example, a consumer might keep buying groceries at the same store in order to earn a prize after collecting 50 books of trading stamps.

- *Variable-ratio reinforcement.*   The person is reinforced after a certain number of responses, but he or she does not know how many responses are required. People in such situations tend to respond at very high and steady rates, and this type of behavior is very difficult to extinguish. This reinforcement schedule is responsible for consumers' attraction to slot machines. They learn that if they keep throwing money into the machine, they will eventually win something (if they don't go broke first).

Cognitive Learning Theory

Cognitive learning occurs as a result of mental processes. In contrast to behavioral theories of learning, cognitive learning theory stresses the importance of internal mental processes. This perspective views people as problem solvers who actively use information from the world around them to master their environment. Supporters of this viewpoint also stress the role of creativity and insight during the learning process.

THE ISSUE OF CONSCIOUSNESS

A lot of controversy surrounds the issue of whether or when people are aware of their learning processes. While behavioral learning theorists emphasize the routine, automatic nature of conditioning, proponents of cognitive learning argue that even these simple effects are based on cognitive factors; that is, expectations are created that a stimulus will be followed by a response (the formation of expectations requires mental activity). According to this school of thought, conditioning occurs because subjects develop conscious hypotheses and then act on them.

On the one hand, there is some evidence for the existence of nonconscious procedural knowledge. People apparently do process at least some information in an automatic, passive way, which is a condition that has been termed *mindlessness.*[8] When we meet someone new or encounter a new product, for example, we have a tendency to respond to the stimulus in terms of existing categories, rather than taking the trouble to formulate different ones. Our reactions are activated by a *trigger feature*, some stimulus that cues us toward a particular pattern. For example, men in one study rated a car in an ad as superior on a variety of characteristics if a seductive woman (the trigger feature) was present, despite the fact that the men did not believe the woman's presence actually had an influence.[9]

Nonetheless, many modern theorists are beginning to regard some instances of conditioning as cognitive processes, especially where expectations are formed about the linkages between stimuli and responses. Indeed, studies using *masking effects*, wherein it is difficult for subjects to learn CS/UCS associations, show substantial reductions in conditioning.[10] For example, an adolescent girl may observe that women on television and in real life seem to be rewarded with compliments and attention when they smell nice and wear alluring clothing. She figures out that the probability of these rewards occurring is greater when she wears perfume and deliberately wears a popular scent to obtain the payoff of social acceptance.

OBSERVATIONAL LEARNING

Observational learning occurs when people watch the actions of others and note the reinforcements they receive for their behaviors. This type of learning is a complex process; people store these observations in memory as they accumulate knowledge, perhaps using this information at a later point to guide their own behaviors. This process of imitating the behavior of others is called *modeling*. For example, a woman shopping for a new kind of perfume may remember the reactions a friend received upon wearing a certain brand several months earlier, and she will base her behavior on her friend's actions.

In order for observational learning in the form of modeling to occur, four conditions must be met.[11] These factors are summarized in Figure 3–3.

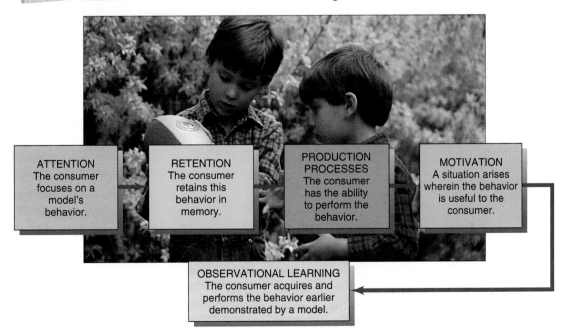

ATTENTION
The consumer focuses on a model's behavior.

RETENTION
The consumer retains this behavior in memory.

PRODUCTION PROCESSES
The consumer has the ability to perform the behavior.

MOTIVATION
A situation arises wherein the behavior is useful to the consumer.

OBSERVATIONAL LEARNING
The consumer acquires and performs the behavior earlier demonstrated by a model.

FIGURE 3–3 ▼ Components of Observational Learning
Photo courtesy of Richard Heinzen/Superstock.

1. The consumer's attention must be directed to the appropriate model who, for reasons of attractiveness, competence, status, or similarity, is desirable to emulate.
2. The consumer must remember what is said or done by the model.
3. The consumer must convert this information into actions.
4. The consumer must be motivated to perform these actions.

MARKETING APPLICATIONS OF LEARNING PRINCIPLES

Understanding how consumers learn is very important to marketers. After all, many strategic decisions are based on the assumption that consumers are continually accumulating information about products and that people can be "taught" to prefer some alternatives over others.

Behavioral Learning Applications

Many marketing strategies focus on the establishment of associations between stimuli and responses. Behavioral learning principles apply to many consumer phenomena, ranging from the creation of a distinctive brand image to the perceived linkage between a product and an underlying need.

HOW MARKETERS TAKE ADVANTAGE OF CLASSICAL CONDITIONING PRINCIPLES

The transfer of meaning from an unconditioned stimulus to a conditioned stimulus explains why "made-up" brand names like Marlboro, Coca-Cola, or IBM can exert such powerful effects on consumers. The association between the Marlboro Man and the cigarette is so strong that in some cases the company no longer even includes the brand name in its ad. When nonsense syllables (meaningless sets of letters) are paired with such evaluative words as beauty or success, the meaning is transferred to the nonsense syllables. This change in the symbolic significance of initially meaningless words shows that complex meanings can be conditioned.[12]

These conditioned associations are crucial to many marketing strategies that rely on the creation and perpetuation of positive **brand equity,** in which a brand has strong positive associations in a consumer's memory and commands a lot of loyalty as a result.[13] As we will see in the next chapter, a product with brand equity holds a tremendous advantage in the marketplace.

Repetition.   One advertising researcher argues that more than three exposures are wasted. The first creates awareness of the product, the second demonstrates its relevance to the consumer, and the third serves as a reminder of the product's benefits.[14] However, even this bare-bones approach implies that repetition is needed to ensure that the consumer is actually exposed to (and processes) the ad at least three times. Marketers attempting to condition an association must ensure that the consumers they have targeted will be exposed to the stimulus a sufficient number of times.

On the other hand, it is possible to have too much of a good thing. Consumers can become so used to hearing or seeing a marketing stimulus that they no longer pay attention to it (see Chapter 2). This problem, known as *advertising wearout,* can

Les histoires de Mario.

Le poisson de Provigo.

One innovative way to employ repetition without causing wearout is illustrated by these related billboard images. Courtesy of Cossette Communications Marketing for Provigo Supermarkers, 1986.

be alleviated by varying the way in which the basic message is presented. For example, the tax-preparation firm of H&R Block is famous for its long-standing "Another of the seventeen reasons to use H&R Block. . . ." campaign.

Conditioning Product Associations.   Advertisements often pair a product with a positive stimulus to create a desirable association. Various aspects of a marketing message, such as music, humor, or imagery, can affect conditioning. In one study, for example, subjects who viewed a slide of pens paired with either pleasant or unpleasant music were more likely to later select the pen that appeared with pleasant music.[15]

The order in which the conditioned stimulus and the unconditioned stimulus is presented can affect the likelihood that learning will occur. Generally speaking, the unconditioned stimulus should be presented prior to the conditioned stimulus. The technique of *backward conditioning,* such as showing a soft drink (the CS) and then playing a jingle (the UCS) is generally not effective.[16] Because sequential presentation is desirable for conditioning to occur, classical conditioning is not very effective in static situations, such as in magazine ads, where (in contrast to TV or radio) the marketer cannot control the order in which the CS and the UCS are perceived.

Just as product associations can be formed, they can be *extinguished.* Because of the danger of extinction, a classical conditioning strategy may not be as effective for products that are frequently encountered, since there is no guarantee they will be accompanied by the CS. A bottle of Pepsi paired with the refreshing sound of a carbonated beverage being poured over ice may seem like a good example of conditioning. Unfortunately, the product would also be seen in many other contexts where this sound was absent, reducing the effectiveness of the conditioning.

By the same reasoning, a novel tune should be chosen over a popular one to pair with a product, since the popular song might also be heard in many situations in which the product is not present.[17] Music videos in particular may serve as effective UCSs because they often have an emotional impact on viewers and this effect may transfer to ads accompanying the video.[18]

This trade ad for King Features promotes the characters from the Blondie comic strip to potential licensers for use in their own advertising, with the expectation that positive attitudes toward these characters will be generalized to their products.
© 1986 by King Features Syndicate, Inc.

Applications of Stimulus Generalization. The process of stimulus generalization is often central to branding and packaging decisions that attempt to capitalize on consumers' positive associations with an existing brand or company name, as exemplified by a haircutting establishment called United Hairlines.[19] In one 20-month period, Procter & Gamble introduced almost 90 new products. Not a single product carried a new brand name. In fact, roughly 80 percent of all new products are actually extensions of existing brands or product lines.[20] Strategies based on stimulus generalization include the following:

MARKETING OPPORTUNITY

The marketing value of an admired stimulus is clearly demonstrated at universities with winning sports teams, where loyal fans snap up merchandise from underwear to toilet seats emblazoned with the school's name—about $2.5 billion a year of college merchandise. This business did not even exist 15 years ago, when schools were reluctant to commercialize their images. Texas A&M was one of the first schools that even bothered to file for trademark protection, and that was only after someone put the Aggie logo on a line of handguns.

Today, it's a different story. Even little-known schools have become merchandising powerhouses, largely due to television exposure of their teams. It hasn't hurt that athletic gear has become part of the fashion landscape and many people buy team-related merchandise to make a fashion rather than an athletic statement. In fact, the University of Michigan's "Fab Five" basketball players had a lot to do with turning long, baggy shorts into a chic item. All of the fuss about sweatshirts, drink coasters, and trash cans is welcomed by many college administrators—welcomed because universities earn about $100 million per year in royalties.[21]

● *Family branding,* in which a variety of products capitalize on the reputation of a company name. Companies such as Campbell's, Heinz, and General Electric rely on their positive corporate images to sell different product lines.

● *Product line extensions,* in which related products are added to an established brand. Dole, which is associated with fruit, was able to introduce refrigerated juices and juice bars, while Sun Maid went from raisins to raisin bread. Other recent extensions include Woolite rug cleaner, Cracker Jack gourmet popping corn, and Ivory shampoo.[22]

● *Licensing,* in which well-known names are "rented" by others. This strategy is increasing in popularity as marketers try to link their products and services with well-established figures. Companies as diverse as McDonald's and Harley-Davidson have authorized the use of their names on products. Even Spam™ lovers can buy underwear, earrings, and other items bearing the logo of the canned "meat product"![23] Japan Airlines recently licensed the rights to use Disney characters, and, in addition to painting Mickey Mouse and Donald Duck on several of its planes, the carrier is requiring its flight attendants to wear mouse ears on some domestic flights![24]

● Marketers increasingly are capitalizing on the public's enthusiasm for movies by developing numerous product tie-ins with blockbusters. Table 3–1 provides some examples of major motion pictures of the recent past and the tie-ins they have spawned. The movie *Jurassic Park* alone generated $1 billion in licensed merchandise sales, with about 5,000 products crawling out of the primordial ooze and onto store shelves.[25]

TABLE 3-1 ▼ Movie Tie-Ins

MOVIE	NUMBER OF PRODUCTS	NOTABLE ITEMS
Aladdin	More than 100	Cave of Wonders Play Set
		Genie boxer shorts
		Children's slippers with curled-up toes
		Burger King "magic" cups (in which a genie appears when a beverage is poured in)
Bram Stoker's Dracula	About 100	$1,500 bustier by special order from Macy's Red lace underpants with rosebud appliqué
		Bat, bug, and spider brooches ($500)
		Coffin lipstick holder with Vampire Red lipstick
Home Alone 2: Lost in New York	65–70	"Home Alone 2" backpack with screaming burglar alarm
		Monster Sap Soap
		The Home Alone Survival Guide (safety tips for children)
Malcolm X	More than 100	"X" caps, T-shirts
		Malcolm X figurine with podium
		Automobile air fresheners

Source: Pat H. Broeske, "See the Movie, Buy the Automobile Air Freshener," *New York Times* (December 6, 1992): H12. Copyright © 1992, The New York Times Company. Reprinted by permission.

The fire that briefly raged for the Flintstones *characters was fanned by one of the more intensive merchandising campaigns in recent memory. About 1,000 products hit the market when the movie was released in May of 1994. These items included a Talking Fred doll from Mattel, Flintstones children's cosmetics, and Licking Dino cookies. The same marketers who were responsible for the phenomenal success of* Jurassic Park *masterminded the* Flintstones *strategy. Previous licensing winners include* Superman, Batman, *and* Teenage Mutant Ninja Turtles, *which together sold more than $7.3 billion of tie-in products. Some duds in the licensing graveyard include characters based on* Popeye, The Jetsons, *and* The Addams Family. (Anthony Ramirez, "Gold in Bedrock?" New York Times [May 22, 1994]: 9–10 [2 pp.]; Glenn Heitsmith, "Licensing a Piece of the Bedrock," PROMO [June 1994]: 33 [6 pp.].) Photo courtesy of Yvonne Hemsey/Gamma-Liason, Inc.*

● *Look-alike packaging,* in which distinctive packaging designs create strong associations with a particular brand. This linkage often is exploited by makers of generic or private-label brands who wish to communicate a quality image by putting their products in very similar packages. As one drugstore executive commented, "You want to tell the consumer that it's close to the national brand. . . . You've got to make it look like, within the law, close to the national brand. They're at least attracted to the package."[26]

Applications of Stimulus Discrimination.   An emphasis on communicating a product's distinctive attributes vis-à-vis its competitors is an important aspect of positioning, in which consumers learn to differentiate a brand from its competitors (see Chapter 2). This is not always an easy task, especially in product categories where the brand names of many of the alternatives look and sound alike. For example, a recent survey showed that many consumers have a great deal of trouble distinguishing among products sold by the top computer manufacturers. With a blur of names like OmniPlex, OptiPlex, Premmia, Premium, ProLinea, ProLiant, etc., this confusion is not surprising.[30]

Companies with a well-established brand image try to encourage stimulus discrimination by promoting the unique attributes of their brands. Thus, the constant reminders for American Express® Travelers Cheques: "Ask for them by name. . . ." On the other hand, a brand name that is used so widely that it is no longer distinc-

ᴍARKETING PITFALL

For a stimulus-response connection to be maintained, a new product must share some important characteristics with the original. Trouble can result if consumers do not make the connection between a brand and its extension. In fact, if attributes of the new products are inconsistent with the consumer's beliefs about the family brand, the overall image of the family brand runs the danger of being diluted.[27]

When Cadillac came out with the smaller Cadillac Cimarron, people who already owned Cadillacs did not regard the new model as a bona fide Cadillac. Arm & Hammer deodorant failed, possibly because consumers identified the product too strongly with something in the back of their refrigerators.[28] An extension even has the potential to weaken the parent brand, as the Carnation Company discovered. The company canceled plans for "Lady Friskies," a contraceptive dog food, after tests indicated it would reduce sales of regular Friskies.[29]

tive becomes part of the *public domain* and can be used by competitors, as has been the case for such products as aspirin, cellophane, yo-yo, and escalator.

HOW MARKETERS TAKE ADVANTAGE OF INSTRUMENTAL CONDITIONING PRINCIPLES

Principles of instrumental conditioning are at work when a consumer is rewarded or punished for a purchase decision. Businesspeople shape behavior by gradually reinforcing consumers for taking appropriate actions. For example, a car dealer might encourage a reluctant buyer to just sit in a floor model, then suggest a test drive, and so on.

Marketers have many ways to reinforce consumers, ranging from a simple thank you after a purchase to substantial rebates and follow-up phone calls. For example, a life insurance company obtained a much higher rate of policy renewal among a group of new customers who received a thank you letter after each payment compared to a control group that did not receive any reinforcement.[31]

A popular technique known as **frequency marketing** reinforces regular purchasers by giving them prizes with values that increase along with the amount purchased. This operant learning strategy was pioneered by the airline industry, which introduced "frequent-flyer" programs in the early 1980s to reward loyal customers. Well over 20 percent of food stores, for example, now offer trading stamps or some other frequent-buyer promotion.

In some industries, these reinforcers take the form of clubs, including a Luv's Baby Club, a Virginia Slims Club, and a Hilton Hotel Club. Club members usually earn bonus points to apply toward future purchases, and some get such privileges as magazines and toll-free numbers and sometimes even invitations to exclusive outings. The George Dickel Tennessee Whiskey Water Conservation Society takes the concept a step further. Members pay $4.95 to own a Duel Kit, which allows them to challenge other whiskey drinkers to a taste test. This kit contains two shot glasses, a blindfold, napkins, and a score card.[32]

How Marketers Take Advantage of Cognitive Learning Principles

Consumers' ability to learn vicariously by observing how the behavior of others is reinforced makes the lives of marketers much easier. Because people do not have to be directly reinforced for their actions, marketers do not necessarily have to reward or punish them for purchase behaviors. Instead, they can show what happens to desirable models who use or do not use their products and know that consumers will often be motivated to imitate these actions at a later time. For example, a perfume commercial may depict a woman surrounded by a throng of admirers who are providing her with positive reinforcement for using the product. Needless to say, this learning process is more practical than providing the same personal attention to each woman who actually buys the perfume!

Consumers' evaluations of models go beyond simple stimulus-response connections. For example, a celebrity's image is often more than a simple reflexive response of good or bad.[33] It is a complex combination of many attributes. In general, the degree to which a model will be emulated depends upon his or her social attractiveness. Attractiveness can be based upon several components, including physical appearance, expertise, or similarity to the evaluator.

These factors will be further addressed in Chapter 6, which discusses personal characteristics that make a communication's source more or less effective in changing consumers' attitudes. In addition, many applications of consumer problem solving are related to ways information is represented in memory and recalled at a later date. This aspect of cognitive learning is the focus of the next section.

This cosmetics ad illustrates the principle of vicarious reinforcement. The model uses the product and is shown reaping the reward—the approval of her boyfriend. Courtesy of Maybelline, Inc.

MARKETING PITFALL

The modeling process is a powerful form of learning, and people's tendencies to imitate others' behaviors can have negative effects. Of particular concern is the potential of television shows and movies to teach violence to children. Children may be exposed to new methods of aggression by models (e.g., cartoon heroes) in the shows they watch. At some later point, when the child becomes angry, these behaviors will be available for actual use. A classic study demonstrates the effect of modeling on children's actions. Kids who watched an adult stomp on, knock down, and otherwise torture a large, inflated "Bobo doll" repeated these behaviors when later left alone in a room with the doll, in contrast to the behaviors of other children who did not witness these acts.[34] The parallel to violent programming is, unfortunately, clear.

THE ROLE OF MEMORY IN LEARNING

Memory involves a process of acquiring information and storing it over time so that it will be available when needed. Contemporary approaches to the study of memory employ an information-processing approach. They assume that the mind is in some ways like a computer; data are input, processed, and output for later use in revised form. In the **encoding** stage, information is entered in a way the system will recognize. In the **storage** stage, this knowledge is integrated with what is already in memory and "warehoused" until needed. During **retrieval,** the person accesses the desired information.[35] The memory process is summarized in Figure 3–4.

WEAR PACO AND BE REMEMBERED.
WHAT IS REMEMBERED IS UP TO YOU.

EAU DE TOILETTE

paco rabanne

This fragrance ad emphasizes that products can evoke memories of earlier experiences. Courtesy of COMPAR.

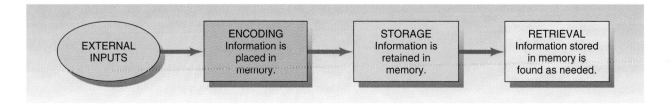

FIGURE 3–4 ▼
The Memory Process

As suggested by Joe's experience at the beginning of the chapter, many of our experiences are locked inside our heads, and they may surface years later if prompted by the right cues. Marketers rely on consumers to retain information they have learned about products and services, trusting that it will later be applied in situations where purchase decisions must be made. During the consumer decision-making process, this *internal memory* is combined with *external memory*—which includes all of the product details on packages, in shopping lists, and through other marketing stimuli—to permit brand alternatives to be identified and evaluated.[36]

Encoding of Information for Later Retrieval

The way information is *encoded,* or mentally programmed, helps to determine how it will be represented in memory. In general, incoming data that are associated with other information already in memory stand a better chance of being retained. For example, brand names that are linked to physical characteristics of a product category (e.g., Coffee Mate creamer or Sani-Flush toilet bowl cleaner) or that are easy to visualize (e.g., Tide detergent or Mercury Cougar cars) tend to be more easily retained in memory than more abstract brand names.[37]

TYPES OF MEMORY

A consumer may process a stimulus simply in terms of its *sensory meaning,* such as its color or shape. When this occurs, the meaning may be activated when the person sees a picture of the stimulus. We may experience a sense of familiarity upon seeing an ad for a new snack food we recently tasted, for example.

In many cases, though, meanings are encoded at a more abstract level. *Semantic meaning* refers to symbolic associations, such as the idea that rich people drink champagne or that fashionable men wear an earring.

Episodic memories are those that relate to events that are personally relevant, such as Joe's experiences at Woodstock.[38] As a result, a person's motivation to retain these memories will likely be strong. Couples often have "their song" that reminds them of their first date or wedding. The memories that might be triggered upon hearing this song would be quite different and unique for them.

Commercials sometimes attempt to activate episodic memories by focusing on experiences shared by many people (e.g., Woodstock—either the 1969 or the 1994 version). Recall of the past may have an effect on future behavior. For example, a college fund-raising campaign can get higher donations by evoking pleasant college memories. Some especially vivid associations are called *flashbulb memories.* These are usually related to some highly significant event. As one example, many people claim to remember exactly what they were doing when President Kennedy was assassinated in the early 1960s.

MEMORY SYSTEMS

According to the information-processing perspective, there are three distinct memory systems: sensory memory, short-term memory (STM), and long-term memory (LTM). Each plays a role in processing brand-related information. The interrelationships of these memory systems are summarized in Figure 3–5.

Sensory memory permits storage of the information we receive from our senses. This storage is very temporary; it lasts a couple of seconds at most. For example, a person might be walking past a donut shop and get a quick, enticing whiff of something baking inside. While this sensation would only last for a few seconds, it would be sufficient to allow the person to determine if he or she should investigate further. If the information is retained for further processing, it passes through an *attentional gate* and is transferred to short-term memory.

Short-term memory also stores information for a limited period of time, and its capacity is limited. Similar to a computer, this system can be regarded as *working memory;* it holds the information we are currently processing. Verbal input may be stored *acoustically* (in terms of how it sounds) or *semantically* (in terms of its meaning).[39]

The information is stored by combining small pieces into larger ones in a process known as "*chunking.*" A chunk is a configuration that is familiar to the person and can be manipulated as a unit. For example, a brand name can be a chunk that summarizes a great deal of detailed information about the brand.

Initially, it was believed that STM was capable of processing between five and nine chunks of information at a time, and for this reason phone numbers were designed to have seven digits.[40] It now appears that three to four chunks is the

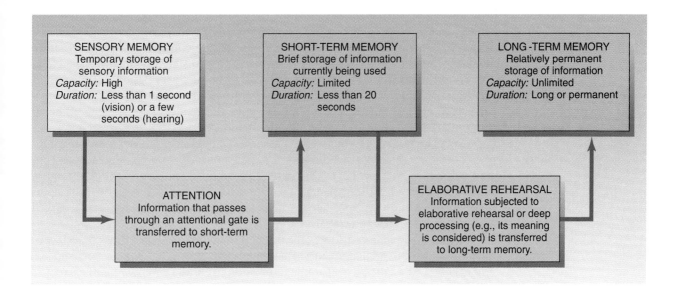

FIGURE 3–5 ▼ **Relationships Among Memory Systems**

optimum size for efficient retrieval (seven-digit phone numbers can be remembered because the individual digits are chunked, so we may remember a three-digit exchange as one piece of information).[41]

Long-term memory is the system that allows us to retain information for a long period of time. In order for information to enter into long-term memory from short-term memory, *elaborative rehearsal* is required. This process involves thinking about the meaning of a stimulus and relating it to other information already in memory. Marketers sometimes assist in the process by devising catchy slogans or jingles that consumers repeat on their own.

Storing of Information in Memory

Relationships among the types of memory are a source of some controversy. The traditional perspective, known as *multiple-store,* assumes that STM and LTM are separate systems. More recent research has moved away from the distinction between the two types of memory, instead emphasizing the interdependence of the systems. This work argues that depending upon the nature of the processing task, different levels of processing occur that activate some aspects of memory rather than others. These approaches are called **activation models of memory.**[42] The more effort it takes to process information (so-called deep processing), the more likely it is that information will be placed in long-term memory.

Activation models propose that an incoming piece of information is stored in an *associative network* containing many bits of related information organized according to some set of relationships. The consumer has organized systems of concepts relating to brands, stores, and so on.

KNOWLEDGE STRUCTURES

These storage units, known as **knowledge structures,** can be thought of as complex spider webs filled with pieces of data. This information is placed into *nodes,* which are connected by *associative links* within these structures. Pieces of information that are seen as similar in some way are chunked together under some more abstract category. New, incoming information is interpreted to be consistent with the structure already in place.[43] According to the *hierarchical processing model,* a message is processed in a bottom-up fashion: Processing begins at a very basic level and is subject to increasingly complex processing operations that require greater cognitive capacity. If processing at one level fails to evoke the next level, processing of the ad is terminated, and capacity is allocated to other tasks.[44]

Links form between nodes as an associative network is developed. For example, a consumer might have a network for "perfumes." Each node represents a concept related to the category. This node can be an attribute, a specific brand, a celebrity identified with a perfume, or even a related product. A network for perfumes might include concepts like the names Chanel, Obsession, and Charlie, as well as attributes like sexy and elegant.

When asked to list perfumes, the consumer would recall only those brands contained in the appropriate category. This group constitutes that person's **evoked set**. The task of a new entrant that wants to position itself as a category member (e.g., a new luxury perfume) is to provide cues that facilitate its placement in the appropriate category. A sample network for perfumes is shown in Figure 3–6.

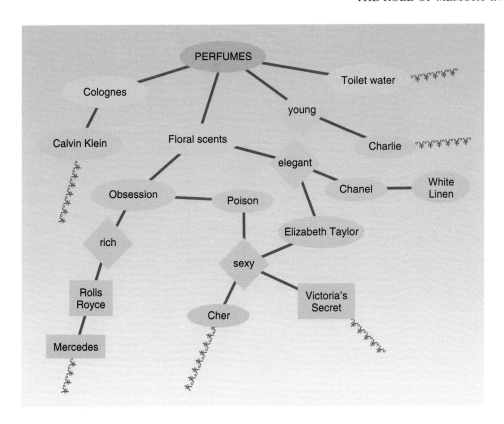

FIGURE 3–6 ▼ An Associative Network for Perfumes

SPREADING ACTIVATION

A meaning can be activated indirectly; energy spreads across nodes of varying levels of abstraction. As one node is activated, other nodes associated with it also begin to be triggered. Meaning thus spreads across the network, bringing up concepts including competing brands and relevant attributes that are used to form attitudes toward the brand.

This process of *spreading activation* allows consumers to shift back and forth between levels of meaning. The way a piece of information is stored in memory depends upon the type of meaning assigned to it. This meaning type will, in turn, determine how and when the meaning is activated. For example, the *memory trace* for an ad could be stored in one or more of the following ways:

- Brand-specific—in terms of claims made for the brand
- Ad-specific—in terms of the medium or content of the ad itself
- Brand identification—in terms of the brand name
- Product category—in terms of how the product works, where it should be used, or experiences with the product
- Evaluative reactions—in terms of whether "that looks like fun"[45]

LEVELS OF KNOWLEDGE

Knowledge is coded at different levels of abstraction and complexity. *Meaning concepts* are individual nodes (e.g., elegant). These may be combined into a larger unit, called a *proposition* (also known as a *belief*). A proposition links two nodes together to form a more complex meaning, which can serve as a single chunk of information. For example, a proposition might be that "Chanel is a perfume for elegant women."

Propositions are, in turn, integrated to produce a complex unit known as a schema. As was noted at the beginning of the chapter, a **schema** is a cognitive framework that is developed through experience. Information that is consistent with an existing schema is encoded more readily.[46] The ability to move up and down among levels of abstraction greatly increases processing flexibility and efficiency. For this reason, young children, who do not yet have well-developed schemas, are not able to make efficient use of purchase information compared to older children.[47]

One type of schema that is relevant to consumer behavior is a *script*, a sequence of procedures that is expected by an individual. For example, consumers learn service scripts that guide expectations and purchasing behavior in business settings. Consumers learn to expect a certain sequence of events, and they may become uncomfortable if the service departs from the script. A service script for your visit to the dentist might include such events as (1) driving to the dentist, (2) reading old magazines in the waiting room, (3) hearing your name called and sitting in the dentist's chair, (4) having the dentist put a funny substance on your teeth, (5) having the dentist clean your teeth, and so on. This desire to follow a script helps to explain why such service innovations as automatic bank machines and self-service gas stations have met with resistance by some consumers, who have trouble adapting to a new sequence of events.[48]

Retrieving of Information for Purchase Decisions

Retrieval is the process whereby information is accessed from long-term memory. As evidenced by the popularity of the game Trivial Pursuit, people have a vast quantity of information stored in their heads that is not necessarily available on demand. Although most of the information entered in long-term memory does not go away, it may be difficult or impossible to retrieve unless the appropriate cues are present.

FACTORS INFLUENCING RETRIEVAL

Some differences in retrieval ability are physiological. Older adults consistently display inferior recall ability for current items, such as prescription information, though events that happened to them when they were younger may be recalled with great clarity.[49]

Other factors are situational, relating to the environment in which the message is delivered. Not surprisingly, recall is enhanced when the consumer pays more attention to the message in the first place. Some evidence indicates that information about a *pioneering brand* (the first brand to enter a market) is more easily retrieved from memory than follower brands because the product's introduction is likely to be distinctive and, for the time being, no competitors divert the consumer's attention.[50] In addition, descriptive brand names are more likely to be recalled than are those that do not provide adequate cues as to what the product is.[51]

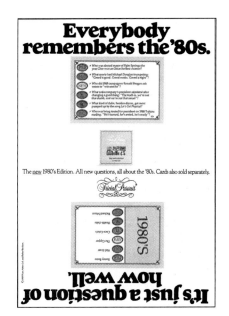

Trivial Pursuit, a popular board game, tests consumers' memories of cultural happenings. TRIVIAL PURSUIT® is a registered trademark of Horn Abbot Ltd., under exclusive license to Parker Brothers and used with permission.

The viewing environment of a marketing message also can affect recall. For example, commercials shown during baseball games yield the lowest recall scores among sports programs because the activity is stop-and-go rather than continuous. Unlike football or basketball, the pacing of baseball gives many opportunities for attention to wander even during play. Similarly, General Electric found that its commercials fare better in television shows with continuous activity, such as stories or dramas, compared to variety shows or talk shows that are punctuated by a series of acts.[52]

State-Dependent Retrieval. In a process termed *state-dependent retrieval,* people are better able to access information if their internal state is the same at the time of recall as it was when the information was learned.

This phenomenon, called the *mood congruence effect,* underscores the desirability of matching a consumer's mood at the time of purchase when planning exposure to marketing communications. A consumer is more likely to recall an ad, for example, if his or her mood or level of arousal at the time of exposure is similar to that in the purchase environment. By recreating the cues that were present when the information was first presented, recall can be enhanced. For example, Life cereal uses a picture of "Mikey" from its commercial on the cereal box itself, which facilitates recall of brand claims and favorable brand evaluations.[53]

Familiarity and Recall. As a general rule, prior familiarity with an item enhances its recall. Indeed, this is one of the basic goals of marketers who are trying to create and maintain awareness of their products. The more experience a consumer has with a product, the better use that person is able to make of product information.[54]

However, there is a possible fly in the ointment: As noted earlier in the chapter, some evidence indicates that extreme familiarity can result in inferior learning and/or recall. When consumers are highly familiar with a brand or an advertisement, they may attend to fewer attributes because they do not believe that any additional effort will yield a gain in knowledge.[55] For example, when consumers are exposed to the technique of *radio replay,* where the audio track from a television ad is replayed on the radio, they do very little critical, evaluative processing and instead mentally replay the video portion of the ad.[56]

Salience and Recall.   The salience of a brand refers to its prominence or level of activation in memory. As noted in Chapter 2, stimuli that stand out in contrast to their environment are more likely to command attention, which, in turn, increases the likelihood they will be recalled. Almost any technique that increases the novelty of a stimulus also improves recall (a result known as the *von Restorff Effect*).[57] This effect explains why unusual advertising or distinctive packaging tends to facilitate brand recall.[58]

As we saw in Chapter 2, introducing a surprise element in an ad (e.g., the Energizer Bunny™ who unexpectedly marches through a commercial) can be particularly effective. This strategy aids recall even if the stimulus is not relevant to the factual information being presented.[59] In addition, so-called *mystery ads,* where the brand is not identified until the end of the ad, are more effective at building associations in memory between the product category and that brand—especially in the case of novel brands.[60]

Pictorial Versus Verbal Cues.   There is some evidence for the superiority of visual memory over verbal memory, but this advantage is unclear because it is more difficult to measure recall of pictures.[61] However, the available data indicate that information presented in picture form is more likely to be recognized later.[62] Certainly, visual aspects of an ad are more likely to grab a consumer's attention. In fact, eye-movement studies indicate that about 90 percent of viewers look at the dominant picture in an ad before they bother to view the copy.[63]

While pictorial ads may enhance recall, however, they do not necessarily improve comprehension. One study found that television news items presented with illustrations (still pictures) as a backdrop result in improved recall for details of the news story, even though understanding of the story's content does not improve.[64] Visual imagery can be especially effective when it includes verbal cues that relate to

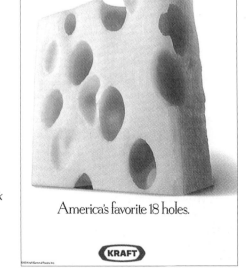

This Kraft cheese ad uses a play on words to link the product to consumers' preexisting knowledge, increasing the chances that brand information will be stored in memory. Kraft® is a registered trademark of Kraft General Foods, Inc. Used with permission.

4

Motivation, Values, and Involvement

·····························   ·

INTRODUCTION

Some people are so involved in an activity that they can be termed *fanatic consumers*. Whether they are training for a triathlon, watching television, or playing music, these people tend to become totally engrossed in an activity to the point where such involvement has been called a "positive addiction." One survey of triathletes (like Basil), for example, found that intense commitment to the sport resulted in a highly modified daily schedule, unwillingness to stop training even if injured, major dietary changes, and—most relevant to marketers—a substantial financial commitment for travel to races, specialized clothing, and health club memberships.[1]

The forces that drive people to buy and use products are generally straightforward, as when a person purchases a pair of running shoes for everyday wear. As hard-core triathletes demonstrate, however, even the consumption of an everyday product like running shoes may also be related to deep-seated experiences. In some cases, these emotional responses create a deep commitment to the product. Sometimes, people are not even fully aware of the forces that drive them toward some products and away from others.

To understand motivation is to understand *why* consumers do what they do. Why do people choose to bungee-jump off a bridge or go white-water rafting in the Yukon, while others spend their leisure time playing chess or gardening? We do everything for a reason, whether to quench a thirst, to kill boredom, or to attain some deep spiritual experience. Marketing students are taught from day one that the goal of marketing is to satisfy consumers' needs. However, this insight is useless unless we can discover *what* those needs are and *why* they exist. A popular beer commercial asks the question, "Why ask why?" In this chapter, we'll find out.

THE MOTIVATION PROCESS

Motivation refers to the processes that cause people to behave as they do. It occurs when a need is aroused that the consumer wishes to satisfy. Once a need has been activated, a state of tension exists that drives the consumer to attempt to reduce or eliminate the need. Marketers try to create products and services that will provide the desired benefits and permit the consumer to reduce this tension.

Figure 4–1 gives an overview of the motivation process. The sections to follow will elaborate on the components in this model, but in general the process works this way: A need is recognized by the consumer. This need may be utilitarian (i.e., a desire to achieve some functional or practical benefit, as when a person requires a pair of durable sneakers), or it may be hedonic (i.e., an experiential need, involving emotional responses or fantasies, as when Basil buys special running shoes for a triathlon event). The desired end state is the consumer's **goal.**

In either case, a discrepancy exists between the consumer's present state and some ideal state. This gulf creates a state of tension. The magnitude of this tension determines the urgency the consumer feels to reduce the tension. This degree of arousal is called a **drive.** A basic need can be satisfied any number of ways, and the specific path a person chooses is influenced by his or her unique set of experiences, cultural upbringing, and so on.

These factors combine to create a **want,** which is one manifestation of a need. For example, hunger is a basic need that must be satisfied by all; the lack of food creates a tension state that can be reduced by the intake of such products as cheeseburgers, double-fudge Oreo cookies, raw fish, or bean sprouts. The specific route to hunger reduction is culturally determined.

Once the goal is attained, tension is reduced, and the motivation recedes (for the time being). Motivation can be described in terms of its strength, or the pull it exerts on the consumer, and its direction, or the particular way the consumer attempts to reduce motivational tension.

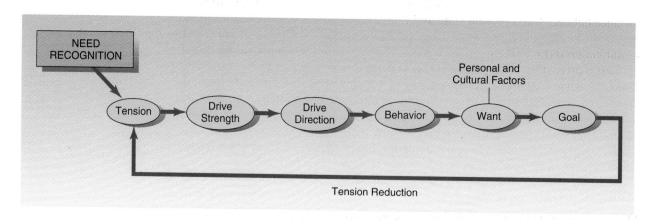

FIGURE 4–1 ▼ An Overview of the Motivation Process

MOTIVATIONAL STRENGTH

The degree to which a person is willing to expend energy to reach one goal as opposed to another reflects his or her underlying motivation to attain that goal. Many theories have been advanced to explain why people behave the way they do. Most share the basic idea that people have some finite amount of energy that must be directed toward certain goals.

Early work on motivation ascribed behavior to instinct, the innate patterns of behavior that are universal in a species. This view is now largely discredited. For one thing, the existence of an instinct is difficult to prove or disprove. The instinct is inferred from the behavior it is supposed to explain (this type of circular explanation is called a *tautology*).[2] It is like saying that a consumer buys products that are status symbols because he or she is motivated to attain status, which is hardly a satisfying explanation.

Drive Theory

Drive theory focuses on biological needs that produce unpleasant states of arousal (e.g., your stomach grumbles during a morning class). We are motivated to reduce the tension caused by this arousal. Tension reduction has been proposed as a basic mechanism governing human behavior.

In marketing, tension refers to the unpleasant state that exists if a person's consumption needs are not fulfilled. A person may be grumpy if he hasn't eaten, or he may be dejected or angry if he cannot afford that new car he wants. This state activates goal-oriented behavior that attempts to reduce or eliminate this unpleasant state and return to a balanced one, called **homeostasis.**

Those behaviors that are successful in reducing the drive by eliminating the underlying need are strengthened and tend to be repeated. (This aspect of the learning process was discussed in Chapter 3.) Your motivation to leave class early in order to grab a snack would be greater if you hadn't eaten in 24 hours than if you had eaten only 2 hours earlier. If you did sneak out and got indigestion after, say, wolfing down a package of Twinkies, this behavior would be less likely to be repeated the next time you wanted a snack. One's degree of motivation, then, depends upon the distance between one's present state and the goal.

Drive theory, however, runs into difficulties when it tries to explain some facets of human behavior that run counter to its predictions. People often do things that *increase* a drive state rather than decrease it. For example, people may delay gratification. If you know you are going out for a lavish dinner, you might decide to forgo a snack earlier in the day even though you are hungry at that time. In other cases, people deliberately watch erotic movies, even though these stimuli often increase sexual arousal rather than diminish it.

Expectancy Theory

Most current explanations of motivation focus on cognitive factors rather than biological ones to understand what drives behavior. **Expectancy theory** suggests that behavior is largely pulled by expectations of achieving desirable outcomes—*positive* *incentives*—rather than pushed from within. We choose one product over another because we expect this choice to have more positive consequences for us. Thus, the term *drive* is used here more loosely to refer to both physical and cognitive processes.

MOTIVATIONAL DIRECTION

Motives have direction as well as strength. They are goal oriented in that specific objectives are desired to satisfy a need. Most goals can be reached by a number of routes, and the objective of marketers is to convince consumers that the alternative they offer provides the best chance to attain the goal. For example, a consumer who decides that he needs a pair of jeans to help him reach his goal of being accepted by others or projecting an appropriate image can choose among Levi's, Wranglers, Guess, Calvin Klein, and many other alternatives, each of which promises to deliver certain benefits.

Needs Versus Wants

The specific way a need is satisfied depends upon the individual's unique history and learning experiences and his or her cultural environment. The particular form of consumption used to satisfy a need is termed a want. For example, two classmates may feel their stomachs rumbling during a lunchtime lecture. If neither person has eaten since the night before, the strength of their respective needs (hunger) would be about the same. However, the way each person goes about satisfying this need might be quite different. The first person may be a health-conscious individual who fantasizes about gulping down a big handful of trail mix, while the second person may be equally aroused by the prospect of a greasy cheeseburger and fries.

This distinction between needs and wants is an important one, because it relates to the issue of whether marketers are actually capable of creating needs. That issue will be considered at the end of the chapter. For now, it is important to note that a marketing strategy is more effective when it aims to influence the direction a consumer will take to satisfy a need rather than to create the need itself. Thus, a marketer will likely be more successful in convincing the "junk food junkie" to reach for the trail mix instead of the burger when hunger hits, rather than *creating* his or her hunger.

Types of Needs

People are born with a need for certain elements necessary to maintain life, such as food, water, air, and shelter. These are called *biogenic needs*. People have many other needs, however, that are not innate. *Psychogenic needs* are acquired in the process of becoming a member of a culture. These include the need for status, power, affiliation, and so on. Psychogenic needs reflect the priorities of a culture, and their effect on behavior will vary in different environments. For example, an American consumer may be driven to devote a good chunk of his income to products that permit him to display his wealth and status, while his Japanese counterpart may work equally hard to ensure that he does not stand out from his group. These differences in cultural values will be discussed in Chapter 15.

Consumers can also be motivated to satisfy either utilitarian or hedonic needs. The satisfaction of utilitarian needs implies that consumers will emphasize the objective, tangible attributes of products, such as miles per gallon in a car; the amount of fat, calories, and protein in a cheeseburger; and the durability of a pair of blue jeans. Hedonic needs are subjective and experiential; that is, consumers may rely on a product to meet their needs for excitement, self-confidence, fantasy, and so on. Of course, consumers may be motivated to purchase a product because it provides *both* types of benefits. For example, a mink coat may be bought because it feels soft and luxurious against the skin and because it keeps one warm on a snowy day.

Motivational Conflicts

A goal has *valence,* which means that it can be positive or negative. A positively valued goal is one toward which consumers direct their behavior; they are motivated to *approach* the goal and will seek out products that will be instrumental in attaining it. Basil uses his athletic equipment to help him improve his triathlon performance, his goal. However, not all behavior is motivated by the desire to approach a goal. As we saw in Chapter 3, sometimes consumers are motivated to *avoid* a negative outcome. They will structure their purchases or consumption activities to reduce the chances of attaining this end result. For example, many consumers work hard to avoid rejection, a negative goal. They will stay away from products that they associate with social disapproval. Products such as deodorants and mouthwash frequently rely upon consumers' negative motivation by depicting the onerous social consequences of underarm odor or bad breath. Basil would most likely be especially vigilant about avoiding junk food as he prepared for an upcoming race.

Because a purchase decision may involve more than one source of motivation, consumers often find themselves in situations where different motives, both positive and negative, conflict with one another. Since marketers are attempting to satisfy consumers' needs, they can also be helpful by providing possible solutions to these dilemmas. As shown in Figure 4–2, three general types of conflicts can occur: approach-approach, approach-avoidance, and avoidance-avoidance.

APPROACH-APPROACH CONFLICT

In an approach-approach conflict, a person must choose between two desirable alternatives. A student might be torn between going home for the holidays and going on a skiing trip with friends. Or, he or she might have to choose between two record albums.

The **theory of cognitive dissonance** is based on the premise that people have a need for order and consistency in their lives and that a state of tension is created when beliefs or behaviors conflict with one another. The conflict that arises when choosing between two alternatives may be resolved through a process of cognitive dissonance reduction, in which people are motivated to reduce this inconsistency (or dissonance) and thus eliminate unpleasant tension.[3]

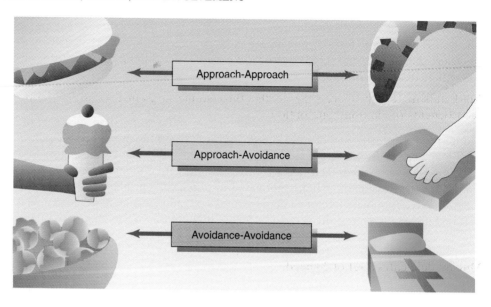

FIGURE 4–2 ▼ **Three Types of Motivational Conflicts**

A state of dissonance occurs when there is a psychological inconsistency between two or more beliefs or behaviors. It often occurs when a consumer must make a choice between two products, in which both alternatives usually possess both good and bad qualities. By choosing one product and not the other, the person gets the bad qualities of the chosen product and loses out on the good qualities of the unchosen one.

This loss creates an unpleasant, dissonant state that the person is motivated to reduce. People tend to convince themselves after the fact that choices they made were smart ones, by finding additional reasons to support the alternatives they chose or perhaps by "discovering" flaws with the options they did not choose. A marketer can resolve an approach-approach conflict by bundling several benefits together. For example, Miller Lite's claim that it is "less filling" *and* "tastes great" allows the drinker to "have his beer and drink it too." We'll explore some other applications of cognitive dissonance theory in the next chapter.

APPROACH-AVOIDANCE CONFLICT

Many of the products and services we desire have negative consequences attached to them, as well. We may feel guilty or ostentatious when buying a status-laden product or feel like a glutton when contemplating a box of Twinkies. When we desire a goal but wish to avoid it at the same time, an approach-avoidance conflict exists.

Some solutions to these conflicts include the proliferation of fake furs, which eliminate guilt about harming animals to make a fashion statement, and the success of diet foods, such as Weight Watchers, that promise good food without the calories. Many marketers try to overcome guilt by convincing consumers that they are deserving of luxuries (e.g., when the model for L'Oréal cosmetics claims, "Because I'm worth it!").

AVOIDANCE-AVOIDANCE CONFLICT

Sometimes consumers find themselves caught "between a rock and a hard place." They may face choices with two undesirable alternatives. A person may be faced with the option of either throwing more money into an old car or buying a new one. Marketers frequently address this conflict through messages that stress the unforeseen benefits of choosing one option (e.g., by emphasizing special credit plans to ease the pain of new-car payments).

Classifying Consumer Needs

Much research has been done on classifying human needs. On the one hand, some psychologists have tried to define a universal inventory of needs that could be traced systematically to explain virtually all behavior. One such effort, developed by Henry Murray, delineates a set of 20 needs that (sometimes in combination) result in specific behaviors. These needs include such dimensions as autonomy (being independent), defendance (defending the self against criticism), and even play (engaging in pleasurable activities).[4]

Others have focused on specific needs (which often are included in general models like Murray's) and their ramifications for behavior. For example, individuals with a high *need for achievement* strongly value personal accomplishment.[5] They place a premium on products and services that signify success because these consumption items provide feedback about the realization of their goals. These consumers are good prospects for products that provide evidence of their achievements. One study of working women found that those who were high in achievement motivation were more likely to choose clothing they considered businesslike, and less likely to be interested in apparel that accentuated their femininity.[6] Some other important needs that are relevant to consumer behavior include the following:

- *Need for affiliation* (to be in the company of other people).[7] This need is relevant to products and services that are consumed in groups, such as team sports, bars, and shopping malls, and that alleviate loneliness.
- *Need for power* (to control one's environment).[8] Many products and services, ranging from "hopped-up" muscle cars and loud boom boxes (large portable radios) to hotels, restaurants, and resorts that promise to respond to the customer's every whim, allow consumers to feel that they have mastery over their surroundings.
- *Need for uniqueness* (to assert one's individual identity).[9] This need is satisfied by products that pledge to accentuate a consumer's distinctive qualities. For example, Cachet perfume claims to be "as individual as you are."

One influential approach to motivation was proposed by the psychologist Abraham Maslow. Maslow's approach is a general one originally developed to understand personal growth and the attainment of "peak experiences."[10] Maslow formulated a hierarchy of needs, in which levels of motives are specified. A hierarchical approach implies that the order of development is fixed—that is, a certain level must be attained before the next, higher one is activated. This universal approach to motivation has been adapted by marketers because it (indirectly) specifies certain types of product benefits people might be looking for, depending upon the different stages in their development and/or their environmental conditions.

These levels are summarized in Figure 4–3. At each level, different priorities exist in terms of the product benefits a consumer is looking for. Ideally, an individual progresses up the hierarchy until his or her dominant motivation is a focus on "ultimate" goals, such as justice and beauty. Unfortunately, this state is difficult to achieve (at least on a regular basis); most of us have to be satisfied with occasional glimpses, or peak experiences. Examples of product appeals tailored to each level are provided in Table 4–1.

The implication of Maslow's hierarchy is that one must first satisfy basic needs before progressing up the ladder (i.e., a starving man is not interested in status symbols, friendship, or self-fulfillment). This hierarchy is not set in stone. Its use in marketing has been somewhat simplistic, especially since the same product or activity can satisfy a number of different needs.

Sex, for example, is characterized as a basic biological drive. While this observation is true throughout most of the animal kingdom, it is obviously a more complicated phenomenon for humans. Indeed, this activity could conceivably fit into every level of Maslow's hierarchy. A sociobiologist, who approaches human behavior in terms of its biological origins, might argue that reproductive behavior provides

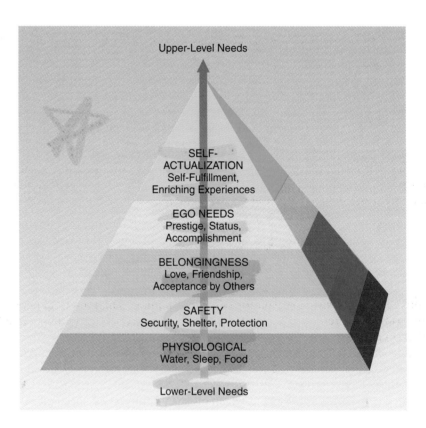

FIGURE 4–3 ▼ **Levels of Needs in the Maslow Hierarchy**

TABLE 4–1 ▼ Maslow's Hierarchy and Marketing Strategies

LEVEL OF HIERARCHY	RELEVANT PRODUCTS	EXAMPLE
Self-Actualization	Hobbies, travel, education	U.S. Army—"Be all you can be."
Ego needs	Cars, furniture, credit cards, stores, country clubs, liquors	Royal Salute Scotch—"What the rich give the wealthy."
Belongingness	Clothing, grooming products, clubs, drinks	Pepsi—"You're in the Pepsi generation."
Safety	Insurance, alarm systems, retirement investments	Allstate Insurance—"You're in good hands with Allstate."
Physiology	Medicines, staple items, generics	Quaker Oat Bran—"It's the right thing to do."

security because it ensures continuation of a person's gene pool and the provision of children to care for the person in old age. Sex can also express love and affiliation at the belongingness level. In addition, sex is often used as a vehicle to attain status, to dominate another, and to satisfy ego needs; it can be a significant determinant of self-respect. Finally, a sexual experience can be self-actualizing in that it may provide an ecstatic, transcendental experience.

Another problem with taking Maslow's hierarchy too literally is that it is culture bound. The assumptions of the hierarchy may be restricted to Western culture. People in other cultures (or, for that matter, in Western culture) may question the order of the levels as specified. A religious person who has taken a vow of celibacy would not necessarily agree that his or her physiological needs must be satisfied for self-fulfillment to occur.

Similarly, many Eastern cultures operate on the premise that the welfare of the group (belongingness needs) are more highly valued than needs of the individual (esteem needs). The point is that this hierarchy, while widely applied in marketing, should be valued because it reminds us that consumers may have different need priorities at different times (i.e., you have to walk before you can run) rather than because it *exactly* specifies a consumer's progression up the ladder of needs.

HIDDEN MOTIVES: PROBING BENEATH THE SURFACE

A motive is an underlying reason for behavior and not something researchers can see or easily measure. Furthermore, the same behavior can be caused by a number of different motives. To compound the problem of identifying motives, the consumer may be unaware of the actual need he or she is attempting to satisfy, or, alternatively, he or she may not be willing to admit that this need exists. Because of these difficulties, motives usually must be *inferred* by the analyst.

Although some consumer needs undoubtedly are utilitarian and fairly straightforward, some researchers feel that a great many purchase decisions are not the result of deliberate, logical decisions. To the contrary, people may do things to satisfy motives of which they are not even aware.

Like many advertisements for home furnishings, this one for Waverly fabrics and wall coverings emphasizes the significance of having a secure and attractive home. The expression "There's no place like home!" is a testament to the importance of security and shelter in Maslow's hierarchy.
Reprinted by permission of Waverly. All rights reserved.

Consumer Behavior on the Couch: Freudian Theory

Sigmund Freud had a profound impact on many basic assumptions of human behavior. His work changed the way we view such topics as adult sexuality, dreams, and psychological adjustment. Freud developed the idea that much of human behavior stems from a fundamental conflict between a person's desire to gratify his or her physical needs and the necessity to function as a responsible member of society. This struggle is carried out in the mind among three systems. (Note that these systems do not refer to physical parts of the brain.)

The **id** is entirely oriented toward immediate gratification—that is, it is the "party animal" of the mind. It operates according to the **pleasure principle;** behavior is guided by the primary desire to maximize pleasure and avoid pain. The id is selfish and illogical. It directs a person's psychic energy toward pleasurable acts without regard for any consequences.

The **superego** is the counterweight to the id. This system is essentially the person's conscience. It internalizes society's rules (especially as communicated by parents) and works to prevent the id from seeking selfish gratification.

Finally, the **ego** is the system that mediates between the id and the superego. It is, in a way, a referee in the fight between temptation and virtue. The ego tries to balance these two opposing forces according to the reality principle. It finds ways to gratify the id that will be acceptable to the outside world. These conflicts occur on an unconscious level, so the person is not necessarily aware of the underlying reasons for behavior.

According to Freudian theory, a person's development hinges on the way these systems interact in childhood. Aspects of Freudian theory are controversial, and his observations are not always accepted literally. For example, the bulk of Freud's insights were based on his own patients, a limited sample composed primarily of affluent Viennese housewives. Many feminists object to Freud's assumption about the inferiority of women, though this idea was widely accepted in his time. Nonetheless, Freud had a profound impact on the fields of psychiatry and clinical psychology.

Some of Freud's ideas have also been adapted by consumer researchers. In particular, his work highlights the potential importance of unconscious motives underlying purchases. The implication is that consumers cannot necessarily tell us their true motivations for choosing a product, even if we can devise a sensitive way to ask them directly.

The Freudian perspective also hints at the possibility that the ego relies on the symbolism in products to compromise between the demands of the id and the prohibitions of the superego. The person channels his or her unacceptable desire into acceptable outlets by using products that signify these underlying desires. This is the connection between product symbolism and motivation: The product stands for, or represents, a consumer's true goal, one that is socially unacceptable or unattainable. By acquiring the product, the person is able to vicariously experience the forbidden fruit.

Most Freudian applications in marketing are related to the sexuality of products. For example, some analysts have speculated that a sports car is a substitute for sexual gratification for many men. Indeed, some men do seem inordinately attached to their cars and may spend many hours lovingly washing and polishing them. The Infiniti ad shown here reinforces the belief that cars symbolically satisfy consumers' sexual needs in addition to their functional ones by describing the J30 model as ". . . what happens when you cross sheet metal and desire."

Others focus on male-oriented symbolism—the so-called phallic symbol—that appeals to women. Although Freud himself joked that "sometimes a cigar is just a cigar," many pop applications of Freud's ideas revolve around the use of objects that resemble sex organs (e.g., cigars, trees, or swords for men and tunnels for women). This focus stems from Freud's analysis of dreams, which were often interpreted as communicating repressed desires through symbols.

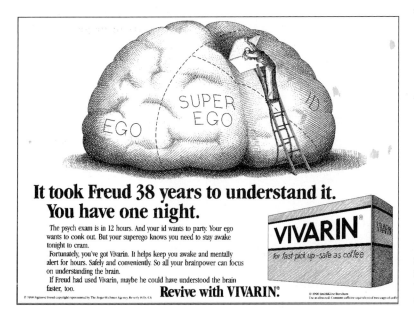

This ad for Vivarin stimulants depicts the three components of Freud's perspective on motivation and the unconscious. *Licensed by The Roger Richman Agency, Inc., Beverly Hills, CA. Courtesy of Grey Advertising, Inc.*

Motivational Research

The first attempts to apply Freudian ideas to understand the deeper meanings of products and advertisements were made in the 1950s, when a perspective known as **motivational research** was developed. This approach is largely based on psycho-analytic (Freudian) interpretations, with a heavy emphasis on unconscious motives. A basic assumption is that socially unacceptable needs are channeled into accept-able outlets. Product use or avoidance is motivated by unconscious forces that often are determined in childhood.

Motivational research relies on *depth interviews* with individual consumers. Instead of asking many consumers a few general questions about product usage and combining these responses with those of many other consumers in a representative statistical sample, this technique uses relatively few consumers but probes deeply into each person's purchase motivations. A depth interview might take several hours and is based on the assumption that the respondent cannot immediately articulate his or her latent, or underlying, motives. These can be derived only after meticulous questioning and interpretation on the part of a carefully trained interviewer.

This technique was pioneered by Ernest Dichter, a psychoanalyst who was trained in Vienna in the early part of the century. Dichter conducted in-depth inter-view studies on over 230 different products, and many of his findings have been incorporated in actual marketing campaigns.[11] For example, Esso (now Exxon) for many years reminded consumers to "Put a tiger in your tank" after Dichter found that people responded well to this powerful animal symbolism containing vaguely suggestive overtones. A summary of major consumption motivations identified using this approach appears in Table 4–2.

CRITICISMS OF MOTIVATIONAL RESEARCH

Motivational research is attacked for two quite opposite reasons. Some feel it does not work, while others feel it works *too* well. On the one hand, social critics have reacted much the same way they have reacted to subliminal perception studies (see Chapter 2). They have attacked this school of thought for giving advertisers the power to manipulate consumers.[12] On the other hand, many consumer researchers

This Infiniti ad stresses the sexual dimension of car ownership. Courtesy of Infiniti Division, Nissan Motor Corporation U.S.A.

TABLE 4–2 ▼ Major Motives for Consumption as Identified by Ernest Dichter

MOTIVE	ASSOCIATED PRODUCTS
Power-masculinity-virility	Power: Sugary products and large breakfasts (to charge oneself up), bowling, electric trains, hot rods, power tools
	Masculinity-virility: Coffee, red meat, heavy shoes, toy guns, buying fur coats for women, shaving with a razor
Security	Ice cream (to feel like loved child again), full drawer of neatly ironed shirts, real plaster walls (to feel sheltered), home baking, hospital care
Eroticism	Sweets (to lick), gloves (to be removed by women as a form of undressing), a man lighting a woman's cigarette (to create a tension-filled moment culminating in pressure, then relaxation)
Moral purity-cleanliness	White bread, cotton fabrics (to connote chastity), harsh household cleaning chemicals (to make housewives feel moral after using), bathing (to be equated with Pontius Pilate, who washed blood from his hands), oatmeal (sacrifice, virtue)
Social acceptance	Companionship: Ice cream (to share fun), coffee
	Love and affection: Toys (to express love for children), sugar and honey (to express terms of affection)
	Acceptance: Soap, beauty products
Individuality	Gourmet foods, foreign cars, cigarette holders, vodka, perfume, fountain pens
Status	Scotch; ulcers, heart attacks, indigestion (to show one has a high-stress, important job!); carpets (to show one does not live on bare earth like peasants)
Femininity	Cakes and cookies, dolls, silk, tea, household curios (to have a light, decorative, and heavy tactile component)
Reward	Cigarettes, candy, alcohol, ice cream, cookies
Master over environment	Kitchen appliances, boats, sporting goods, cigarette lighters
Disalienation (a desire to feel connectedness to things)	Home decorating, skiing, morning radio broadcasts (to feel "in touch" with the world)
Magic-mystery	Soups (having healing powers), paints (change the mood of a room), carbonated drinks (magical effervescent property), vodka (romantic history), unwrapping of gifts

Source: Adapted from Jeffrey F. Durgee, "Interpreting Dichter's Interpretations: An Analysis of Consumption Symbolism in *The Handbook of Consumer Motivations*," *Marketing and Semiotics: Selected Papers from the Copenhagen Symposium,* eds. Hanne Hartvig-Larsen, David Glen Mick, and Christian Alstead (Copenhagen, 1991).

feel the research has lacked sufficient rigor and validity, since interpretations are subjective and indirect.[13] Because conclusions are based on the analyst's own judgment and are derived from discussions with a small number of people, some researchers are dubious as to the degree to which these results can be generalized to a large market. In addition, because the original motivational researchers were heavily influenced by orthodox Freudian theory, their interpretations usually carried strong sexual overtones. This emphasis tends to overlook other plausible causes for behavior.

THE POSITIVE SIDE OF MOTIVATIONAL RESEARCH

Motivational research has great appeal to at least some marketers for several reasons, some of which are detailed here.

Motivational research tends to be less expensive than large-scale, quantitative surveys because interviewing and data-processing costs are relatively minimal.

The knowledge derived from motivational research can possibly help to develop marketing communications that appeal to deep-seated needs and thus provide a more powerful hook to relate a product to consumers. Even if they are not necessarily valid for all consumers in a target market, these insights can be valuable when used in an exploratory way. For example, the rich imagery that may be associated with a product can be used creatively when developing advertising copy.

Some of the findings seem intuitively plausible after the fact. For example, motivational studies concluded that coffee is associated with companionship, that people avoid prunes because they remind them of old age, and that men fondly equate the first car they owned as an adolescent with the onset of their sexual freedom.

Other interpretations are hard for some people to swallow, such as the observations that, to a woman, baking a cake symbolizes giving birth or that men are reluctant to give blood because they feel their vital fluids are being drained. On the other hand, some people do refer to a pregnant woman as "having a bun in the oven," and Pillsbury claims that "nothing says lovin' like something from the oven." Motivational research for the American Red Cross did find that men (but not women) tend to drastically overestimate the amount of blood that is taken during a donation. This group counteracted the fear of loss of virility by symbolically equating the act of giving blood with fertilization: "Give the gift of life." Despite its drawbacks, motivational research continues to be employed as a useful diagnostic tool. Its validity is enhanced, however, when used in conjunction with the other research techniques available to the consumer researcher.

NEEDS AND WANTS: DO MARKETERS MANIPULATE CONSUMERS?

One of the most common and stinging criticisms of marketing is that marketing techniques (especially advertising) are responsible for convincing consumers that they "need" many material things and that they will be unhappy and somehow inferior people if they do not have these "necessities." The issue is a complex one and is

This ad was created by the American Association of Advertising Agencies to counter charges that ads create artificial needs. Courtesy of American Association of Advertising Agencies.

certainly worth considering: Do marketers give people what they want, or do they tell people what they should want?

Philosophers have approached this issue when considering the concept of free will. It has been argued that in order to claim that consumers are acting autonomously in response to ads, the capacity for free will and free action must be present. That is, the consumer must be capable of *independently* deciding what to do and not be prevented from carrying out that decision. This situation is probably true for purely informative advertising, wherein only the product or store information required to make a rational decision is provided. The case for persuasive advertising, in which imagery or underlying motivations are tapped, is not as clear.[14] Three issues related to the complex relationship between marketing practices and consumers' needs are considered here.

Do Marketers Create Artificial Needs?

The marketing system has come under fire from both ends of the political spectrum. On the one hand, some members of the religious right believe that advertising contributes to the moral breakdown of society by presenting images of hedonistic pleasure, thus encouraging the pursuit of secular humanism. On the other hand, some leftists argue that the same deceitful promises of material pleasure function to buy off people who would otherwise be revolutionaries working to change the system.[15] Through advertising, the system creates demand that only its products can satisfy.

A need is a basic biological motive, while a want represents one way that society has taught us that the need can be satisfied. For example, while thirst is biologically based, we are taught to want Coca-Cola to satisfy that thirst rather than, say, goat's milk. Thus, the need is already there; marketers simply recommend ways to satisfy it. A basic objective of advertising is to create awareness that these needs exist, rather than to create them. In some circumstances, however, the marketer can

This ad from the early 1920s for Listerine mouthwash is an example of a marketing strategy that highlights a need and then offers a solution. In this case, Edna's failure to get married is blamed on "halitosis" (bad breath). The answer is Listerine. Courtesy of Warner Lambert, Inc.

engineer an environment to make it more probable that a need will be activated. This occurs, for example, when movie theaters sell popcorn and bars supply free peanuts to patrons in order to stimulate thirst.

Is Advertising Necessary?

As social critic Vance Packard wrote over 30 years ago, "Large-scale efforts are being made, often with impressive success, to channel our unthinking habits, our purchasing decisions, and our thought processes by the use of insights gleaned from psychiatry and the social sciences."[16]

The economist John Kenneth Galbraith feels that radio and television are important tools to accomplish this manipulation of the masses. Since virtually no literacy is required to use these media, they allow repetitive and compelling communications to reach almost everyone.

Goods are arbitrarily linked to desirable social attributes. One influential critic even argued that the problem is that we are not materialistic enough—that is, we do not sufficiently value goods for the utilitarian functions they deliver but instead focus on the irrational value of goods for what they symbolize. According to this view, for example, "Beer would be enough for us, without the additional promise that in drinking it we show ourselves to be manly, young at heart, or neighborly. A washing machine would be a useful machine to wash clothes, rather than an indication that we are forward-looking or an object of envy to our neighbors."[17]

Products are designed to meet existing needs, and advertising only helps to communicate their availability. Marketing overcomes some of the disadvantages of labor specialization, where most consumers are unfamiliar with the characteristics of mass-produced goods.[18] According to the economics-of-information perspective, advertising is an important source of consumer information.[19] This view emphasizes the economic cost of the time spent searching for products. Accordingly, advertising is a service for which consumers are willing to pay since the information it provides reduces search time.

*M*ARKETING PITFALL

The charge that businesses create artificial needs is relevant in the case of gasoline marketing. Oil companies have attempted to convince consumers of the need for premium gasolines, even though this need has been questioned by many people. As one automotive engineer noted, " 'Oil company advertising has led people to the conclusion that more expensive fuels will make their car [sic] start easier, get more gas mileage, and last longer, . . .' But in most cases this is untrue. . . . Your engine has to be designed to use that extra octane. . . . Otherwise, . . . the extra cost is just lining the pockets of the oil companies." An oil industry executive wrote, "When prices go up a bit, people will come to their senses and premium volumes will diminish. . . ." But for now, people buy higher-octane fuel for reasons that have nothing to do with car engines; one, he theorized, is "the use of premium as an expression of self-worth."[20] Is the need for higher octane a genuine one or something manufactured by the oil companies by associating premium gasoline with power, status, manliness, and so on?

MULTICULTURAL DIMENSIONS

As Eastern Europe opens up to capitalism, some fear that consumers are being exploited as Western advertisements bombard them for products they didn't know they needed. In Poland, for example, previously taboo items like women's sanitary napkins are being advertised for the first time, and new markets are being created for products such as pet food.

The actions of one Polish entrepreneur illustrate how a consumer's need for social approval can be channeled into a want for a product. Beginning with an ad campaign featuring Miss Poland, he single-handedly created a market for electronic hair removers (Polish women usually do not shave their legs). He also persuaded a leading Polish fashion designer to announce that hairy legs were out of fashion in Europe, and he organized local beauty contests to find the best legs. At last report, he was selling 30,000 hair removers a month.[21]

Do Marketers Promise Miracles?

Consumers are led to believe through advertising that products have magical properties; that is, products will do special and mysterious things for them that will transform their lives. They will be beautiful, have power over others' feelings, be successful, be relieved of all ills, and so on. In this respect, advertising functions as mythology does in primitive societies; it provides simple, anxiety-reducing answers to complex problems.

The effectiveness of advertising is overstated. There is little evidence that advertising creates patterns of consumption (though it may accelerate them). Instead, the marketing system creates a new way to satisfy an old need.

This cartoon lampoons the widely held belief that marketers manipulate consumers by making us feel inadequate about ourselves. Then they bombard us with products and services we don't really want or need with the promise that we will be better people, more attractive, more successful, and so on if only we will buy them. How valid is this criticism?
Copyright © 1994 by Bill Watterston.
Courtesy of Universal Press Syndicate.

need to deal with similar information at a future time will be more likely to start forming attitudes in anticipation of this event.[8]

Two people can each have the same attitude toward some object for very different reasons. As a result, it can be helpful for a marketer to know *why* an attitude is held before attempting to change it. The following are attitude functions as identified by Katz:

- *Utilitarian function.*   The utilitarian function is related to the basic principles of reward and punishment. We develop some of our attitudes toward products simply on the basis of whether these products provide pleasure or pain. If a person likes the taste of a cheeseburger, that person will develop a positive attitude toward cheeseburgers. Ads that stress straightforward product benefits (e.g., you should drink Diet Coke "just for the taste of it") appeal to the utilitarian function.

- *Value-expressive function.*   Attitudes that perform a value-expressive function express the consumer's central values or self-concept. A person forms a product attitude not because of its objective benefits, but because of what the product says about him or her as a person (e.g., "What sort of man reads *Playboy?*"). Value-expressive attitudes are highly relevant to lifestyle analyses, where consumers cultivate a cluster of activities, interests, and opinions to express a particular social identity.

- *Ego-defensive function.*   Attitudes that are formed to protect the person, either from external threats or internal feelings, perform an ego-defensive function. An early marketing study indicated that housewives in the 1950s resisted the use of instant coffee because it threatened their conception of themselves as capable homemakers.[9] Products that promise to help a man project a "macho" image (e.g., Marlboro cigarettes) may be appealing to his insecurities about his masculinity. Another example of this function is deodorant campaigns that stress the dire, embarrassing consequences of being caught with underarm odor in public.

This company coaches students who are about to take standardized admissions tests. Its appeal is based on an instrumental attitude function: increasing one's chances of getting admitted to a good school. Courtesy of Kaplan Educational Centers.

● *Knowledge function.* Some attitudes are formed as the result of a need for order, structure, or meaning. This need is often present when a person is in an ambiguous situation or is confronted with a new product (e.g., "Bayer wants you to know about pain relievers").

An attitude can serve more than one function, but in many cases a particular one will be dominant. By identifying the dominant function a product serves for consumers (i.e., what *benefits* it provides), marketers can emphasize these benefits in their communications and packaging. Ads relevant to the function prompt more favorable thoughts about what is being marketed and can result in a heightened preference for both the ad and the product.

One study determined that for most people coffee serves more of a utilitarian function than a value-expressive function. As a consequence, subjects responded more positively to copy for a coffee (which was fictitious) that read, "The delicious, hearty flavor and aroma of Sterling Blend coffee comes from a blend of the freshest coffee beans" (i.e., utilitarian appeal) than they did to copy that read, "The coffee you drink says something about the type of person you are. It can reveal your rare, discriminating taste" (i.e., value-expressive function).[10]

The ABC Model of Attitudes and Hierarchies of Effects

Most researchers agree that an attitude has three components: affect, behavior, and cognition. **Affect** refers to the way a consumer *feels* about an attitude object. **Behavior** involves the person's intentions to do something with regard to an attitude object (but, as will be discussed at a later point, an intention does not always result in an actual behavior). **Cognition** refers to the *beliefs* a consumer has about an attitude object. These three components of an attitude can be remembered as the *ABC model of attitudes*.

This model emphasizes the interrelationships among knowing, feeling, and doing. Consumers' attitudes toward a product cannot be determined by simply identifying their beliefs about it. For example, a researcher may find that shoppers "know" a particular camcorder has an 8:1 power zoom lens, auto-focus, and a flying erase head, but such findings do not indicate whether they feel these attributes are good, bad, or irrelevant or whether they would actually buy the camcorder.

While all three components of an attitude are important, their relative importance will vary depending upon a consumer's level of motivation with regard to the attitude object. The differences in drink choices among the three friends at the bar illustrate how these elements can be combined in different ways to create attitudes. Attitude researchers have developed the concept of a **hierarchy of effects** to explain the relative impact of the three components. Each hierarchy specifies that a fixed sequence of steps occurs en route to an attitude. Three different hierarchies are summarized in Figure 5–1.

THE STANDARD LEARNING HIERARCHY

Nancy's choice of a favorite drink closely resembles the process by which most attitudes have been assumed to be constructed. A consumer approaches a product decision as a problem-solving process. First, he or she forms beliefs about a product by accumulating knowledge (beliefs) regarding relevant attributes. Next, the consumer

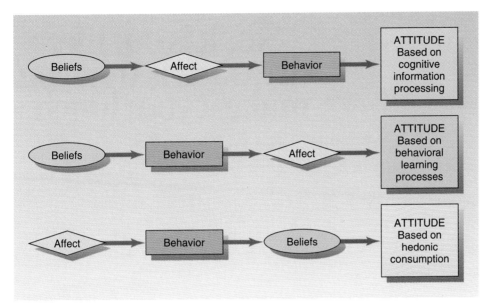

FIGURE 5–1 ▼ **Three Hierarchies of Effects**

evaluates these beliefs and forms a feeling about the product (affect). Over time, Nancy integrated information about alternative vodka brands and formed a preference for one kind.

Finally, based on this evaluation, the consumer engages in a relevant behavior, such as buying the product. This careful choice process often results in the type of brand loyalty displayed by Nancy; the consumer "bonds" with the product over time and is not easily persuaded to experiment with other brands. The standard learning hierarchy assumes that a consumer is highly involved in making a purchase decision.[11] The person is motivated to seek out a lot of information, carefully weigh alternatives, and come to a thoughtful decision. As we saw in Chapter 4, this process is likely to occur if the decision is important to the consumer or in some way central to the consumer's self-concept.

THE LOW-INVOLVEMENT HIERARCHY

In sharp contrast to Nancy, Jan's interest in the attitude object (a particular brand of alcoholic beverage) is at best lukewarm. She has collected only a minimal amount of information before acting and has an emotional response only after consuming the beverage. Jan is typical of a consumer who forms an attitude via the *low-involvement hierarchy of effects*. In this sequence, the consumer initially does not have a strong preference for one brand over another, but he or she instead acts on the basis of limited knowledge and then forms an evaluation only after the fact.[12] The attitude is likely to come about through behavioral learning, where the consumer's choice is reinforced by good or bad experiences with the product after purchase.

The possibility that consumers simply don't care enough about many decisions to carefully assemble a set of product beliefs and then evaluate them is important because it implies that all of the concern about influencing beliefs and carefully communicating information about product attributes may largely be wasted. Consumers aren't necessarily going to pay attention anyway; they are more likely to respond to simple stimulus-response connections when making purchase decisions. For example, a consumer choosing among paper towels might remember that "Bounty is the

Steak is our life.
All we ask is that you
make it your lunch.

Smith & Wollensky.
The quintessential New York City steakhouse.
49th St. & 3rd Ave. (212) 753-1530.

Winner of The *Wine Spectators* 1987 Grand Award.

This ad for New York's famous Smith & Wollensky restaurant emphasizes that marketers and others associated with a product or service are often more involved with it than are their consumers. Courtesy of Smith & Wollensky Steakhouse, 797 3rd Avenue, NYC.

quicker picker-upper" rather than bothering to systematically compare all of the brands on the shelf.

The notion of low involvement on the part of consumers is a bitter pill for some marketers to swallow. Who wants to admit that what they market is not very important or involving? A brand manager for, say, a brand of bubble gum or cat food may find it hard to believe that consumers don't put that much thought into purchasing her product since she spends many of her waking (and perhaps sleeping) hours thinking about it.

For marketers, the ironic silver lining to this low-involvement cloud is that under these conditions, consumers are not motivated to process a lot of complex brand-related information. Instead, they will be swayed by principles of behavioral learning, such as the simple responses caused by conditioned brand names, point-of-purchase displays, and so on. This results in what we might call the involvement paradox: that is, the *less* important the product is to consumers, the *more* important are many of the marketing stimuli (e.g., packages, jingles) that must be devised to sell it.

THE EXPERIENTIAL HIERARCHY

Researchers in recent years have begun to stress the significance of emotional response as a central aspect of an attitude. According to the *experiential hierarchy of effects,* consumers act on the basis of their emotional reactions (just as Terri felt strongly about drunk drivers). Although the factors of beliefs and behavior still are recognized as playing a part, a consumer's overall evaluation of an attitude object is considered by many to be the core of an attitude.

This perspective highlights the idea that attitudes can be strongly influenced by intangible product attributes, such as package design, and by consumers' reactions toward accompanying stimuli, such as advertising and even the brand name. As dis-

It's cold. You're hurting.
And three rookies
will kill for your job.

How does it feel?

Sports
Illustrated
Get the feeling.

This Sports Illustrated *ad, which emphasizes feelings, underscores the importance of affect in forming attitudes.* John Iacono/Sports Illustrated.

cussed in Chapter 4, resulting attitudes will be affected by consumers' hedonic motivations, such as how the product makes them feel or the fun its use will provide.

One important debate about the experiential hierarchy concerns the *independence* of cognition and affect. On the one hand, the *cognitive-affective model* argues that an affective judgment is but the last step in a series of cognitive processes. Earlier steps include the sensory registration of stimuli and the retrieval of meaningful information from memory to categorize these stimuli.[13]

On the other hand, the *independence hypothesis* takes the position that affect and cognition involve two separate, partially independent systems; affective responses do not always require prior cognitions.[14] A number one song on the *Billboard* "Top 40" may possess the same attributes as many other songs (e.g., dominant bass guitar, raspy vocals, persistent downbeat), but beliefs about these attributes cannot explain why one song becomes a classic while another sharing the same characteristics winds up in the bargain bin at the local record store. The independence hypothesis does not *eliminate* the role of cognition in experience. It simply balances this traditional, rational emphasis on calculated decision making by paying more attention to the impact of aesthetic, subjective experience. This type of holistic processing is more likely to occur when the product is perceived as primarily expressive or delivers sensory pleasure rather than utilitarian benefits.[15]

There's More to Marketing Than Product Attitudes

Marketers who are concerned with understanding consumers' attitudes have to contend with an even more complex issue: In decision-making situations, people form attitudes toward objects other than the product itself that can influence their ultimate selections. One additional factor to consider is *attitudes toward the act of buying* in general. As we'll see later in the chapter, sometimes people simply are

Some advertising campaigns try to increase their entertainment value by producing spots that strongly resemble soap operas. MCI created a fictional company, called Gramercy Press, and presents different segments that show how employees are adjusting to the Information Age. Courtesy of MCI Communications, Business Markets Div., and Messner, Vetere, Berger, McNanee, Schmetterer, NYC.

reluctant, embarrassed, or just plain too lazy to expend the effort to actually obtain a desired product or service.

In addition, consumers' reactions to a product, over and above their feelings about the product itself, are influenced by their evaluations of its advertising. Our evaluation of a product can be determined solely by our appraisal of how it's depicted in marketing communications—that is, we don't hesitate to form attitudes toward products we've never even seen in person, much less used.

The **attitude toward the advertisement (A_{ad})** is defined as a predisposition to respond in a favorable or unfavorable manner to a particular advertising stimulus during a particular exposure occasion. Determinants of A_{ad} include the viewer's attitude toward the advertiser, evaluations of the ad execution itself, the mood evoked by the ad, and the degree to which the ad affects viewers' arousal levels.[16] A viewer's feelings about the context in which an ad appears can also influence brand attitudes. For example, attitudes about an ad and the brand depicted will be influenced if the

$\mathcal{M}$ARKETING PITFALL

In a study of irritating advertising, researchers examined over 500 prime-time network commercials that had registered negative reactions by consumers. The most irritating commercials were for feminine-hygiene products, hemorrhoid medications or laxatives, and women's underwear. The researchers identified the following factors as prime offenders:[17]

- A sensitive product is shown (e.g., hemorrhoid medicine), and its use or package is emphasized.
- The situation is contrived or overdramatized.
- A person is put down in terms of appearance, knowledge, or sophistication.
- An important relationship, such as a marriage, is threatened.
- There is a graphic demonstration of physical discomfort.
- Uncomfortable tension is created by an argument or by an antagonistic character.
- An unattractive or unsympathetic character is portrayed.
- A sexually suggestive scene is included.
- The commercial suffers from poor casting or execution.

consumer sees the ad while watching a favorite TV program.[18] The effects demonstrated by A_{ad} emphasize the importance of an ad's entertainment value in the purchase process.[19]

The feelings generated by advertising have the capacity to directly affect brand attitudes. Commercials can evoke a wide range of emotional responses, from disgust to happiness. These feelings can be influenced both by the way the ad is done (i.e., the specific advertising *execution*) and by the consumer's reactions to the advertiser's motives. For example, many advertisers who are trying to craft messages for adolescents and young adults are encountering problems because this age group, having grown up in a "marketing society," tends to be skeptical about attempts to get them to buy things.[20] These reactions can, in turn, influence memory for advertising content.[21] At least three emotional dimensions have been identified in commercials: pleasure, arousal, and intimidation.[22] Specific types of feelings that can be generated by an ad include the following:[23]

- *Upbeat feelings*—amused, delighted, playful
- *Warm feelings*—affectionate, contemplative, hopeful
- *Negative feelings*—critical, defiant, offended

FORMING ATTITUDES

We all have lots of attitudes, and we don't usually question how we got them. Certainly, a person isn't born with the conviction that, say, Pepsi is better than Coke or that heavy-metal music liberates the soul. Where do these attitudes come from?

This ad for EggStro'dinaire, an egg substitute, illustrates that ads are capable of communicating negative feelings. Courtesy of Food Service Division, Sandoz Nutrition, Minneapolis, MN 55416.

An attitude can form in several different ways, depending upon the particular hierarchy of effects in operation. It can occur because of *classical conditioning,* wherein an attitude object, such as the Pepsi name, is repeatedly paired with a catchy jingle ("You're in the Pepsi Generation . . ."). Or, it can be formed through *instrumental conditioning,* in which consumption of the attitude object is reinforced (e.g., Pepsi quenches one's thirst). Or, the learning of an attitude can be the outcome of a very complex cognitive process. For example, a teenager may come to model the behavior of friends and media figures who drink Pepsi because she believes that this act will allow her to fit in with the desirable images of the Pepsi Generation.

It is thus important to distinguish among types of attitudes, since not all are formed the same way.[24] For example, a highly brand-loyal consumer like Nancy, the Stolichnaya drinker, has an enduring, deeply held positive attitude toward an attitude object, and this involvement will be difficult to weaken. On the other hand, another consumer like Jan, the occasional wine drinker, may be more fickle: she may have a mildly positive attitude toward a product but be quite willing to abandon it when something better comes along. This section will consider the differences between strongly and weakly held attitudes and briefly review some of the major theoretical perspectives that have been developed to explain how attitudes form and relate to one another in the minds of consumers.

Levels of Commitment to an Attitude

Consumers vary in their *commitment* to an attitude; the degree of commitment is related to their level of involvement with the attitude object, as follows:[25]

● *Compliance:* At the lowest level of involvement, compliance, an attitude is formed because it helps in gaining rewards or avoiding punishments from others. This attitude is very superficial; it is likely to change when the person's behavior is no longer monitored by others or when another option becomes available. A person may drink Pepsi because this brand is sold in the cafeteria and it is too much trouble to go elsewhere for a Coca-Cola.

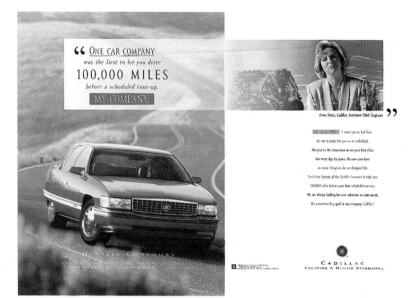

By describing Cadillac as "my company," the woman featured in this ad is exhibiting a high level of attitudinal commitment to her employer. Courtesy of Cadillac.

● *Identification:* A process of identification occurs when attitudes are formed in order for the consumer to be similar to another person or group. Advertising that depicts the social consequences of choosing some products over others is relying on the tendency of consumers to imitate the behavior of desirable models.

● *Internalization:* At a high level of involvement, deep-seated attitudes are internalized and become part of the person's value system. These attitudes are very difficult to change because they are so important to the individual. For example, many consumers had strong attitudes toward Coca-Cola and reacted quite negatively when the company attempted to switch to the New Coke formula. This allegiance to Coke was obviously more than a minor preference for these people; the brand had become intertwined with their social identities, taking on patriotic and nostalgic properties.

The Consistency Principle

Have you ever heard someone say, "Pepsi is my favorite soft drink. It tastes terrible," or "I love my husband. He's the biggest idiot I've ever met"? Probably you have not heard these statements too often because these beliefs or evaluations are not consistent with one another. According to the **principle of cognitive consistency,** consumers value *harmony* among their thoughts, feelings, and behaviors, and they are motivated to maintain uniformity among these elements. This desire means that, if necessary, consumers will *change* their thoughts, feelings, or behaviors to make them consistent with their other experiences. The consistency principle is an important reminder that attitudes are not formed in a vacuum. A significant determinant of the way an attitude object will be evaluated is how it fits with other, related attitudes already held by the consumer.

COGNITIVE DISSONANCE THEORY REVISITED

In the last chapter, we discussed the role played by cognitive dissonance when consumers are trying to choose between two desired products. Cognitive dissonance theory also has other important ramifications for attitudes, since people often are confronted with situations in which there is some conflict between their attitudes and behaviors.[26]

The theory proposes that, much like hunger or thirst, people are *motivated* to reduce this negative state by making things fit with one another. The theory focuses on situations where two *cognitive elements* are inconsistent with one another.

A cognitive element can be something a person believes about himself, a behavior he performs, or an observation about his surroundings. For example, the two cognitive elements "I know smoking cigarettes causes cancer" and "I smoke cigarettes" are *dissonant* with one another. This psychological inconsistency creates a feeling of discomfort that the smoker is motivated to reduce. The magnitude of dissonance depends upon both the importance and number of dissonant elements.[27] In other words, the pressure to reduce dissonance is more likely to be observed in high-involvement situations in which the elements are more important to the individual.

Dissonance reduction can occur either by eliminating, adding, or changing elements. For example, the person could stop smoking (eliminating) or remember great-aunt Sophie, who smoked until the day she died at age 90 (adding). Alternatively, he might question the research that links cancer and smoking (changing), perhaps by believing industry-sponsored studies that try to refute this connection.

Dissonance theory can help to explain why evaluations of a product tend to increase *after* it has been purchased, i.e., postpurchase dissonance. The cognitive element "I made a stupid decision" is dissonant with the element "I am not a stupid person," so people tend to find even more reasons to like something after it becomes theirs.

This ad for Woman's Day *attempts to counter the role consistency plays in shaping attitudes: Consumers often distort information so that it fits with what they already know or believe. Courtesy of* Woman's Day *(Hachette Magazines Inc.).*

1. A government agency wants to encourage the use of designated drivers by people who have been drinking. What advice could you give the organization about constructing persuasive communications? Discuss some factors that might be important, including the structure of the communications, where they should appear, and who should deliver them. Should fear appeals be used, and if so, how?

2. Are infomercials ethical? Should marketers be allowed to use any format they want to present product-related information?

3. Discuss some conditions where it would be advisable to use a comparative advertising strategy.

4. Why would a marketer consider saying negative things about his or her product? When is this strategy feasible? Can you find examples of it?

5. A marketer must decide whether to incorporate rational or emotional appeals in its communications strategy. What factors would favor choosing one approach over the other?

6. Collect ads that rely on sex appeal to sell products. How often are benefits of the actual products communicated to the reader?

7. To observe the process of counterargumentation, ask a friend to talk out loud while watching a commercial. Ask him or her to respond to each point in the ad or to write down reactions to the claims made. How much skepticism regarding the claims can you detect?

8. Make a log of all the commercials shown on one network television channel over a six-hour period. Categorize each according to product category and whether they are presented as drama or argument. Describe the types of messages used (e.g., two-sided arguments), and keep track of the types of spokespeople (e.g., television actors, famous people, or animated characters). What can you conclude about the dominant forms of persuasion tactics currently employed by marketers?

9. Collect examples of ads that rely on the use of metaphors or resonance. Do you feel these ads are effective? If you were working with the products, would you feel more comfortable with ads that use a more straightforward, "hard-sell" approach? Why or why not?

ABC NEWS CONNECTION

It Slices, It Dices, It's an Infomercial!

What would life be like without such "necessities" as a Vega-Matic or a complete set of Ginzu knives? Producers of infomercials don't intend to let us find out. These extended commercials, often masquerading as talk shows or news programs, continue to bombard the airwaves. While many of the products sold on "direct-response television" in the early days made dubious claims about their ability to promote weight loss or make long-lost hair grow back, the industry is evolving as mainstream corporations begin to get into the act.

Still, problems remain. One pitfall is that infomercials may dupe consumers into changing their attitudes toward advertised items by making them believe that the information they are receiving is more credible and objective than is really the case.

By presenting product information in a news or talk show format, receivers of these persuasive communications may not counterargue as heavily as if the message were clearly identified as coming from a commercial sponsor. For example, in a controversial campaign for Maxwell House coffee, TV newscasters Linda Ellerbee and Willard Scott plugged the product in a setting resembling a news show. This format attempted to capitalize on the actors' backgrounds to produce the inference that their reports were news rather than commercials.[1] So, look carefully the next time you are channel-surfing and happen on an adoring crowd applauding a demonstration of the latest juicer, glass maker, or other "must-have" product. The money you save may be your own.

SIMMONS CONNECTION

Attitudes and Behavior

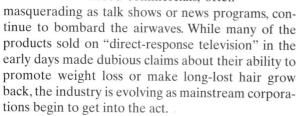

Although this exercise is assigned for Chapter 6, it draws upon material that students have studied in Chapter 5, as well. The Simmons datafile contains items from the Buying Style inventory—these tap attitudes that should be very relevant to their shopping behavior. Some of these attitudes relate to environmental issues. Most of the products listed in the datafile have a negative impact on the environment;

for example, disposable diapers place a burden on landfill sites. Others represent environmentally safer alternatives—for example, cloth diapers.

What evidence do you find that consumers select products consistent with their attitudes concerning the environment? Are some attitudes more or less consistent with behavior than others? Why do you think this is the case?

---

[1] See James Cox, "Star-Struck Advertisers Lean on Celebs," *USA Today* (June 20, 1990): 80.

NOTES

1. Quoted in Cyndee Miller, "The Fur Flies as Fashion Foes Pelt It Out Over Animal Rights," *Marketing News* 2 (December 4, 1989): 2.

2. Nina Darnton, "Revolt of the Fur Bearers," *Newsweek* (January 6, 1992): 49.

3. Quoted in Miller, "The Fur Flies as Fashion Foes Pelt It Out Over Animal Rights": 8.

4. Darnton, "Revolt of the Fur Bearers."

5. Vida Roberts, "Phony Express: Faux Fur a Reality in Fashion World," *Asbury Park Press* (September 18, 1994): D2.

6. For extensive development of consumers' reactions to persuasive communications, see Marian Friestad and Peter Wright, "The Persuasion Knowledge Model: How People Cope with Persuasion Attempts," *Journal of Consumer Research* 21, 1 (June 1994): 1–31; David M. Boush, Marian Friestad, and Gregory M. Rose, "Adolescent Skepticism Toward TV Advertising and Knowledge of Advertiser Tactics," *Journal of Consumer Research* 21, 1 (June 1994): 165–75.

7. Gert Assmus, "An Empirical Investigation into the Perception of Vehicle Source Effects," *Journal of Advertising* 7 (winter 1978): 4–10; for a more thorough discussion of the pros and cons of different media, see Stephen Baker, *Systematic Approach to Advertising Creativity* (New York: McGraw-Hill, 1979).

8. Carl I. Hovland and W. Weiss, "The Influence of Source Credibility on Communication Effectiveness," *Public Opinion Quarterly* 15 (1952): 635–50.

9. Herbert Kelman, "Processes of Opinion Change," *Public Opinion Quarterly* 25 (spring 1961): 57–78; Susan M. Petroshius and Kenneth E. Crocker, "An Empirical Analysis of Spokesperson Characteristics on Advertisement and Product Evaluations," *Journal of the Academy of Marketing Science* 17 (summer 1989): 217–26.

10. Kenneth G. DeBono and Richard J. Harnish, "Source Expertise, Source Attractiveness, and the Processing of Persuasive Information: A Functional Approach," *Journal of Personality and Social Psychology* 55, 4 (1988): 541–6.

11. Hershey H. Friedman and Linda Friedman, "Endorser Effectiveness by Product Type," *Journal of Advertising Research* 19, 5 (1979): 63–71.

12. S. Ratneshwar and Shelly Chaiken, "Comprehension's Role in Persuasion: The Case of Its Moderating Effect on the Persuasive Impact of Source Cues," *Journal of Consumer Research* 18 (June 1991): 52–62.

13. "Jim Palmer Pitches Style for Jockey," *New York Times* (August 29, 1982).

14. "Robber Makes It Biggs in Ad," *Advertising Age* (May 29, 1989): 26.

15. Tim Triplett, "Big Names Crowd the Infomercial Airwaves," *Marketing News* (March 28, 1994): 1 (2 pp.).

16. Rick Marin, "The Stepford Channel," *New York Times* (October 4, 1992): 1v.

17. Barry Meier, "TV Commercials That Go On and On," *New York Times* (January 27, 1990): 54.

18. Alice H. Eagly, Andy Wood, and Shelly Chaiken, "Causal Inferences About Communicators and Their Effect in Opinion Change," *Journal of Personality and Social Psychology* 36, 4 (1978): 424–35; see also David J. Moore, John C. Mowen, and Richard Reardon, "Multiple Sources in Advertising Appeals: When Product Endorsers Are Paid by the Advertising Sponsor," *Journal of the Academy of Marketing Science* 22, 3 (1994): 234–43.

19. Karen K. Dion, "What is Beautiful is Good," *Journal of Personality and Social Psychology* 24 (December 1972): 285–90.

20. Michael J. Baker and Gilbert A. Churchill, Jr., "The Impact of Physically Attractive Models on Advertising Evaluations," *Journal of Marketing Research* 14 (November 1977): 538–55; Marjorie J. Caballero and William M. Pride, "Selected Effects of Salesperson Sex and Attractiveness in Direct Mail Advertisements," *Journal of Marketing* 48 (January 1984): 94–100; W. Benoy Joseph, "The Credibility of Physically Attractive Communicators: A Review," *Journal of Advertising* 11, 3 (1982): 15–24; Lynn R. Kahle and Pamela M. Homer, "Physical Attractiveness of the Celebrity Endorser: A Social Adaptation Perspective," *Journal of Consumer Research* 11, 4 (1985): 954–61; Judson Mills and Eliot Aronson, "Opinion Change as a Function of Communicator's Attractiveness and Desire to Influence," *Journal of Personality and Social Psychology* 1 (1965): 173–7.

21. Leonard N. Reid and Lawrence C. Soley, "Decorative Models and the Readership of Magazine Ads," *Journal of Advertising Research* 23, 2 (1983): 27–32.

22. Marjorie J. Caballero, James R. Lumpkin, and Charles S. Madden, "Using Physical Attractiveness as an Advertising Tool: An Empirical Test of the Attraction Phenomenon," *Journal of Advertising Research* (August/September 1989): 16–22.

23. Baker and Churchill, Jr., "The Impact of Physically Attractive Models on Advertising Evaluations"; George E. Belch, Michael A. Belch, and Angelina Villareal, "Effects of Advertising Communications: Review of Research," in *Research in Marketing* 9 (Greenwich, CT: JAI Press, 1987): 59–117; A. E. Courtney and T. W. Whipple, *Sex Stereotyping in Advertising* (Lexington, MA: Lexington Books, 1983).

24. Kahle and Homer, "Physical Attractiveness of the Celebrity Endorser."

25. Baker and Churchill, Jr., "The Impact of Physically Attractive Models on Advertising Evaluations."

26. Michael A. Kamins, "Celebrity and Noncelebrity Advertising in a Two-Sided Context," *Journal of Advertising Research* 29 (June/July 1989): 34; Joseph M. Kamen, A. C. Azhari, and J. R. Kragh, "What a Spokesman Does for a Sponsor," *Journal of Advertising Research* 15, 2 (1975): 17–24; Lynn Langmeyer and Mary Walker, "A First Step to Identify the Meaning in Celebrity Endorsers," in *Advances in Consumer Research* 18, eds. Rebecca H. Holman and Michael R. Solomon (Provo, UT: Association for Consumer Research, 1991): 364–71.

27. Jeffrey Burroughs and Richard A. Feinberg, "Using Response Latency to Assess Spokesperson Effectiveness," *Journal of Consumer Research* 14 (September 1987): 295–9.

28. Carolyn Tripp, Thomas D. Jensen, and Les Carlson, "The Effects of Multiple Product Endorsements by Celebrities on Consumers' Attitudes and Intentions," *Journal of Consumer Research* 20, 4 (March 1994): 535–47.

29. Quoted in Douglas C. McGill, "Star Wars in Cola Advertising," *New York Times* (March 22, 1989): D1.

30. Larry Armstrong, "Still Starstruck," *Business Week* (July 4, 1994): 38; Jeff Giles, "The Risks of Wishing Upon a Star," *Newsweek* (September 6, 1993): 38.

31. Cyndee Miller, "Celebrities Hot Despite Scandals," *Marketing News* (March 28, 1994): 1 (3 pp.).

32. W. Jeffrey Burroughs, Mary-Ann Hooten, and Patricia Knowles, "Celebrity-Product Congruence and Endorser Effectiveness," *Proceedings of the American Marketing Association Summer Educators' Conference* (August 1994): 395; see also James Lynch and Drue Schuler, "The Matchup Effect of Spokesperson and Product Congruence: A Schema Theory Interpretation," *Psychology & Marketing* 11, 5 (September/October 1994): 417–45; M. Walker, L. Langmeyer, and D. Langmeyer, "Celebrity Endorsers: Do You Get What You Pay For?" *Journal of Consumer Marketing* 9 (1992): 69–76.

33. Thomas R. King, "Credibility Gap: More Consumers Find Celebrity Ads Unpersuasive," *Wall Street Journal* (July 5, 1989): B5; Bruce Haring, "Company Totes Up Popularity Quotients," *Billboard Magazine* 101 (1989): 12.

34. Marie Okabe, "Fading Yen for Foreign Stars in Ads," *Singapore Straits-Times* (1986).

35. Haring, "Company Totes Up Popularity Quotients."

36. Kevin Goldman, "Catch a Falling Star: Big Names Plummet from List of Top 10 Celebrity Endorsers," *Wall Street Journal* (October 19, 1994): B1.

37. Anthony R. Pratkanis, Anthony G. Greenwald, Michael R. Leippe, and Michael H. Baumgardner, "In Search of Reliable Persuasion Effects: III. The Sleeper Effect Is Dead, Long Live the Sleeper Effect," *Journal of Personality and Social Psychology* 54 (1988): 203–18.

38. Herbert C. Kelman and Carl I. Hovland, "Reinstatement of the Communication in Delayed Measurement of Opinion Change," *Journal of Abnormal Psychology* 4, 48 (1953): 327–35.

39. Darlene Hannah and Brian Sternthal, "Detecting and Explaining the Sleeper Effect," *Journal of Consumer Research* 11 (September 1984): 632–42.

40. David Mazursky and Yaacov Schul, "The Effects of Advertisement Encoding on the Failure to Discount Information: Implications for the Sleeper Effect," *Journal of Consumer Research* 15 (June 1988): 24–36.

41. David W. Stewart and David H. Furse, "The Effects of Television Advertising Execution on Recall, Comprehension, and Persuasion," *Psychology & Marketing* 2 (fall 1985): 135–60.

42. R. C. Grass and W. H. Wallace, "Advertising Communication: Print vs. TV," *Journal of Advertising Research* 14 (1974): 19–23.

43. Elizabeth C. Hirschman and Michael R. Solomon, "Utilitarian, Aesthetic, and Familiarity Responses to Verbal Versus Visual Advertisements," in *Advances in Consumer Research* 11, ed. Thomas C. Kinnear (Provo, UT: Association for Consumer Research, 1984): 426–31.

44. Andrew A. Mitchell and Jerry C. Olson, "Are Product Attribute Beliefs the Only Mediator of Advertising Effects on Brand Attitude?" *Journal of Marketing Research* 18, 3 (1981): 318–32.

45. Terry L. Childers and Michael J. Houston, "Conditions for a Picture-Superiority Effect on Consumer Memory," *Journal of Consumer Research* 11 (September 1984): 643–54.

46. Andrew A. Mitchell, "The Effect of Verbal and Visual Components of Advertisements on Brand Attitudes and Attitude Toward the Advertisement," *Journal of Consumer Research* 13 (June 1986): 12–24.

47. John R. Rossiter and Larry Percy, "Attitude Change Through Visual Imagery in Advertising," *Journal of Advertising Research* 9, 2 (1980): 10–6.

48. Jolita Kiselius and Brian Sternthal, "Examining the Vividness Controversy: An Availability-Valence Interpretation," *Journal of Consumer Research* 12 (March 1986): 418–31.

49. Scott B. Mackenzie, "The Role of Attention in Mediating the Effect of Advertising on Attribute Importance," *Journal of Consumer Research* 13 (September 1986): 174–95.

50. Robert B. Zajonc, "Attitudinal Effects of Mere Exposure," Monograph, *Journal of Personality and Social Psychology* 8 (1968): 1–29.

51. George E. Belch, "The Effects of Television Commercial Repetition on Cognitive Response and Message Acceptance," *Journal of Consumer Research* 9 (June 1982): 56–65; Marian Burke and Julie Edell, "Ad Reactions Over Time: Capturing Changes in the Real World," *Journal of Consumer Research* 13 (June 1986): 114–8; Herbert Krugman, "Why Three Exposures May Be Enough," *Journal of Advertising Research* 12 (December 1972): 11–4.

52. Robert F. Bornstein, "Exposure and Affect: Overview and Meta-Analysis of Research, 1968–1987," *Psychological Bulletin* 106, 2 (1989): 265–89; Arno Rethans, John Swasy, and Lawrence Marks, "Effects of Television Commercial Repetition, Receiver Knowledge, and Commercial Length: A Test of the Two-Factor Model," *Journal of Marketing Research* 23 (February 1986): 50–61.

53. Linda L. Golden and Mark I. Alpert, "Comparative Analysis of the Relative Effectiveness of One- and Two-Sided Communication for Contrasting Products," *Journal of Advertising* 16 (1987); Kamins, "Celebrity and Noncelebrity Advertising in a Two-Sided Context"; Robert B. Settle and Linda L. Golden, "Attribution Theory and Advertiser Credibility," *Journal of Marketing Research* 11 (May 1974): 181–5.

54. See Alan G. Sawyer, "The Effects of Repetition of Refutational and Supportive Advertising Appeals," *Journal of Marketing Research* 10 (February 1973): 23–33; George J. Szybillo and Richard Heslin, "Resistance to Persuasion: Inoculation Theory in a Marketing Context," *Journal of Marketing Research* 10 (November 1973): 396–403; Ayn E. Crowley and Wayne D. Hoyer, "An Integrative Framework for Understanding Two-Sided Persuasion," *Journal of Consumer Research* 20, 4 (March 1994): 561–74; Cornelia Pechmann, "Predicting When Two-Sided Ads Will be More Effective Than One-Sided Ads: The Role of Correlational and Correspondent Inferences," *Journal of Marketing Research* 29 (November 1992): 441–53.

55. Lawrence M. Fisher, "Winery's Answer to Critics: Print Good and Bad Reviews," *New York Times* (January 9, 1991): D5.

56. Golden and Alpert, "Comparative Analysis of the Relative Effectiveness of One- and Two-Sided Communication for Contrasting Products."

57. G. Belch, M. Belch, and Villareal, "Effects of Advertising Communications."

58. Frank R. Kardes, "Spontaneous Inference Processes in Advertising: The Effects of Conclusion Omission and Involvement on Persuasion," *Journal of Consumer Research* 15 (September 1988): 225–33.

59. G. Belch, M. Belch and Villareal, "Effects of Advertising Communications."

60. Cornelia Dröge and Rene Y. Darmon, "Associative Positioning Strategies Through Comparative Advertising: Attribute vs. Overall Similarity Approaches," *Journal of Marketing Research* 24 (1987): 377–89; D. Muehling and N. Kangun, "The Multidimensionality of Comparative Advertising: Implications for the FTC," *Journal of Public Policy and Marketing* (1985): 112–28; Beth A. Walker and Helen H. Anderson, "Reconceptualizing Comparative Advertising: A Framework and Theory of Effects," in *Advances in Consumer Research* 18, eds. Rebecca H. Holman and Michael R. Solomon (Provo, UT: Association for Consumer Research, 1991): 342–7; William L. Wilkie and Paul W. Farris, "Comparison Advertising: Problems and Potential," *Journal of Marketing* 39 (October 1975): 7–15; R. G. Wyckham, "Implied Superiority Claims," *Journal of Advertising Research* (February/March 1987): 54–63.

61. Stephen A. Goodwin and Michael Etgar, "An Experimental Investigation of Comparative Advertising: Impact of Message Appeal, Information Load, and Utility of Product Class," *Journal of Marketing Research* 17 (May 1980): 187–202; Gerald J. Gorn and Charles B. Weinberg, "The Impact of Comparative Advertising on Perception and Attitude: Some Positive Findings," *Journal of Consumer Research* 11 (September 1984): 719–27; Terence A. Shimp and David C. Dyer, "The Effects of Comparative Advertising Mediated by Market Position of Sponsoring Brand," *Journal of Advertising* 3 (summer 1978): 13–9; R. Dale Wilson, "An Empirical Evaluation of Comparative Advertising Messages: Subjects, Responses to Perceptual Dimensions," in *Advances in Consumer Research* 3, ed. B. B. Anderson (Ann Arbor, MI: Association for Consumer Research, 1976): 53–7; Randall L. Rose, Paul W. Miniard, Michael J. Barone, Kenneth C. Manning, and Brian D. Till, "When Persuasion Goes Undetected: The Case of Comparative Advertising," *Journal of Marketing Research* 30 (August 1993): 315–30.

62. Dröge and Darmon, "Associative Positioning Strategies Through Comparative Advertising: Attribute vs. Overall Similarity Approaches."

63. Dottie Enrico, "Guaranteed! Greatest Advertising Story Ever Told!" *Newsday* (October 16, 1991): 43; Bruce Buchanan and Doron Goldman, "Us vs. Them: The Minefield of Comparative Ads," *Harvard Business Review* 38,7 (May/June 1989): 50.

64. Michael Lev, "For Car Buyers, Technology or Zen," *New York Times* (May 22, 1989): D1.

65. "Connecting Consumer and Product," *New York Times* (January 18, 1990): D19.

66. Edward F. Cone, "Image and Reality," *Forbes* (December 14, 1987): 226.

67. H. Zielske, "Does Day-After Recall Penalize Feeling Ads?" *Journal of Advertising Research* 22 (1982): 19–22.

68. Cone, "Image and Reality."

69. G. Belch, M. Belch, and Villareal, "Effects of Advertising Communications"; Courtney and Whipple, *Sex Stereotyping in Advertising;* Michael S. LaTour,

"Female Nudity in Print Advertising: An Analysis of Gender Differences in Arousal and Ad Response," *Psychology & Marketing* 7, 1 (1990): 65–81; B. G. Yovovich, "Sex in Advertising—The Power and the Perils," *Advertising Age* (May 2, 1983): M4–M5.

70. Marc G. Weinberger and Harlan E. Spotts, "Humor in U.S. Versus U.K. TV Commercials: A Comparison," *Journal of Advertising* 18, 2 (1989): 39–44.

71. Thomas J. Madden, "Humor in Advertising: An Experimental Analysis" (working paper No. 8327, University of Massachusetts, 1984); Thomas J. Madden and Marc G. Weinberger, "The Effects of Humor on Attention in Magazine Advertising," *Journal of Advertising* 11, 3 (1982): 8–14; Weinberger and Spotts, "Humor in U.S. Versus U.K. TV Commercials."

72. David Gardner, "The Distraction Hypothesis in Marketing," *Journal of Advertising Research* 10, (1970): 25–30.

73. Kevin Goldman, "Knock, Knock. Who's There? The Same Old Funny Ad Again," *Wall Street Journal* (November 2, 1993): B10.

74. "Funny Ads Provide Welcome Relief During These Gloom and Doom Days," *Marketing News* (April 17, 1981): 3.

75. Lynette S. Unger and James M. Stearns, "The Use of Fear and Guilt Messages in Television Advertising: Issues and Evidence," in *1983 AMA Educators' Proceedings,* eds. Patrick E. Murphy et al. (Chicago: American Marketing Association, 1983): 16–20.

76. *Lurzer's Archiv* (Frankfurt, 1994).

77. Kevin Goldman, "Everybody's Afraid of the Big Bad Boss," *New York Times* (January 12, 1994): B1 (2 pp.).

78. Michael L. Ray and William L. Wilkie, "Fear: The Potential of an Appeal Neglected by Marketing," *Journal of Marketing* 34, 1 (1970): 54–62; Tony L. Henthorne, Michael S. LaTour, and Rajan Nataraajan, "Fear Appeals in Print Advertising: An Analysis of Arousal and Ad Response," *Journal of Advertising* 22, 2 (June 1993): 59–70; Thomas Giese, Dana-Nicoleta Lascu, and Terry M. Weisenberger, "Intended and Unintended Consequences of the Use of Fear and Guilt Appeals in Marketing Communications," *Proceedings of the Southern Marketing Association* (1993): 12.

79. Ronald Paul Hill, "An Exploration of the Relationship Between AIDS-Related Anxiety and the Evaluation of Condom Advertisements," *Journal of Advertising* 17, 4 (1988): 35–42.

80. Randall Rothenberg, "Talking Too Tough on Life's Risks?" *New York Times* (February 16, 1990): D1.

81. Barbara B. Stern, "Medieval Allegory: Roots of Advertising Strategy for the Mass Market," *Journal of Marketing* 52 (July 1988): 84–94.

82. Judith Waldrop, "They're Coming to Take You Away (Fear as a Form of Persuasion)," *American Demographics* (June 15, 1988): 2; John F. Tanner, Jr., James

B. Hunt, and David R. Eppright, "The Protection Motivation Model: A Normative Model of Fear Appeals," *Journal of Marketing* 55 (July 1991): 36–45.

83. Brian Sternthal and C. Samuel Craig, "Fear Appeals: Revisited and Revised," *Journal of Consumer Research* 1 (December 1974): 22–34.

84. Stern, "Medieval Allegory."

85. Andrew E. Serwer, "Crime Stoppers Making a Killing," *Fortune* (April 4, 1994): 109 (3 pp.).

86. Kevin Goldman, "NRA Says Its Ads Aimed at Women are Educational," *Wall Street Journal* (September 28, 1993): B6.

87. "A Drive to Woo Women and Invigorate Sales," *New York Times* (April 2, 1989).

88. Carrie Goerne, "Gun Companies Target Women: Foes Call it Marketing to Fear," *Marketing News* (August 31, 1992): 1.

89. Edward F. McQuarrie and David Glen Mick, "On Resonance: A Critical Pluralistic Inquiry into Advertising Rhetoric," *Journal of Consumer Research* 19 (September 1992): 180–97.

90. See Linda M. Scott, "The Troupe: Celebrities as Dramatis Personae in Advertisements," in *Advances in Consumer Research* 18, eds. Rebecca H. Holman and Michael R. Solomon (Provo, UT: Association for Consumer Research, 1991): 355–63; Barbara Stern, "Literary Criticism and Consumer Research: Overview and Illustrative Analysis," *Journal of Consumer Research* 16 (1989): 322–34; Judith Williamson, *Decoding Advertisements* (Boston: Marion Boyars, 1978).

91. John Deighton, Daniel Romer, and Josh McQueen, "Using Drama to Persuade," *Journal of Consumer Research* 16 (December 1989): 335–43.

92. Richard E. Petty, John T. Cacioppo, and David Schumann, "Central and Peripheral Routes to Advertising Effectiveness: The Moderating Role of Involvement," *Journal of Consumer Research* 10, 2 (1983): 135–46.

93. Jerry C. Olson, Daniel R. Toy, and Philip A. Dover, "Do Cognitive Responses Mediate the Effects of Advertising Content on Cognitive Structure?" *Journal of Consumer Research* 9, 3 (1982): 245–62.

94. Julie A. Edell and Andrew A. Mitchell, "An Information Processing Approach to Cognitive Responses," in *Research Frontiers in Marketing: Dialogues and Directions,* ed. S. C. Jain (Chicago: American Marketing Association, 1978).

95. See Mary Jo Bitner and Carl Obermiller, "The Elaboration Likelihood Model: Limitations and Extensions in Marketing," in *Advances in Consumer Research* 12, eds. Elizabeth C. Hirschman and Morris B. Holbrook (Provo, UT: Association for Consumer Research, 1985): 420–5; Meryl P. Gardner, "Does Attitude Toward the Ad Affect Brand Attitude

Under a Brand Evaluation Set?" *Journal of Marketing Research* 22 (1985): 192–8; C. W. Park and S. M. Young, "Consumer Response to Television Commercials: The Impact of Involvement and Background Music on Brand Attitude Formation," *Journal of Marketing Research* 23 (1986): 11–24; Petty, Cacioppo, and Schumann, "Central and Peripheral Routes to Advertising Effectiveness"; for a discussion of how different kinds of involvement interact with the ELM, see Robin A. Higie, Lawrence F. Feick, and Linda L. Price, "The Importance of Peripheral Cues in Attitude Formation for Enduring and Task-Involved Individuals," in *Advances in Consumer Research* 18, eds. Rebecca H. Holman and Michael R. Solomon (Provo, UT: Association for Consumer Research, 1991): 187–93.

96. J. Craig Andrews and Terence A. Shimp, "Effects of Involvement, Argument Strength, and Source Characteristics on Central and Peripheral Processing in Advertising," *Psychology & Marketing* 7 (fall 1990): 195–214.

97. Richard E. Petty, John T. Cacioppo, Constantine Sedikides, and Alan J. Strathman, "Affect and Persuasion: A Contemporary Perspective," *American Behavioral Scientist* 31, 3 (1988): 355–71.

THE ROAD NOT TAKEN

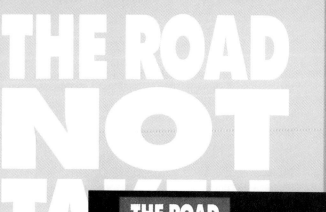

THE ROAD NOT TAKEN.

Want to know the perfect hood ornament? A man. If ever there was a single product that captured the spirit of the American male it's the automobile. And if ever there was a magazine that did it, it's Playboy. So how come the two of us can't get together?

40 years ago we created the ideal vehicle for Detroit to talk to men, but a billion ads and a zillion readers later there's an astonishing absence of Motown messages for all those guys driven by what they see, hear, discover and believe in Playboy. Guys who go from zero to sixty on features like Automotive Report, articles like *Gotti's Fall*, and Interviews that put an Anne Rice, Betty Friedan or Barry Bonds in the passenger seat.

Yes, we're a frankly male oriented book dedicated to all the dimensions of the male mind, heart and glands, but aren't you folks in the same business? Don't you sell adrenaline? Sensuality? Fantasy? You offer the exhilaration–and acceleration–of the possible. That's what men want, that's what you give them, and that's what Playboy has always been about. A journey through all the fascinating highways, byways and hideaways in the male personality.

Almost 10 million men take that journey every month. It's a shame they're not driving your car.

40TH ANNIVERSARY PLAYBOY OPEN UP YOUR MIND.

© PLAYBOY 1994

Rhoda has been trying to concentrate on the report her client is expecting by five o'clock. Rhoda has always worked hard to maintain this important account for the firm, but today she keeps getting distracted thinking about her date last night with Rob. Although things seemed to go okay, why couldn't she shake the feeling that Rob regarded her more as a friend than as a potential romantic partner?

Leafing through *Glamour* and *Cosmopolitan* during her lunch hour, Rhoda is struck by all of the articles about ways to be more attractive by dieting, exercise, and wearing sexy clothes. Rhoda begins to feel depressed as she looks at the models in the many advertisements for perfumes, apparel, and makeup. Each woman is more glamorous and beautiful than the next. She could swear that some of them must have had breast implants and other assorted "adjustments." Women just don't look that way in real life.

In her down mood, Rhoda even entertains the thought that maybe she should look into cosmetic surgery. Even though she's never considered herself unattractive, who knows! Maybe a new nose or larger breasts are what it will take to turn Rob around. On second thought, though, is he even worth it? . . .

7

The Self

∙∙∙∙∙∙∙∙∙∙∙∙∙∙∙∙∙∙∙∙∙∙∙∙∙∙∙∙∙∙∙∙∙∙∙∙∙∙∙

PERSPECTIVES ON THE SELF

Rhoda is not alone in feeling that her physical appearance and possessions affect her "value" as a person. Consumers' insecurities about their appearance are rampant: It has been estimated that 72 percent of men and 85 percent of women are unhappy with at least one aspect of their appearance.[1] Many products, from cars to cologne, are bought because people are trying to highlight or hide some aspect of the self. This chapter focuses on the self, and we'll consider how consumers' feelings about themselves shape their consumption practices, particularly as they strive to fulfill their society's expectations about how males or females should look and act.

Exposure to ads can trigger a process of *social comparison,* wherein the person tries to evaluate his or her self by comparing it to other people's and those of media images. This form of comparison appears to be a basic human motive, and many marketers have tapped into this need by supplying idealized images of happy, attractive people who just happen to be using their products. A recent study illustrates this process of social comparison. It showed that female college students do tend to compare their physical appearance with that of models who appear in advertising. Furthermore, the study participants who were exposed to beautiful women in advertisements afterwards expressed lowered satisfaction with their *own* appearance, as compared to other participants who did not view ads with models.[2] Another study demonstrated that young women's perceptions of their body shapes and sizes can be altered after being exposed to as little as 30 minutes of television programming.[3]

The 1980s were called the "Me Decade" because, for many, this time was marked by an absorption with the self. While it seems natural to think about each consumer as having a self, this concept is actually a relatively new way of regarding people and their relationships to society. The idea that each single human life is unique, rather than a part of a group, only developed in late medieval times (between the 11th and 15th centuries). The notion that the self is an object to be pampered is even more recent. In addition, the emphasis on the unique nature of the self is much greater in Western societies.[4] Many Eastern cultures instead stress the importance of a collective self, in which the person's identity is derived in large measure from his or her social group.

The self can be understood from many different theoretical vantage points. From a psychoanalytic, or Freudian, perspective, the self is a system of competing forces riddled with conflict (see Chapter 4). As we saw in Chapter 3, behaviorists tend to regard the self as a collection of conditioned responses. From a cognitive orientation, the self is an information-processing system, an organizing force that serves as a nucleus around which new information is processed.[5]

Self-Concept

The **self-concept** refers to the attitude a person holds toward him- or herself. Just as a consumer has an attitude toward Pepsi or democracy, the self is also a subject of evaluation. An overall self-attitude is frequently positive, but not always; there are certainly parts of the self that are evaluated more positively than others. For example, Rhoda felt better about her professional identity than she did about her feminine identity.

COMPONENTS OF THE SELF-CONCEPT

Compared to other attitudes, the self-concept is a very complex structure. It is composed of many attributes, some of which are given greater emphasis in determining overall self-attitude. Attributes of self-concept can be described along such dimensions as their content (e.g., facial attractiveness versus mental aptitude), positivity or negativity (i.e., self-esteem), intensity, stability over time, and accuracy (i.e., the degree to which one's self-assessment corresponds to reality).[6] As will be seen later in the chapter, consumers' self-assessments can be quite distorted, especially with regard to their physical appearance.

SELF-ESTEEM

Self-esteem refers to the positivity of one's attitude toward oneself. People with low self-esteem do not expect that they will perform very well, and they will try to avoid embarrassment, failure, or rejection. In developing a new line of snack cakes, for example, Sara Lee found that consumers low in self-esteem preferred portion-controlled snack items because they felt they lacked self-control.[7] In contrast, people with high self-esteem expect to be successful, will take more risks, and are more willing to be the center of attention.[8] Self-esteem often is related to acceptance by others. For example, high school students who "hang out" in high-status "crowds" have higher self-esteem than their classmates.[9]

Self-esteem advertising attempts to change product attitudes by stimulating positive feelings about the self.[10] One strategy is to challenge the consumer's self-esteem and then show a linkage to a product. For example, the Marine Corps uses this strategy with its theme "If you have what it takes. . . ." Another strategy is to flatter the consumer, as when Virginia Slims cigarettes says, "You've come a long way, baby." Sometimes such compliments are derived by comparing the consumer to others. For instance, many consumers are socialized to consider body odors repulsive and are motivated to protect their self-image by denying the existence of these odors in themselves. This attitude explains the success of the theme for Dial soap's advertising: "Aren't you glad you use Dial? Don't you wish everyone did?"[11] Other examples of self-esteem appeals appear in Table 7–1.

REAL AND IDEAL SELVES

Self-esteem is influenced by a process where the consumer compares his or her actual standing on some attribute to some ideal. A consumer might ask, "Am I as attractive as I would like to be?" "Do I make as much money as I should?" and so on. The **ideal self** is a person's conception of how he or she would like to be, while the **actual self** is our more realistic appraisal of the qualities we do and don't have.

The ideal self is partly molded by elements of the consumer's culture, such as heroes or people depicted in advertising, that serve as models of achievement or appearance.[12] Products may be purchased because they are believed to be instrumental in helping the consumer achieve these goals. Some products are chosen because they are perceived to be consistent with the consumer's actual self, while others are used to help in reaching the standard set by the ideal self.

While most people experience a discrepancy between their real and ideal selves, for some consumers this gap is larger than for others. These people are especially good targets for marketing communications that employ *fantasy appeals*.[13] A **fantasy** or daydream is a self-induced shift in consciousness, which is sometimes a way of compensating for a lack of external stimulation or coping with problems in the real world.[14]

Many products and services are successful because they appeal to consumers' tendencies to fantasize. These marketing strategies allow us to extend our vision of ourselves by placing us in unfamiliar, exciting situations or by permitting us to "try

TABLE 7–1 ▼ Examples of Self-Esteem Appeals in Advertising

PRODUCT	AD THEME
Virginia Slims cigarettes	"You've come a long way, baby."
Clairol hair coloring	"You're not getting older, you're getting better."
Michelob beer	"You know where you're going."
Budweiser beer	"For all you do, this Bud's for you."
Pepsi Cola	"You're feeling good about yourself and you're drinking Diet Pepsi—and it shows."
McDonald's	"You deserve a break today."
Salem cigarettes	"You've got what it takes."
Republic Airlines	"Perks; you've earned them."

Source: Adapted from Jeffrey F. Durgee, "Self-Esteem Advertising," *Journal of Advertising* 14, 4 (1986): 21. Reprinted with permission.

MARKETING OPPORTUNITY

The aging of the population and the market saturation of material goods for many affluent consumers is fueling a demand for fantasy experiences. People with ample disposable income appear to be running out of material things to buy, so their attention is instead turning inward toward an emphasis on consuming experiences rather than status-laden goods. "Experience vacations," as they are called in the travel industry, combine physical and mental exertion and often have a large sensory component. Popular excursions include mountain climbing, going on safaris, and exploring primitive countries. These trips now account for between five percent and ten percent of the money spent by Americans on travel. The typical adventure traveler is an affluent male approaching middle age.[15]

A number of hotels and resorts are targeting the emerging fantasy market. The Hyatt Regency Waikaloa in Hawaii offers man-made islands, lagoons, and waterfalls, as well as gondola transportation and deer, exotic birds, and porpoises. A seven-story floating resort is opening on the Great Barrier Reef off the coast of Australia. Jules' Undersea Lodge in Florida is a luxury hotel built into the shell of a former underwater sea lab. The more down-to-earth fantasizer can stay at a hotel in Iowa that features a "Lovers' Leap" suite, where guests sleep in a red 1973 Delta 88 Royale convertible.[16]

on" interesting or provocative roles. Nissan played on this theme in its commercials for the 240SX model. As illustrated by the storyboard shown here, a male driver imagines that his girlfriend instead of his dog is with him and then makes a more unlikely substitution, fantasizing that model Christie Brinkley has taken her place.

Multiple Selves

In a way, each consumer is really a number of different people. We have as many selves as we do different social roles. Depending upon the situation, we act differently, use different products and services, and even vary in terms of how much we like ourselves. A person may require a different set of products to play a desired role: She may choose a sedate, understated perfume when she is being her professional self but splash on something more provocative on Saturday night as she becomes her femme fatale self. The *dramaturgical perspective* on consumer behavior views people much like actors who play different roles. We each play many roles, and each has its own script, props, and costumes.[17]

ROLE IDENTITIES

Depending on the characteristics of a situation and the other people with whom one is interacting, different roles are played. The self can be thought of as having different components or *role identities,* and only some of these are active at any given time. Some identities (e.g., husband, boss, or student) are more central to the self than others, but other identities (e.g., stamp collector, dancer, or advocate for the homeless) may be dominant in specific situations. For example, executives in a

If I had a Nissan 240SX . . . it would be a red coupe.

Wait! A silver fastback. And I'd go for a spin up Route 7, the twisty part.

Just me and Astro . . .

no, Amy.

Heck, Christie Brinkley!

Wow! Yeah, me and Christie . . .

in my silver—no, red 240SX . . . driving into the sunset.

This storyboard for a Nissan 240SX ad illustrates the use of the fantasy theme, which allows consumers to try on new roles and extend their vision of the ideal self. Reprinted by permission of Nissan Motor Corporation USA and Christie Brinkley.

This Sony Walkman ad uses a variety of props to emphasize its appeal to all sides of a consumer's personality. Courtesy of Sony Corporation of America.

survey done in the United States, the United Kingdom, and some Pacific Rim countries said that different aspects of their personalities come into play depending on whether they are making purchase decisions at home or at work. Not surprisingly, they report being less time conscious, more emotional, and less disciplined in their home roles.[18]

SYMBOLIC INTERACTIONISM

If each person potentially has many social selves, how does each develop, and how do we decide which self to "activate" at any point in time? The sociological tradition of **symbolic interactionism** stresses that relationships with other people play a large part in forming the self.[19] This perspective maintains that people exist in a symbolic environment and the meaning attached to any situation or object is determined by the interpretation of these symbols. As members of society, we learn to agree on shared meanings. Thus, we "know" that a red light means stop, the "golden arches" means fast food, and "blondes have more fun."

Like other social objects, the meanings of consumers themselves are defined by social consensus. The consumer interprets his or her own identity, and this assessment is continually evolving as he or she encounters new situations and people. In symbolic interactionist terms, we *negotiate* these meanings over time. Essentially, the consumer poses the question, "Who am I in this situation?" The answer to this question is greatly influenced by those around us and is really an answer to the question, "Who do other people think I am?" We tend to pattern our behavior on the perceived expectations of others in a form of *self-fulfilling prophecy*. By acting the way we *assume* others expect us to act, we often wind up confirming these perceptions.

This process of imagining the reactions of others toward us is known as "taking the role of the other," or the **looking-glass self.**[20] According to this view, a process of *reflexive evaluation* occurs when the individual attempts to define the self, and it operates as a sort of psychological sonar: We take readings of our own identity by "bouncing" signals off of others. The looking-glass image we receive will differ depending upon whose views we are considering. Like the images in distorted mirrors in a fun house, our appraisal of who we are can vary, depending upon whose perspective we are taking. A confident career woman like Rhoda may sit morosely at a bar or discotheque imagining that others see her as an unattractive woman with little sex appeal (whether these perceptions are true or not).

Self-Consciousness

There are times when people seem to be painfully aware of themselves. If you have ever walked into a class in the middle of a lecture and noticed that all eyes were on you, you can understand this feeling of self-consciousness. In contrast, consumers sometimes behave with little self-consciousness. For example, people may do things in a stadium, during a riot, or at a fraternity party that they would never do if they were highly conscious of their behavior.[21]

Some people seem, in general, to be more sensitive to the image they communicate to others (on the other hand, we all know people who act as if they're oblivious to the impression they are making!). A heightened concern about the nature of one's public "image" also results in more concern about the social appropriateness of products and consumption activities.

Several measures have been devised to quantify this tendency. Consumers who score high on a scale of public self-consciousness, for example, are also more interested in clothing and tend to be heavier users of cosmetics.[22] A similar measure is *self-monitoring*. High self-monitors are more attuned to how they present themselves in their social environments, and their product choices are influenced by their estimates of how these items will be perceived by others.[23] Self-monitoring is assessed by consumers' extents of agreement with such items as "I guess I put on a show to impress or entertain others" or "I would probably make a good actor."[24]

PERSONALITY

To understand the nature of the self, some theorists focus on the concept of **personality,** which refers to a person's unique psychological makeup and how it consistently influences the way a person responds to his or her environment. In recent years, the nature of the personality construct has been hotly debated. Many studies have found that people tend not to behave consistently across different situations and that they do not seem to exhibit stable personalities. In fact, some researchers feel that people do not exhibit a consistent personality across different situations; they argue that this is merely a convenient way to think about other people.

This argument is a bit hard to accept intuitively, possibly because we tend to see others in a limited range of situations, and so, to us, most people do act consistently. On the other hand, we each know that we are not all that consistent; we may be wild and crazy at times and the model of respectability at others. While certainly not all psychologists have abandoned the idea of personality, many now recognize that a person's underlying characteristics are but one part of the puzzle and that situational factors often play a very large role in determining behavior.[25] This realization underscores the potential importance of segmenting according to situations, a concept discussed in Chapter 9. Still, some aspects of personality continue to be included in marketing strategies. These dimensions are usually employed in concert with a person's choices of leisure activities, political outlook, aesthetic tastes, and other individual factors to segment consumers in terms of *lifestyles,* a process described more fully in Chapter 16.

Classic Personality Theories

Many approaches to understanding the complex concept of personality can be traced to psychological theorists who began to develop these perspectives in the early part of the century. These perspectives were qualitative, in the sense that they were largely based on analysts' interpretations of patients' accounts of dreams, traumatic experiences, and encounters with others.

Much of this work was significantly influenced by Sigmund Freud's psychoanalytic theory of personality. Some of Freud's ideas were discussed in Chapter 4, since they are so important in understanding the deep-seated needs that may motivate consumers to acquire brands with "personalities" that somehow satisfy these underlying desires.

NEO-FREUDIAN THEORIES

Recall that much of Freud's emphasis was on how people found socially acceptable ways to satisfy sexual desires. Although Freud opened the door to the realization that explanations for behavior may lurk beneath the surface, many of his co-workers and students felt that an individual's personality was more influenced by how he or she handled relationships with others. These theorists are often called *neo-Freudian* (meaning following from or being influenced by Freud).

One of the most prominent neo-Freudians was a psychoanalyst named Karen Horney. She proposed that people can be described as moving toward others (compliant), away from others (detached), or against others (aggressive).[26] Some research indicates that these three types prefer different kinds of products. For example, one study found that compliant people are more likely to gravitate toward name-brand products, detached types are more likely to be tea drinkers, while males classified as aggressive prefer brands with a strong masculine orientation (e.g., Old Spice deodorant).[27] Other well-known neo-Freudians include Alfred Adler, who proposed that many actions are motivated by people's desires to overcome feelings of inferiority relative to others, and Harry Stack Sullivan, who focused on how personality evolves to reduce anxiety in social relationships.[28]

JUNGIAN THEORY

Carl Jung was also a disciple of Freud's (and was being groomed by Freud to be his successor). However, Jung was unable to accept Freud's emphasis on sexual aspects of personality, and this was a contributing factor in the eventual dissolution of their relationship. Jung went on to develop his own method of psychotherapy, which became known as *analytical psychology.* This approach emphasized both the individual's development as a creative person (his or her future) and his or her individual and racial history (his or her past) in the formation of personality.

Jung believed that people are shaped by the cumulative experiences of past generations. A central part of his perspective was an emphasis on what Jung called the *collective unconscious,* which is a storehouse of memories inherited from our ancestral past. For example, Jung would argue that many people are afraid of the dark because their distant ancestors had good reason to exhibit this fear. These shared memories create **archetypes,** or universally shared ideas and behavior patterns. Archetypes involve themes, such as birth, death, or the devil, that appear frequently in myths, stories, and dreams.

Jung's ideas may seem a bit far-fetched, but advertising messages often do invoke (at least intuitively) archetypes to link products with underlying meanings. For example, some of the archetypes identified by Jung and his followers include the old wise man and the earth mother.[29] These images appear frequently in marketing messages that use such characters as wizards, revered teachers, or even Mother Nature to convince people of the merits of products.

Trait Theory

One approach to personality is to focus on the quantitative measurement of **traits,** or identifiable characteristics that define a person. For example, people can be distinguished by the degree to which they are socially outgoing (the trait of *extroversion*). Some specific traits that are relevant to consumer behavior include *innovativeness* (the degree to which a person likes to try new things), *materialism* (amount of emphasis placed on acquiring and owning products), *self-consciousness* (the degree to which a person deliberately monitors and controls the image of the self that is projected to others), and *need for cognition* (the degree to which a person likes to think about things and, by extension, to expend the necessary effort to process brand information).[30]

Since large numbers of consumers can be categorized in terms of their standing on various traits, these approaches can, in theory, be used for segmentation purposes. If a car manufacturer, for example, could determine that drivers who fit a trait profile are more likely to prefer a car with certain features, this match could be used to great advantage. The notion that consumers buy products that are extensions of their personalities makes intuitive sense. This idea is endorsed by many marketing managers, who try to create brand personalities that will appeal to different types of consumers.

However, the use of standard personality-trait measurements to predict product choices has met with mixed success at best. In general, marketing researchers simply have not been able to predict consumers' behaviors on the basis of measured personality traits. A number of explanations have been offered for these equivocal results.[31]

- Many of the scales are not sufficiently valid or reliable; they do not adequately measure what they are supposed to measure, and their results may not be stable over time.

- Personality tests are often developed for specific populations (e.g., mentally ill people); these tests are then "borrowed" and applied to the general population where their relevance is questionable.

- The tests often are not administered under the appropriate conditions; they may be given in a classroom or over a kitchen table by people who are not properly trained.

- The researchers often make changes in the instruments to adapt them to their own situations, in the process deleting or adding items and renaming variables.

These ad hoc changes dilute the validity of the measures and also reduce researchers' ability to compare results across consumer samples.

● Many trait scales are intended to measure gross, overall tendencies (e.g., emotional stability or introversion); these results are then used to make predictions about purchases of specific brands.

● In many cases, a number of scales are given with no advance thought about how these measures should be related to consumer behavior. The researchers then use a shotgun approach, following up on anything that happens to look interesting.

Although the use of personality measures by marketing researchers was largely abandoned after many studies failed to yield meaningful results, some researchers have not abandoned the early promise of this line of work. More recent efforts (many in Europe) have been focused on benefiting from past mistakes. These researchers are using more specific measures of personality traits that they have reason to believe are relevant to economic behavior. They are trying to increase the validity of these measures, primarily by using multiple measures of behavior rather than relying on the common practice of trying to predict purchasing responses from a single item on a personality test.

In addition, they have toned down their expectations of what personality traits can tell them about consumers. They now recognize that traits are only part of the solution, and personality data must be incorporated with information about people's social and economic conditions in order to be useful.[32] As a result, some more recent research has had better success at relating personality traits to such consumer behaviors as alcohol consumption among young men or shoppers' willingness to try new, healthier food products.[33]

CONSUMPTION AND SELF-CONCEPT

By extending the dramaturgical perspective a bit further, one can easily see how the consumption of products and services contributes to the definition of the self. For an actor to play a role convincingly, he or she needs the correct props, stage setting, and so on. Consumers learn that different roles are accompanied by *constellations* of products and activities that help to define these roles.[34] Some "props" are so important to the roles we play that they can be viewed as a part of the *extended self,* a concept to be discussed shortly.

Products That Shape the Self: You Are What You Consume

The reflected self helps to shape self-concept, which implies that people see themselves as they imagine others see them. Since what others see includes a person's clothing, jewelry, furniture, car, and so on, it stands to reason that these products also help to determine the perceived self. A consumer's products place him or her into a social role, which helps to answer the question "Who am I now?"

People use an individual's consumption behaviors to help them make judgments about who that person is. In addition to considering a person's clothes, grooming habits, and so on, we make inferences about personality based on a person's choice of leisure activities (e.g., squash versus bowling), food preferences (e.g., vegetarians versus "steak-and-potatoes" people), cars, home-decorating choices, and so on. People who are shown pictures of someone's living room, for example, are able to make surprisingly accurate guesses about that consumer's personality.[35] In the same way that a consumer's use of products influences others' perceptions, the same products can help to determine his or her *own* self-concept and social identity.[36]

A consumer exhibits *attachment* to an object to the extent that it is used by that person to maintain his or her self-concept.[37] Objects can act as a sort of security blanket by reinforcing our identities, especially in unfamiliar situations. For example, students who decorate their dorm rooms with personal items are less likely to drop out of college. This coping process may protect the self from being diluted in a strange environment.[38]

The use of consumption information to define the self is especially important when an identity is yet to be adequately formed, as occurs when a consumer plays a new or unfamiliar role. **Symbolic self-completion theory** predicts that people who have an incomplete self-definition tend to complete this identity by acquiring and displaying symbols associated with it.[39] Adolescent boys, for example, may use "macho" products like cars and cigarettes to bolster their developing masculinity; products are a sort of "social crutch" to be leaned upon during a period of uncertainty.

Product atttachment is perhaps most apparent when these treasured objects are lost or stolen. One of the first acts performed by institutions that want to repress individuality and encourage group identity, such as prisons or convents, is to confiscate personal possessions.[40] Victims of burglaries and natural disasters commonly report feelings of alienation, of depression, or of being "violated." One consumer's comment after being robbed is typical: "It's the next worst thing to being bereaved; it's like being raped."[41] Burglary victims exhibit a diminished sense of community and fewer feelings of privacy and take less pride in their houses' appearance than do their neighbors.[42]

In emphasizing the notion that looking the right way gives one confidence, this Yes Clothing ad relies on symbolic self-completion theory to appeal to consumers. © Philippe Berthome for No Comment!

Self/Product Congruence

Because many consumption activities are related to self-definition, it is not surprising to learn that consumers demonstrate consistency between their values and attitudes and the things they buy.[43] **Self-image congruence models** predict that products will be chosen when their attributes match some aspect of the self.[44] These models assume a process of cognitive matching between these attributes and the consumer's self-image.[45]

While results are somewhat mixed, the ideal self appears to be more relevant as a comparison standard for highly expressive social products, such as perfume. In contrast the actual self is more relevant for everyday, functional products. These standards are also likely to vary by usage situation. For example, a consumer might want a functional, reliable car to commute to work every day but a flashier model with more "zing" when going out on a date in the evening.

Research tends to support the idea of congruence between product usage and self-image. One of the earliest studies to examine this process found that car owners' ratings of themselves tended to match their perceptions of their cars. Pontiac drivers, for example, saw themselves as more active and flashier than did Volkswagen drivers.[46] Congruity also has been found between consumers and their most-preferred brands of beer, soap, toothpaste, and cigarettes relative to their least-preferred brands, as well as between consumers' self-images and their favorite stores.[47] Some specific attributes that have been found to be useful in describing some of the matches between consumers and products include rugged/delicate, excitable/calm, rational/emotional, and formal/informal.[48]

While these findings make some intuitive sense, we cannot blithely assume that consumers will always buy products whose "personality" characteristics match their own. It is not clear that consumers really see aspects of themselves in down-to-earth, functional products that don't have very complex or humanlike images. It is one thing to consider a brand personality for an expressive, image-oriented product like perfume and quite another to impute human characteristics to a toaster.

Another problem is the old "chicken-and-egg" question: Do people buy products because they are seen as similar to the self, or do they *assume* that these products must be similar because they have bought them? The similarity between a person's self-image and the images of products purchased does tend to increase with ownership, so this explanation cannot be ruled out.

The Extended Self

As noted earlier, many of the props and settings consumers use to define their social roles in a sense become a part of their selves. Those external objects that we consider a part of us comprise the **extended self.** In some cultures, people literally incorporate objects into the self—that is, they lick new possessions, take the names of conquered enemies (or, in some cases, eat them), or bury the dead with their possessions.[49]

We don't usually go that far, but many people do cherish possessions as if they were a part of them. Many material objects, ranging from personal possessions and pets to national monuments or landmarks, help to form a consumer's identity. Just about everyone can name a valued possession that has a lot of the self "wrapped up" in it, whether it is a beloved photograph, a trophy, an old shirt, a car, or a cat. Indeed, it is often possible to construct a pretty accurate "biography" of someone just by cataloguing the items on display in his or her bedroom or office.

In one study on the extended self, people were given a list of items that ranged from electronic equipment, facial tissues, and television programs to parents, body parts, and favorite clothes. They were asked to rate each in terms of its closeness to the self. Objects were more likely to be considered a part of the extended self if "psychic energy" was invested in them by expending effort to obtain them or because they were personalized and kept for a long time.[50]

Four levels of the extended self are used by consumers to define themselves. These range from very personal objects to places and things that allow people to feel as if they are rooted in their environments.[51]

- *Individual level.* Consumers include many of their personal possessions in self-definition. These products can include jewelry, cars, clothing, and so on. The saying "You are what you wear" reflects the belief that one's things are a part of what one is.

- *Family level.* This part of the extended self includes a consumer's residence and the furnishings in it. The house can be thought of as a symbolic body for the family and is often a central aspect of identity.

- *Community level.* It is common for consumers to describe themselves in terms of the neighborhood or town from which they come. For farm families or residents with close ties to a community, this sense of belonging is particularly important.

- *Group level.* Our attachments to certain social groups also can be considered a part of self. A consumer may feel that landmarks, monuments, or sports teams are a part of the extended self.

SEX ROLES

Sexual identity is a very important component of a consumer's self-concept. People often conform to their culture's expectations about what those of their sex should do. Of course, these guidelines change over time, and they can differ radically across societies. It's unclear to what extent sex differences are innate versus culturally shaped, but it is clear they're certainly evident in many consumption decisions!

Consider the sex differences market researchers have observed when comparing the food preferences of men versus women. Men are more likely to eat meat; as one food writer put it, "Boy food doesn't grow. It is hunted or killed." Women eat more fruit (however, men prefer fruit cocktail and raisins to a larger degree than women do). Men are more likely to eat Frosted Flakes or Corn Pops, while women prefer multigrain cereals. Men are big root beer drinkers; women account for the bulk of sales of bottled water. And, the sexes differ sharply in the quantities of food they eat: When researchers at Hershey's discovered that women eat smaller amounts of candy, the company created a white chocolate confection called Hugs, one of the most successful food introductions of all time. On the other hand, men are more likely to take their food and drink in larger servings. When Lipton advertised its iced tea during the Super Bowl, it told its (predominantly male) viewers, "This ain't no sippin' tea," and encouraged them to "gulp, guzzle, and chug it."[52]

Gender Differences in Socialization

A society's assumptions about the proper roles of men and women is communicated in terms of the ideal behaviors that are stressed for each sex (in advertising, among other places). It's likely, for instance, that many women eat smaller quantities because they have been "trained" to be more delicate and dainty.

Every society creates a set of expectations regarding the behaviors appropriate for men and women. For example, an activity such as Christmas shopping is widely regarded as "women's work."[53] In many societies, males are controlled by *agentic goals,* which stress self-assertion and mastery. Females, on the other hand, are taught to value *communal goals,* such as affiliation and the fostering of harmonious relations.[54]

MACHO MARKETERS

The field of marketing has historically been largely defined by men, so it still tends to be dominated by male values. Competition rather than cooperation is stressed, and the language of warfare and domination is often used. Strategists often use distinctly masculine concepts: "market penetration" or "competitive thrusts," for example. Academic marketing articles also emphasize agentic rather than communal goals. The most pervasive theme is power and control over others. Other themes include instrumentality (i.e., manipulating people for the good of an organization) and competition.[55] This bias may diminish in coming years, as more marketing researchers begin to stress such factors as emotions and aesthetics in purchase decisions, and as increasing numbers of women major in marketing!

GENDER VERSUS SEXUAL IDENTITY

Sex-role identity is a state of mind as well as body. A person's biological gender (i.e., male or female) does not totally determine whether he or she will exhibit **sex-typed traits,** or characteristics that are stereotypically associated with one sex or the other. A consumer's subjective feelings about his or her sexuality are crucial, as well.[56]

Unlike maleness and femaleness, masculinity and femininity are *not* biological characteristics. A behavior considered masculine in one culture may not be viewed as such in another. For example, the norm in the United States is that males should be "strong" and repress tender feelings (e.g., "Real men don't eat quiche") and male friends avoid touching each other (except in "safe" situations, such as on the football field). In some Latin and European cultures, however, it is common for men to hug one another. Each society determines what "real" men and women should and should not do.

SEX-TYPED PRODUCTS

Many products (in addition to quiche) also are *sex typed;* they take on masculine or feminine attributes, and consumers often associate them with one sex or another.[57] The car, for example, has long been thought of as a masculine product. The sex typing of products is often created or perpetuated by marketers (e.g., Princess telephones, boys' and girls' toys, and Luvs color-coded diapers). Some sex-typed products are listed in Table 7–2.

This ad for Bijan illustrates how sex role identities are culturally bound by contrasting the expectations of how women should appear in two different countries. Courtesy of Bijan. Photographer Jim Koch.

Androgyny

Masculinity and femininity are not opposite ends of the same dimension. **Androgyny** refers to the possession of both masculine and feminine traits.[58] Researchers make a distinction between sex-typed people, who are stereotypically masculine or feminine, and androgynous people, whose mixture of characteristics allows them to function well in a variety of social situations.

Differences in sex-role orientation can influence responses to marketing stimuli, although evidence for the strength of this factor is mixed.[59] For example,

MASCULINE	FEMININE
Pocket knife	Scarf
Tool kit	Baby oil
Shaving cream	Bedroom slippers
Briefcase	Hand lotion
Camera (35 mm)	Clothes dryer
Stereo system	Food processor
Scotch	Wine
IRA account	Long-distance phone service
Wall paint	Facial tissue

Source: Adapted from Kathleen Debevec and Easwar Iyer, "Sex Roles and Consumer Perceptions of Promotions, Products, and Self: What Do We Know and Where Should We Be Headed," in *Advances in Consumer Research,* ed. Richard J. Lutz (Provo, UT: Association for Consumer Research 13, 1986): 210–4.

TABLE 7–2 ▼ Sex-Typed Products

research evidence indicates that females are more likely to undergo more elaborate processing of message content, so they tend to be more sensitive to specific pieces of information when forming a judgment, while males are more influenced by overall themes.[60] In addition, women with a relatively strong masculine component in their sex-role identity prefer ad portrayals that include nontraditional women.[61] Some research indicates that sex-typed people are more sensitive to the sex-role depictions of characters in advertising, although women appear to be more sensitive to gender-role relationships than are men.

In one study, subjects read two versions of a beer advertisement, couched in either masculine or feminine terms. The masculine version contained phrases like "X beer has the strong, aggressive flavor that really asserts itself with good food and good company . . .," while the feminine version made claims like "Brewed with tender care, X beer is a full-bodied beer that goes down smooth and gentle. . . ." People who rated themselves as highly masculine or highly feminine preferred the version that was described in very masculine or feminine terms (respectively).[62] Sex-typed people, in general, are more concerned with ensuring that their behavior is consistent with their culture's definition of gender appropriateness.

Female Sex Roles

Sex roles for women are changing rapidly. Social changes, such as the dramatic increase in the proportion of women working outside of the home, have led to an upheaval in the way women are regarded by men, in the way they regard themselves, and in the products they choose to buy. Modern women now play a greater role in decisions regarding traditionally male purchases. For example, women now buy almost half of all condoms sold.[63]

One of the most marked changes in sex roles is occurring in Japan. Traditional Japanese wives stay home and care for children, while their husbands work late and entertain clients. The good Japanese wife is expected to walk two paces behind her husband. However, these patterns are changing as women are less willing to live vicariously through their husbands. More than half of Japanese women aged 25 to 29 are either working or looking for jobs.[64] Japanese marketers and advertisers are beginning to depict women in professional situations (though still usually in subservient roles) and even to develop female market segments for such traditionally male products as automobiles.

SEGMENTING WORKING WOMEN

In the 1949 movie *Adam's Rib,* Katharine Hepburn played a stylish and competent lawyer. This film was one of the first to show that a woman can have a successful career and still be happily married. Historically, married women have worked outside of the home, especially during wartime. However, the presence of women in positions of authority is a fairly recent phenomenon. The evolution of a new managerial class of women has forced marketers to change their traditional assumptions about women as they target this growing market.

Ironically, it seems that, in some cases, marketers have overcompensated for their former emphasis on women as housewives. Many attempts to target the vast female working market tend to depict all working women in glamorous, executive positions. This portrayal ignores the facts that the majority of working women do not hold such jobs and that many work because they have to, not for self-fulfillment. This

The character of Rosie the Riveter was created during World War II to symbolize the efforts of American women to take the place of men on factory production lines.

diversity means that all women should not be expected to respond to marketing campaigns that stress professional achievement or the glamour of the working life. Adult women can be segmented into at least four groups.

1. Housewives who do not plan to work outside of the home.
2. Housewives who plan to work at some point. (The women in this group may be staying at home only temporarily—until small children grow old enough to enter school, for example—and are thus not to be grouped with those housewives who have voluntarily chosen a domestic lifestyle.)
3. Career-oriented working women who value professional success and the trappings of achievement.
4. "Just-a-job" women who work primarily because they need the money.[65]

Whether or not they work outside of the home, many women have come to value greater independence and respond positively to marketing campaigns that stress the freedom to make their own lifestyle decisions. The American Express Company has been targeting women for a long time, but the company found that its "Do-you-know-me?" campaign did not appeal to women as much as to men. A campaign aimed specifically at women instead featured confident women using their American Express cards. By depicting women in active situations, the company greatly increased its share of the woman's credit card market.[66]

The desire for independence by women has also affected the marketing of the automobile, a product that epitomizes mobility. Men traditionally were primarily responsible for choosing and purchasing cars; but this situation is changing radically, and carmakers are scrambling to keep up with it. While most car advertising is still male oriented, women are increasingly depicted as serious buyers. More than six in ten new car buyers under the age of 50 are female.[67] Advertising for the 1995-model-year cars is filled with images of female consumers in the driver's seat. In one representative spot for the Mercedes-Benz E420, a woman accelerates to beat a truck, as the voice-over says, "I am engine. Hear me roar," a reference to the Helen Reddy song, "I Am Woman."[68]

THE DEPICTION OF WOMEN IN ADVERTISING

As implied by the ads for Virginia Slims cigarettes—"You've come a long way, baby!"—attitudes about the female sex role have changed remarkably in this century. Still, women continue to be depicted by advertisers and the media in stereotypical ways. Analyses of ads in such magazines as *Time, Newsweek, Playboy,* and even *Ms.* have shown that the large majority of women included were presented as sex objects or in traditional roles.[69] Similar findings have been obtained in the United Kingdom.[70] One of the biggest culprits may be rock videos, which tend to reinforce traditional women's roles. The women portrayed in these videos are usually submissive, and their primary attribute is high physical attractiveness. Recent evidence also indicates an increase in the amount of lingerie and nudity contained in rock videos.[71]

Ads may also reinforce negative stereotypes. Women often are portrayed as stupid, as submissive, as temperamental, or as sexual objects who exist solely for the pleasure of men. An ad for Newport cigarettes illustrates how the theme of female submission may be perpetuated. The copy "Alive with pleasure!" is accompanied by a photo of a woman in the woods, playfully hanging from a pole being carried by two men. The underlying message may be interpreted as two men bringing home their captured prey.[72]

Although women continue to be depicted in traditional roles, this situation is changing as advertisers scramble to catch up with reality. For example, Avon Products is trying to shed its old-fashioned image by focusing on the concerns of contemporary women. As one recent ad proclaims, "After all, you have more on your mind than what's on your lips. And Avon thinks that's beautiful."[73] Women are now as likely as men to be central characters in television commercials. Still, while males increasingly are depicted as spouses and parents, women are still more likely than men to be seen in domestic settings. Also, about 90 percent of all narrators in com-

MARKETING PITFALL

The R. J. Reynolds Tobacco Company created controversy with its "Smooth-Character" campaign for Camel cigarettes. Designed to update the brand's image for a younger audience, ads feature "Old Joe," the company's traditional spokescamel, who presents tips on how to become a "smooth character." One tip suggested a way to impress a person at the beach: ". . . run into the water, grab someone and drag her back to shore. . . . The more she kicks and screams, the better." Several women's rights groups complained, and the ad was pulled.[74]

The Joe Camel campaign has been the subject of debate since its introduction in 1987, with critics charging that it glorifies smoking and encourages younger people to take up the habit. RJR Nabisco's latest attempt to broaden the brand's appeal includes the introduction of "Josephine Camels," female characters who hang out with Old Joe in a bar, shooting pool and smoking cigarettes. The ad shows another male camel getting his back rubbed by a female camel who is wearing a miniskirt and T-shirt. One of the advertising executives involved with the campaign explained, "They [the female camels] may take some people by surprise. But some could think Joe is like Michael Jordan, in that he is too cool and unapproachable. This ad is about inclusion."[75]

to conduct more information search. Women are more inclined to search than are men, as are those who place greater value on style and the image they present.[21]

THE CONSUMER'S PRIOR EXPERTISE

Should prior product knowledge make it more or less likely that a consumer will engage in a search? Products experts and novices use very different procedures during decision making. Novices who know little about a product should be the most motivated to find out more about it; however, experts, who are more familiar with the product category, should be able to better understand the meaning of any new product information they might acquire.

So, who searches more? The answer is neither: Search tends to be greatest among those consumers who are *moderately* knowledgeable about the product. There is an inverted-U-shaped relationship between knowledge and external search effort, as shown in Figure 8–4. People with very limited expertise may not feel they are capable of searching extensively. In fact, they may not even know where to start. Billy, who did not spend a lot of time researching his purchase, is representative of this situation. He visited one store and only looked at brands with which he was already familiar. In addition, he focused on only a small number of product features. On the other hand, people who are extremely knowledgeable in the area can rely heavily on their own memories for information (internal search), so they may not search very much, either.[22]

The type of search undertaken by people with varying levels of expertise differs, as well. Because experts have a better sense of what information is relevant to the decision, they tend to engage in *selective search,* which means their efforts are more focused and efficient. In contrast, novices are more likely to rely upon the opinions of others and upon "nonfunctional" attributes, such as brand name and price, to distinguish among alternatives. They may also process information in a "top-down" rather than a "bottom-up" manner, focusing less on details than on the big picture. For instance, they may be more impressed by the sheer amount of tech-

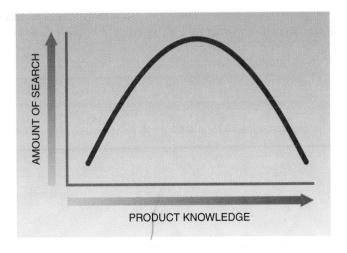

FIGURE 8–4 ▼ The Relationship Between Amount of Information Search and Product Knowledge

nical information presented in an ad than by the actual significance of the claims made.[23]

PERCEIVED RISK

As a rule, purchase decisions that involve extensive search also entail some kind of **perceived risk,** or the belief that the product has potentially negative consequences. Perceived risk may be present if the product is expensive or is complex and hard to understand. Alternatively, perceived risk can be a factor when a product choice is visible to others and we run the risk of embarrassment if the wrong choice is made.

Figure 8–5 lists five basic kinds of risk—including both objective factors (e.g., physical danger) and subjective factors (e.g., social embarrassment)—as well as the products subject to each type. As this figure notes, consumers with greater "risk capital" are less affected by perceived risks associated with the products. For example, a highly self-confident person would be less worried about the social risk inherent in a product, while a more vulnerable, insecure consumer might be reluctant to take a chance on a product that might not be accepted by peers. Consumers who are con-

FIGURE 8–5 ▼ Five Types of Perceived Risk

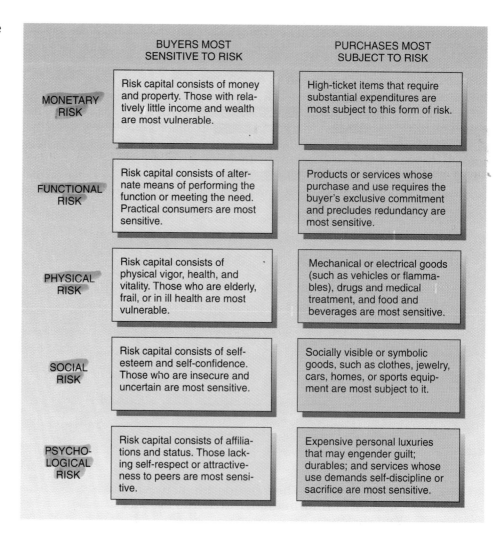

	BUYERS MOST SENSITIVE TO RISK	PURCHASES MOST SUBJECT TO RISK
MONETARY RISK	Risk capital consists of money and property. Those with relatively little income and wealth are most vulnerable.	High-ticket items that require substantial expenditures are most subject to this form of risk.
FUNCTIONAL RISK	Risk capital consists of alternate means of performing the function or meeting the need. Practical consumers are most sensitive.	Products or services whose purchase and use requires the buyer's exclusive commitment and precludes redundancy are most sensitive.
PHYSICAL RISK	Risk capital consists of physical vigor, health, and vitality. Those who are elderly, frail, or in ill health are most vulnerable.	Mechanical or electrical goods (such as vehicles or flammables), drugs and medical treatment, and food and beverages are most sensitive.
SOCIAL RISK	Risk capital consists of self-esteem and self-confidence. Those who are insecure and uncertain are most sensitive.	Socially visible or symbolic goods, such as clothes, jewelry, cars, homes, or sports equipment are most subject to it.
PSYCHOLOGICAL RISK	Risk capital consists of affiliations and status. Those lacking self-respect or attractiveness to peers are most sensitive.	Expensive personal luxuries that may engender guilt; durables; and services whose use demands self-discipline or sacrifice are most sensitive.

Minolta features a No-Risk Guarantee as a way to reduce the perceived risk in buying an office copier. Newsweek, *December 6, 1993. Courtesy of Minolta Corporation.*

cerned or anxious about health and well-being would be more worried about safety features when purchasing a new car, which is the theme of the Mercedes-Benz ad shown here.

EVALUATION OF ALTERNATIVES

Much of the effort that goes into a purchase decision occurs at the stage at which a choice must be made from the available alternatives. After all, modern consumer society abounds with choices. In some cases, there may literally be hundreds of different brands (as in cigarettes) or different variations of the same brand (as in shades of lipstick), each screaming for our attention.

This Mercedes-Benz ad responds to the perceived risk associated with physical danger by stressing that safety is a key feature of its luxury automobiles. © Copyright of Mercedez-Benz AG; photograph provided courtesy of Mercedes-Benz AG.

Just for fun, ask a friend to name all of the brands of perfume she can think of. The odds are she will reel off three to five names rather quickly and then stop to think awhile before coming up with a few more. It is likely that perfumes in the first set of brands are those with which she is highly familiar, and she probably wears one or more of these. The list may also contain one or two brands that she does not like and would perhaps like to forget. Note also that there are many, many more brands on the market than she named.

If your friend were to go to the store to buy perfume, it is likely that she would consider buying some or most of the brands she listed initially. She might also consider a few more possibilities if these were forcefully brought to her attention while at the store—for example, if she were "ambushed" by an employee who sprays scent samples on shoppers, which is a common occurrence in some department stores.

Identifying Alternatives

How do we decide what criteria are important, and how do we narrow down product alternatives to an acceptable number and eventually choose one over the others? The answer varies depending upon the decision-making process used. A consumer engaged in extended problem solving may carefully evaluate several brands, while someone making a habitual decision may not consider any alternatives to his normal brand.

The alternatives actively considered during a consumer's choice process are his or her **evoked set.** The evoked set is composed of those products already in memory (the retrieval set) plus those prominent in the retail environment. For example, recall that Billy did not know much about the technical aspects of television sets and he had only a few major brands in memory. Of these, two were acceptable possibilities and one was not. The alternatives that the consumer is aware of but would not consider buying are his or her *inept set,* while those not entering the game at all comprise the *inert set.* These categories are depicted in Figure 8–6.

FIGURE 8–6 ▼ Identifying Alternatives: Getting in the Game

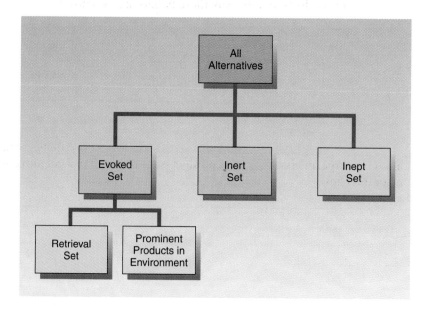

Consumers often consider a surprisingly small number of alternatives in their evoked set. One study combined results from several large-scale investigations of consumers' evoked sets and found that, although there are some marked variations by product category and across countries, the number of products included in these sets is limited. For example, the average size of the evoked set for an American beer consumer was less than three, while Canadian consumers typically considered seven brands. In contrast, while auto buyers in Norway studied two alternatives, American consumers on average looked at more than eight models before making a decision.[24]

For obvious reasons, a marketer who finds that her or his brand is not in the evoked set of many consumers in the target market has cause to worry. A product is not likely to be placed in the evoked set after it has previously been considered and rejected. Indeed, a new brand is more likely to be added to the evoked set than is an existing brand that was previously considered but passed over, even after additional positive information is provided for that brand.[25] For marketers, this unwillingness to give a rejected product a second chance underscores the importance of ensuring that it performs well from the time it is introduced.

Product Categorization

Remember that when consumers process product information, they do not do so in a vacuum. Instead, a product stimulus is evaluated in terms of what people already know about the product or those things it is similar to. A person evaluating a particular 35 mm camera will most likely compare it to other 35 mm cameras rather than to a Polaroid camera, and the consumer would certainly not compare it to a slide projector or VCR. Since the category in which a product is placed determines the other products it will be compared to, categorization is a crucial determinant of how a product is evaluated.

The products in a consumer's evoked set are likely to be those that share some similar features. It is important to understand how this knowledge is represented in a consumer's **cognitive structure,** which refers to a set of factual knowledge (i.e., beliefs) about products and the way these beliefs are organized.[26] These knowledge structures were discussed in Chapter 4. One reason this knowledge is important is that marketers want to ensure that their products are correctly grouped. For example, when Toyota and Nissan introduced their expensive Lexus and Infiniti sports cars, they intended them to be compared with other sports cars rather than to cars in an evoked set of "cheap but reliable Japanese cars."

LEVELS OF CATEGORIZATION

Not only do people group things into categories, but these groupings occur at different levels of specificity. Typically, a product is represented in a cognitive structure at one of three levels. To understand this idea, consider how someone might respond to the following questions about an ice cream cone: What other products share similar characteristics? and Which would be considered as alternatives to eating a cone?

The questions may be more complex than they first appear. At one level, a cone is similar to an apple because both could be eaten as a dessert. At another level, a cone is similar to a piece of pie since both are eaten for dessert and both are fattening. At still another level, a cone is similar to an ice cream sundae. Both are eaten for dessert, are made of ice cream, and are fattening.

It is easy to see that the items a person associates with, say, the category "fattening dessert" influence the choices he or she will make for what to eat after dinner. The middle level, known as a *basic level category,* is typically the most useful in classifying products, since items grouped together at this level tend to have a lot in common with each other but still permit a range of alternatives to be considered. The broader *superordinate category* is more abstract, while the more specific *subordinate category* often includes individual brands.[27] These three levels are depicted in Figure 8–7. Of course, not all items fit equally well into a category. Apple pie is a better example of the subordinate category "pie" than is rhubarb pie, even though both are legitimate kinds of pies. Apple pie is thus more prototypical and would tend to be considered first, especially by category novices. In contrast, pie experts will tend to have knowledge about category examples that are both typical and atypical.[28]

STRATEGIC IMPLICATIONS OF PRODUCT CATEGORIZATION

Product categorization has many strategic implications. The way a product is grouped with others has very important ramifications both for determining its competitors for adoption and what criteria will be used to make this choice.

Positioning and Repositioning. The success of a positioning strategy often hinges on the marketer's ability to convince the consumer that his or her product should be considered within a given category. For example, the orange juice industry tried to reposition orange juice as a drink that could be enjoyed all day long ("It's not just for breakfast anymore"). On the other hand, soft drink companies are now attempting to do the opposite by portraying sodas as suitable for breakfast consumption. They are trying to make their way into consumers' "breakfast drink" category, along with orange juice, grapefruit juice, coffee, and so on.

Defining Competitors. At the abstract, superordinate level, many different product forms compete for membership. Both bowling and the ballet may be considered subcategories of "entertainment" by some people, but many would not necessarily consider the substitution of one of these activities for the other. Products and services that, on the surface, are quite different actually compete with each other at a broad level, often for consumers' discretionary dollars. While bowling or ballet

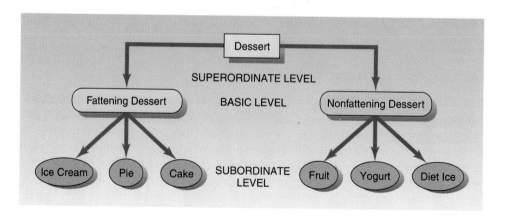

FIGURE 8–7 ▼ **Levels of Abstraction in Dessert Categories**

This ad for Sunkist lemon juice attempts to establish a new category for the product by repositioning it as a salt substitute. Courtesy of Sunkist Growers, Inc.

may not be a likely tradeoff for many people, it is feasible, for example, that a symphony might try to lure away season ticketholders to the ballet by positioning itself as an equivalent member of the category "cultural event."[29]

Consumers are often faced with choices between noncomparable categories, in which a number of attributes exist that cannot be directly related to one another (i.e., the old problem of comparing apples and oranges). The comparison process is easier when consumers can derive an overlapping category that encompasses both items (e.g., entertainment, value, or usefulness) and then rate each alternative in terms of that superordinate category.[30]

Prototypicality.   If a product is a really good example of a category, it is more familiar to consumers and, as a result, is more easily recognized and recalled.[31] Judgments about category attributes tend to be disproportionately influenced by the characteristics of category exemplars.[32] In a sense, brands that are strongly associated with a category get to "call the shots" by defining the evaluative criteria that should be used to evaluate all category members.

Stimulating Interest.   Being a bit less than prototypical is not necessarily a bad thing. Products that are moderately unusual within their product category may stimulate more information processing and positive evaluations, since they are neither so familiar that they will be taken for granted nor so discrepant that they will be dismissed.[33] Further, a brand that is strongly discrepant may occupy a unique niche position, while those that are moderately discrepant remain in a differentiated position within the general category.[34]

Locating Products.   Product categorization can also affect consumers' expectations regarding the places they can locate a desired product. If products do not clearly fit into categories (e.g., is a rug furniture?), consumers' abilities to find them or make sense of them may be affected. For instance, a frozen dog food that had to be thawed and cooked failed in the market, partly because people could not adapt to the idea of buying dog food in the frozen foods section.

Choosing Among Alternatives

Once the relevant options from a category have been assembled, a choice must be made among them.[35] Recall the decision rules that guide choice can range from employment of very simple and quick strategies to complicated processes requiring a lot of attention and cognitive processing. The choice can be influenced by integrating information from such sources as prior experience with the product, information present at the time of purchase, and beliefs about the brands that have been created by advertising.[36]

EVALUATIVE CRITERIA

When Billy was looking at different television sets, recall that he focused on one or two product features and that several others were completely ignored. He narrowed down his choices by only considering two specific brand names, and from the Prime Wave and Precision models, he chose the one that featured stereo capability.

The **evaluative criteria** are the dimensions used to judge the merits of competing options. In comparing alternative products, Billy could have chosen from among any number of criteria, ranging from very functional attributes (does this TV come with remote control?) to experiential ones (does this TV's sound reproduction make me imagine I'm in a concert hall?). The specific evaluative criteria used vary among people and also across cultures.

Another important point is that criteria on which products differ carry more weight in the decision process. If all brands being considered rate equally well on one attribute (e.g., if all TVs come with remote controls), consumers will have to find other attributes to use to make a choice. Those attributes that are actually used to differentiate among choices are *determinant attributes*.

Marketers can play a role in educating consumers about which criteria should be used as determinant attributes. For example, consumer research by Church & Dwight indicated that many consumers view the use of natural ingredients as a

Claiming the product is "full of strength," this ad for Pucko, a Swedish chocolate drink, emphasizes an evaluation criterion based on nutritional value, whereas American consumers might evaluate a similar product based on taste or calorie content. Photographer Kurt Wass. Courtesy of Forsman and BodenFors.

determinant attribute; the result was promotion of a toothpaste made from baking soda, which the company already manufactured for its Arm & Hammer brand.[37] Sometimes marketers take an additional step: They try to "invent" a determinant attribute by highlighting a product benefit consumers hadn't realized was important (and in fact may not be!). Recently, Pepsi-Cola attempted this by stamping freshness dates on soda cans. The company spent about $25 million on an advertising and promotional campaign to convince consumers that there's nothing quite as horrible as a stale can of soda—even though it has been estimated that 98 percent of all cans are consumed well before this could be a problem.[38] Still, the company is optimistic that people will appreciate having this information at their fingertips. Indeed, Pepsi's gamble appears to have paid off: Six months after introducing the campaign, an independent survey found that 61 percent of respondents felt that freshness dating is an important attribute![39]

The decision about which attributes to use is the result of *procedural learning,* in which a person undergoes a series of cognitive steps before making a choice. These steps include identifying important attributes, remembering whether competing brands differ on those attributes, and so on. In order for a marketer to effectively recommend a new decision criterion, his or her communication should convey three pieces of information.[40]

1. It should point out that there are significant differences among brands on the attribute.

2. It should supply the consumer with a decision-making rule, such as, "If [deciding among competing brands], *then* [use the attribute as a criterion]."

3. It should convey a rule that can be easily integrated with how the person has made this decision in the past. Otherwise, the recommendation is likely to be ignored because it requires too much mental work.

Consumers consider sets of product attributes by using different rules, depending upon the complexity of the decision, their involvement in it, and so on. One way

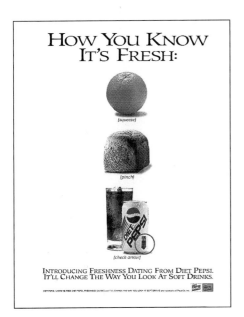

The Pepsi-Cola Company is adding what it hopes will be a determinant attribute by introducing freshness dating on its cans. Newsweek, April 11, 1994. Courtesy of Pepsi-Cola Company.

to differentiate among decision rules is to divide them into those that are *compensatory* versus those that are *noncompensatory*, as discussed below. As an aid in the discussion, the attributes of the TV sets that Billy considered are summarized in Table 8–3.

NONCOMPENSATORY DECISION RULES

Simple decision rules are **noncompensatory,** and a product with a low standing on one attribute cannot make up for this position by being better on another attribute. In other words, people simply eliminate all options that do not meet some basic standards. A consumer like Billy who uses the decision rule "Only buy well-known brand names" would not consider a new brand, even if it were equal or superior to existing ones. When people are less familiar with a product category or not very motivated to process complex information, they tend to use simple, noncompensatory rules.[41]

The Lexicographic Rule. When the *lexicographic rule* is used, the brand that is the best on the most important attribute is selected. If two or more brands are seen as being equally good on that attribute, the consumer then compares them using the second most important attribute. This selection process goes on until the tie is broken. In Billy's case, since both the Prime Wave and Precision models were tied on his most important attribute (a 27-inch screen), the Precision model was chosen because of its rating on this second-most-important attribute—its stereo capability.

The Elimination-by-Aspects Rule. Again, brands are evaluated on the most important attribute under the *elimination-by-aspects rule.* In this case, though, specific cutoffs are imposed. For example, if Billy had been more interested in having a sleep timer on his TV (i.e., if it had a higher importance ranking), he might have stipulated that his choice "must have a sleep timer." Since the Prime Wave model had one and the Precision did not, the Prime Wave would have been chosen.

The Conjunctive Rule. While the two former rules involve processing by attribute, the *conjunctive rule* entails processing by brand. As with the elimination-by-aspects procedure, cutoffs are established for each attribute. A brand is chosen if it meets all of the cutoffs, while failure to meet any one cutoff means it will be rejected. If none of the brands meets all of the cutoffs, the choice may be delayed, the decision rule may be changed, or the cutoffs themselves may be modified.

TABLE 8–3 ▼ **Hypothetical Alternatives for a TV Set**

ATTRIBUTE	IMPORTANCE RANKING	BRAND RATINGS		
		PRIME WAVE	PRECISION	KAMASHITA
Size of screen	1	Excellent	Excellent	Excellent
Stereo broadcast capability	2	Poor	Excellent	Good
Brand reputation	3	Excellent	Excellent	Poor
On-screen programming	4	Excellent	Poor	Poor
Cable-ready capability	5	Good	Good	Good
Sleep timer	6	Excellent	Poor	Good

If Billy had stipulated that all attributes had to be rated as "good" or better, he would not have been able to choose any of the options. He might then have modified his decision rule, conceding that it was not possible to attain these high standards in the price range he was considering. In this case, Billy could perhaps decide that it was not so important to have on-screen programming, so the Precision model could again be considered.

COMPENSATORY DECISION RULES

Unlike noncompensatory decision rules, **compensatory rules** give a product a chance to make up for its shortcomings. Consumers who employ these rules tend to be more involved in the purchase and thus are willing to exert the effort to consider the entire picture in a more exacting way. The willingness to let good and bad product qualities balance out can result in quite different choices. For example, if Billy were not as concerned about having stereo reception, he might have chosen the Prime Wave model using a compensatory rule. But because this brand did not feature this highly ranked attribute, it doesn't stand a chance when he uses a noncompensatory rule.

Simple Compensation.   Two basic types of compensatory rules have been identified. When using the *simple additive rule,* the consumer merely chooses the alternative having the largest number of positive attributes. This choice is most likely to occur when his or her ability or motivation to process information is limited. One drawback to this approach for the consumer is that some of these attributes may not be very meaningful or important. An ad containing a long list of product benefits may be persuasive, despite the fact that many of the benefits included are actually standard within the product class.

Complex Compensation.   The more complex version is known as the *weighted additive rule.*[42] When using this rule, the consumer also takes into account the relative importance of positively rated attributes, essentially multiplying brand ratings by importance weights. If this process sounds familiar, it should. The calculation process strongly resembles the multi-attribute attitude model described in Chapter 5.

Heuristics: Mental Shortcuts

Instead of carefully calculating importance weights, consumers often employ decision rules that allow them to use some dimensions as substitutes for others. Especially where limited problem solving occurs prior to making a choice, consumers often fall back upon **heuristics,** or mental rules of thumb, that lead to a speedy decision. These rules range from the very general (e.g., "Higher-priced products are higher-quality products" or "I buy the same brand I bought last time") to the very specific (e.g., "I buy Domino, the brand of sugar my mother always bought").[43]

For example, Billy relied on certain assumptions as substitutes for a prolonged information search. In particular, he assumed the selection at Zany Zach's would be more than sufficient, so he did not bother to shop at any of Zach's competitors. This assumption served as a shortcut to more extensive information processing.[44] Sometimes these shortcuts may not be in consumers' best interests. A consumer who personally knows one or two people who have had problems with a particular make of car, for example, might assume he or she would have similar trouble with it and thus overlook the model's overall excellent repair record.[45] The influence of such assumptions may be enhanced if the product has an unusual name, which makes it *and* the experiences with it more distinctive.[46]

RELYING ON A PRODUCT SIGNAL

One frequently used shortcut is the tendency to infer hidden dimensions of products from observable attributes. The aspect of the product that is visible acts as a *signal* of some underlying quality. Such inferences explain why someone trying to sell a used car takes great pains to be sure the car's exterior is clean and shiny: Potential buyers often judge the vehicle's mechanical condition by its appearance.[47]

When product information is incomplete, judgments are often derived from beliefs about *covariation,* or associations among events.[48] For example, a consumer may form an association between product quality and the length of time a manufacturer has been in business. Other signals or attributes believed to coexist with good or bad products include well-known brand names, country of origin, price, and the retail outlets that carry the product.

Unfortunately, consumers tend to be poor estimators of covariation. Their beliefs persist despite evidence to the contrary. Similar to the consistency principle discussed in Chapter 5, people tend to see what they are looking for. They will look for product information that confirms their guesses. In one experiment, consumers sampled four sets of products to determine if price and quality were related. Those who believed in this relationship prior to the study elected to sample higher-priced products, thus creating a sort of self-fulfilling prophecy.[49]

MARKET BELIEFS AS HEURISTICS

Consumers often form specific beliefs about relationships in the marketplace. These beliefs then become the shortcuts—whether or not they are accurate—that guide their decisions.[50] Our friend Billy's decisions were influenced by his **market beliefs.** Recall, for instance, that he chose to shop at a large "electronics supermarket" because he assumed the selection would be better (though the prices would be lower). A large number of market beliefs have been identified. Some of these are listed in Table 8–4. How many do you share?

PRICE AS A HEURISTIC

Do higher prices mean higher quality? The assumption of a *price-quality relationship* is one of the most pervasive market beliefs.[51] Novice consumers may, in fact, consider price as the only relevant product attribute. Experts also consider this information, although in the case of experts price tends to be used for its informational value, especially for products (e.g., virgin wool) that are known to have wide quality variations in the marketplace. When this quality level is more standard or strictly regulated (e.g., Harris Tweed sport coats), experts do not weigh price in their decisions. For the most part, this belief is justified; you do tend to get what you pay for. However, let the buyer beware: The price-quality relationship is not always justified.[52]

BRAND NAMES AS A HEURISTIC

Branding is a marketing strategy that often functions as a heuristic. People form preferences for favorite brands and then may literally never change their minds in the course of their lifetimes. A study of the market leaders in 30 product categories

TABLE 8–4 ▼ Common Market Beliefs

Brand	All brands are basically the same.
	Generic products are just name brands sold under a different label at a lower price.
	The best brands are the ones that are purchased the most.
	When in doubt, a national brand is always a safe bet.
Store	Specialty stores are great places to familiarize yourself with the best brands; but once you figure out what you want, it's cheaper to buy it at a discount outlet.
	A store's character is reflected in its window displays.
	Sales people in specialty stores are more knowledgeable than other sales personnel.
	Larger stores offer better prices than small stores.
	Locally owned stores give the best service.
	A store that offers a good value on one of its products probably offers good values on all of its items.
	Credit and return policies are most lenient at large department stores.
	Stores that have just opened usually charge attractive prices.
Prices/Discounts/Sales	Sales are typically run to get rid of slow-moving merchandise.
	Stores that are constantly having sales don't really save you money.
	Within a given store, higher prices generally indicate higher quality.
Advertising and Sales Promotion	"Hard-sell" advertising is associated with low-quality products.
	Items tied to "giveaways" are not a good value (even with the freebee).
	Coupons represent real savings for customers because they are not offered by the store.
	When you buy heavily advertised products, you are paying for the label, not for higher quality.
Product/Packaging	Largest-sized containers are almost always cheaper per unit than smaller sizes.
	New products are more expensive when they're first introduced; prices tend to settle down as time goes by.
	When you are not sure what you need in a product, it's a good idea to invest in the extra features, because you'll probably wish you had them later.
	In general, synthetic goods are lower in quality than goods made of natural materials.
	It's advisable to stay away from products when they are new to the market; it usually takes the manufacturer a little time to work the bugs out.

Source: Adapted from Calvin P. Duncan, "Consumer Market Beliefs: A Review of the Literature and an Agenda for Future Research," in *Advances in Consumer Research* 17, ed. Marvin E. Goldberg, Gerald Gorn, and Richard W. Pollay (Provo, UT: Association for Consumer Research, 1990): 729–35.

by the Boston Consulting Group found that 27 of the brands that were number one in 1930 are still number one today. These brands include such perennial favorites as Ivory soap, Campbell's soup, and Gold Medal flour.[53]

A brand that exhibits that kind of staying power is treasured by marketers, and for good reason. Brands that dominate their markets are as much as 50 percent more profitable than are their nearest competitors.[54] A survey of 3,000 consumers on brand power in Japan, Europe, and the United States combined awareness and esteem scores to produce the following list of the most positively regarded brand names around the world.[55]

1. Coca-Cola
2. IBM
3. Sony
4. Porsche
5. McDonald's
6. Disney
7. Honda
8. Toyota
9. Seiko
10. BMW

Consumers' attachments to certain brands, such as Marlboro, Coca-Cola, Gerber, and Levi's, are so powerful that this loyalty is often considered a positive product attribute in and of itself. Brand equity can actually be quantified in terms of *goodwill,* defined as the difference between the market value and the book value of a brand. Recently, the British company Grand Metropolitan actually decided to record brand names it had acquired on its balance sheets and include these intangible assets in its financial reports to shareholders.[56] Marlboro is the most valuable brand name in the world. It was recently valued at $31.2 billion.[57]

Many people tend to buy the same brand just about every time they go to the store. This consistent pattern is often due to **inertia,** where a brand is bought out of habit merely because less effort is required. If another product comes along that is for some reason easier to buy (e.g., it is cheaper or the original product is out of stock), the consumer will not hesitate to do so. A competitor who is trying to change a buying pattern based on inertia often can do so rather easily, because little resistance to brand switching will be encountered if some reason to do so is apparent. Since there is little to no underlying commitment to the product, such promotional tools as point-of-purchase displays, extensive couponing, or noticeable price reductions may be sufficient to "unfreeze" a consumer's habitual pattern.

This kind of fickleness will not occur if true **brand loyalty** exists. In contrast to inertia, brand loyalty is a form of repeat-purchasing behavior reflecting a conscious decision to continue buying the same brand. This concept thus refers to a pattern of purchases over time where actual decision making occurs.[58] For brand loyalty to exist, a pattern of repeat purchasing must be accompanied by an underlying positive attitude toward the brand. Brand loyalty may be initiated by customer preference based on objective reasons, but after the brand has been around for a long time and is heavily advertised, it can also create an emotional attachment, either by being incorporated into the consumer's self-image or because it is associated with prior experiences.[59] Purchase decisions based on brand loyalty are thus simplified and may even become habitual.

Compared to an inertia situation where the consumer passively accepts a brand, a brand-loyal consumer is actively (sometimes passionately) involved with his or her favorite. Because of the emotional bonds that can be created between brand-loyal consumers and products, "true-blue" users react more vehemently when these products are altered, redesigned, or eliminated.[60] Recall, for example, the

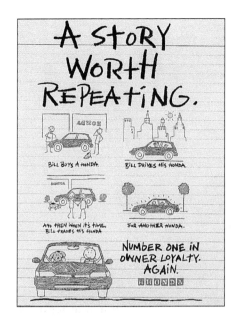

This Honda ad emphasizes the high brand loyalty of Honda owners and so portrays the act of choosing a new car as one of simple, habitual decision making. © 1992 by American Honda Motor Co., Inc. Courtesy of Rubin Poster and Associates.

national call-in campaigns, boycotts, and other protests when Coca-Cola replaced its tried-and-true formula with New Coke.

Although brand loyalty is alive and well for some better-known products, its power seems to be on the decline. Marketers increasingly are struggling with the problem of *brand parity,* which refers to consumers' beliefs that there are no significant differences among brands. For example, more than one-half of consumers worldwide consider all brands of beer and cigarettes to be about the same, and more than 70 percent believe that all paper towels, soaps, and snack chips are alike.[61]

A *Wall Street Journal* survey of American consumers reported that most consumers switch brands for many of the products they use. Of consumers surveyed, 12 percent said they were not brand loyal in any of the 25 product categories included, while only 2 percent were loyal in 16 or more categories. As shown in Figure 8–8, brand loyalty was particularly low for such products as canned vegetables and athletic shoes and tended to be highest for categories such as ketchup and cigarettes that have distinctive flavors. The comments of one 31-year-old homemaker are typical: "The only . . . thing I'm really loyal to is my Virginia Slims cigarettes. Coke and Pepsi are all the same to me, and I usually buy whatever brand of coffee happens to be on sale."[62]

This erosion of brand loyalty is due to a number of factors, including an increase in the volume of short-term promotions and the flood of new products that have hit the market in recent years. Also, many people simply are not that knowledgeable about even well-known brand alternatives, especially for very expensive products that they buy infrequently, if at all. In one large survey, consumers were asked to name the "finest, most elegant" brand in a number of categories. The response "don't know" topped the list in several, including men's and women's clothing and perfumes.[63]

COUNTRY OF ORIGIN AS A HEURISTIC

Modern consumers choose among products made in many countries. Americans may buy Brazilian shoes, Japanese cars, clothing imported from Taiwan, or

McDonald's success at attracting its core market of families with kids varies dramatically by time of day. The restaurant chain earns 55 percent of its revenues during lunchtime, and only 20 percent at dinner. The company has tried luring the dinner crowd with test offerings such as pizza, pasta, and skinless roast chicken, but these attempts failed. The problem: McDonald's has such a strong lunch and breakfast image that people have trouble viewing it as a dinner place, where they want a more relaxed situation. Although about 500 U.S. outlets continue to sell McPizza, for now the company has sent its dinner plans back to the test kitchen. Source: Marcia Berss, "Empty Tables," Forbes (December 6, 1993): 232(2). Photo courtesy of David Young Wolfe/Photo Edit.

whether the context is positive or negative (e.g., a street riot versus a street festival, such as Mardi Gras). Maintaining an "up" feeling in a pleasant context is one factor behind the success of theme parks like Disney World, which try to provide consistent doses of carefully calculated stimulation to patrons.[31]

A specific mood is some combination of these two factors. For example, the state of happiness is high in pleasantness and moderate in arousal, while elation would be high on both dimensions.[32] In general, a mood state (either positive or negative) biases judgments of products and services in that direction.[33] Put simply, consumers like things better when they are in a good mood. When in positive moods, consumers process ads with less elaboration. They pay less attention to specifics of the messages and rely more on heuristic processing (see Chapter 8).[34]

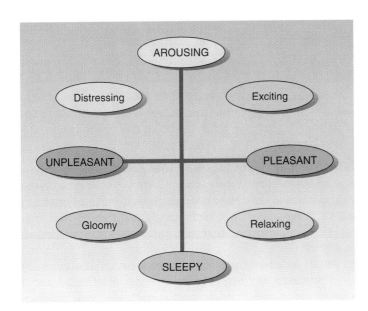

FIGURE 9–3 ▼ Dimensions of Emotional States Source: James Russell and Geraldine Pratt, "A Description of the Affective Quality Attributed to Environment," *Journal of Personality and Social Psychology* 38 (August 1980): 311–22. © Copyright 1980 by the American Psychological Association. Adapted by permission.

Moods can be affected by store design, the weather, or other factors specific to the consumer. In addition, music and television programming can affect mood, which has important consequences for commercials.[35] When consumers hear happy music or watch happy programs, they have more positive reactions to commercials and products, especially when the marketing appeals are aimed at arousing emotional reactions.[36]

Shopping Motives

People often shop even though they do not necessarily intend to buy anything at all; others have to be dragged to a mall. Shopping is a way to acquire needed products and services, but social motives for shopping also are important. Thus, shopping is an activity that can be performed for either utilitarian (functional or tangible) or hedonic (pleasurable or intangible) reasons.[37]

These different motives are illustrated by scale items used by researchers to assess people's underlying reasons for shopping. One item that measures hedonic value is the statement "During the trip, I felt the excitement of the hunt." When that type of sentiment is compared to a functionally related statement, such as "I accomplished just what I wanted to on this shopping trip," the contrast between these two dimensions is clear.[38] Hedonic shopping motives can include the following:[39]

- *Social experiences.* The shopping center or department store has replaced the traditional town square or county fair as a community gathering place. Many people (especially in suburban or rural areas) may have no place else to go to spend their leisure time.

- *Sharing of common interests.* Stores frequently offer specialized goods that allow people with shared interests to communicate.

- *Interpersonal attraction.* Shopping centers are natural places to congregate. The shopping mall has become a central hangout for teenagers. It also represents a controlled, secure environment for other groups, such as the elderly.

- *Instant status.* As every salesperson knows, some people savor the experience of being waited on, even though they may not necessarily buy anything. One men's clothing salesman offered this advice: ". . . remember their size, remember what you sold them last time. Make them feel important! If you can make people feel important, they are going to come back. Everybody likes to feel important!"[40]

- *The thrill of the chase.* Some people pride themselves on their knowledge of the marketplace. Unlike Mark, they may relish the process of haggling and bargaining, viewing it almost as a sport.

Many people seem to be falling out of love with shopping. In 1987, a survey done for Neiman-Marcus and American Express found that 50 percent of the respondents liked shopping as much as they liked watching television and 17 percent found shopping as pleasurable as romance! Just two years later, though, more than half of the respondents in another survey said that they hated browsing in stores as much as they loathed housework.[41]

Which way is it? Do people hate to shop or love it? It depends. Consumers can be segmented in terms of their **shopping orientation,** or general attitudes about shopping. These orientations may vary depending on the particular product categories and store types considered. Mark hates to shop for a car, but he may love to browse in record stores. Several shopping types have been identified.[42]

- *Economic consumer*—a rational, goal-oriented shopper who is primarily interested in maximizing the value of his or her money.
- *Personalized consumer*—a shopper who tends to form strong attachments to store personnel ("I shop where they know my name").
- *Ethical consumer*—a shopper who likes to help out the underdog and will support locally owned stores against big chains.
- *Apathetic consumer*—one who does not like to shop and sees it as a necessary but unpleasant chore.
- *Recreational shopper*—a person who views shopping as a fun, social activity (a preferred way to spend leisure time).

THE PURCHASE ENVIRONMENT

We see bumper stickers and T-shirts everywhere: "Shop 'til you drop," "When the going gets tough, the tough go shopping," and "Born to shop." Like it or not, shopping is a dominant activity for many consumers. On the average, American consumers spend about six percent of their waking hours shopping.[43] According to data reported by Nielsen North America's 40,000 household consumer panel, consumers on average made just under 87 trips in 1993 to the grocery store alone.[44]

The competition for shoppers is getting rougher amongst retailers. Between 1974 and 1984, total retail square footage in the United States grew by 80 percent, but the population grew by only 12 percent. About 200 million square feet of shopping mall space is added every year.[45] Retailers must now offer something extra to lure shoppers, whether that something is excitement or just plain bargains.[46]

Nonstore Shopping

The competition for customers is becoming even more intense as nonstore alternatives that bring retail services to the home continue to multiply. Popular nonstore alternatives include mail-order catalogs, television shopping networks, salespersons who make house calls (e.g., the Avon lady), and home shopping parties (e.g., Tupperware parties). The growth of computerized home shopping systems (e.g., Prodigy) has been somewhat slow in the United States, compared to France, where the Minitel System offers about 8,000 information services and is connected to more than 3.7 million home terminals.[47] Another emerging trend is to bring retailing to the office, as demonstrated by the Spiegel ad shown here. This approach makes sense, because people are working longer hours and earning more money but are leaving themselves less free time in which to spend it.

Finding that many of its female customers are no longer home during the day, even Avon has expanded its distribution network to the office, where representatives make presentations during lunch and coffee breaks. Similarly, Tupperware features "rush hour parties" at the end of the workday and now finds that about 20 percent of its sales are made outside of homes. An employee of Mary Kay cosmetics, another company adopting this strategy, offered another explanation for its success:

"Working women buy more in the office because they are not looking at the wallpaper that needs replacing. They feel richer away from home."[48]

The Shopping Experience

Store-loyal consumers are prized by retailers. They will routinely visit a small set of stores without considering others or doing much in the way of comparative prepurchase search. However, consumers now have an abundance of choices regarding where to shop, including the nonstore alternatives. For this reason, people do not tend to be as store loyal as they once were.[49]

RETAILING AS THEATER

Shopping malls have tried to gain the loyalty of shoppers by appealing to their social motives, as well as providing access to desired goods. The mall is often a focal point in a community. In the United States, 94 percent of adults visit a mall at least once a month. More than half of all retail purchases (excluding autos and gasoline) are made in a mall.[50]

Malls are becoming giant entertainment centers, almost to the point where their traditional retail occupants seem like an afterthought. It is now typical to find such features as carousels, miniature golf, or batting cages in a suburban mall. As one retailing executive put it, "Malls are becoming the new mini-amusement parks."[51] The importance of creating a positive, vibrant, and interesting image has led innovative marketers to blur the line between shopping and theater. Both shopping malls and individual stores must create environments that stimulate people and allow them to shop and be simultaneously entertained.[52] The following are among the best "performers."[53]

- Bloomingdale's department store is noted for its elaborate storewide promotions, often based upon the culture of selected countries. During such an event,

Recognizing that modern women have many time pressures, Spiegel brings retailing to the office.
© *Copyright 1991, Spiegel, Inc.*

,the entire store is transformed, with each department featuring unusual merchandise from the country. The promotion is accompanied by lavish parties, food, and entertainment associated with that country.

- Babyland (the home of Cabbage Patch dolls) does not have a sales staff. Instead, the company offers "doctors," "nurses," and "adoption officers." Dolls are never "sold"; they are adopted. Every 15 minutes, Bunny Bees hover over the cabbage patch and inseminate the cabbages. These cabbages quiver and the leaves open, displaying newborn Cabbage Patch babies.

- Ralph Lauren's Madison Avenue store is in a refurbished mansion, and the decor is consistent with the company's image of aristocratic gentility and the good life. The store is furnished with expensive antiques and tapestries, and cocktails and canapés are served in the evening. Even cleaning supplies are carried in Lauren shopping bags by maintenance staff.

STORE IMAGE

With so many stores competing for customers, how do consumers pick one over another? Like products, stores may be thought of as having "personalities." Some stores have very clearly defined images (either good or bad). Others tend to blend into the crowd. They may not have anything distinctive about them and may be overlooked for this reason. This personality, or **store image,** is composed of many different factors. Store features, coupled with such consumer characteristics as shopping orientation, help to predict which shopping outlets people will prefer.[54] Some of the important dimensions of a store's profile are location, merchandise suitability, and the knowledge and congeniality of the sales staff.[55]

Store Gestalt.　When shoppers think about stores, they may not say, "Well, that place is fairly good in terms of convenience, the salespeople are acceptable, and services are good." They are more likely to say, "That place gives me the creeps," or "I always enjoy shopping there." Consumers evaluate stores in terms of both their spe-

The Nike Town Store in Portland, Oregon, provides an innovative, futuristic atmosphere designed to enhance the shopping experience. © Christopher Kean.

cific attributes *and* a global evaluation, or *gestalt* (see Chapter 2).[56] This overall feeling may have more to do with such intangibles as interior design and the types of people one finds in the store than with such aspects as return policies or credit availability. As a result, some stores are likely to consistently be in consumers' evoked sets, while others will never be considered.[57]

Atmospherics.   Because a store's gestalt is now recognized to be a very important aspect of the retailing mix, attention is increasingly paid to **atmospherics,** or the "conscious designing of space and its various dimensions to evoke certain effects in buyers."[58] These dimensions include colors, scents, and sounds. For example, stores done in red tend to make people tense, while a blue decor imparts a calmer feeling.[59]

Many elements of store design can be cleverly controlled to attract customers and produce desired effects on consumers. Light colors impart a feeling of spaciousness and serenity, and signs in bright colors create excitement. In one subtle but effective application, fashion designer Norma Kamali replaced fluorescent lights with pink ones in department store dressing rooms. The light had the effect of flattering the face and banishing wrinkles, making female customers more willing to try on (and buy) the company's bathing suits.[60]

In addition to visual stimuli, all sorts of cues can influence behaviors.[61] For example, patrons of country-and-western bars drink more when the jukebox music is slower. According to a researcher, "Hard drinkers prefer listening to slower paced, wailing, lonesome, self-pitying music. . . ."[62] Similarly, music can affect eating habits. Another study found that diners who listened to loud, fast music ate more food. In contrast, those who listened to Mozart or Brahms ate less and more slowly. The researchers concluded that diners who choose soothing music at mealtimes can increase weight loss by at least five pounds a month![63]

In-Store Decision Making

Despite all their efforts to "presell" consumers through advertising, marketers increasingly are recognizing the significant degree to which many purchases are influenced by the store environment. It has been estimated that about two out of every three supermarket purchases are decided in the aisles. The proportion of unplanned purchases is even higher for some product categories. It is estimated that 85 percent of candy and gum, almost 70 percent of cosmetics, and 75 percent of oral-hygiene purchases are unplanned.[64]

SPONTANEOUS SHOPPING

When a shopper is prompted to buy something while in the store, one of two different processes may be at work.

Unplanned Buying.   Unplanned buying may occur when a person is unfamiliar with a store's layout or perhaps when under some time pressure. Or, a person may be reminded to buy something by seeing it on a store shelf. About one-third of unplanned buying has been attributed to the recognition of new needs while within the store.[65]

Impulse Buying.   When the person experiences a sudden urge that he or she cannot resist, **impulse buying** occurs.[66] For this reason, so-called impulse items, such as candy and gum, are conveniently placed near the checkout. Similarly, many supermarkets have installed wider aisles to encourage browsing, and the widest tend to contain products with the highest margin. Items with low markup that are purchased regularly tend to be stacked high in narrower aisles, to allow shoppers to speed through.[67]

Planning Versus Impulse Shopping.   Shoppers can be categorized in terms of how much advance planning they do. *Planners* tend to know what products and specific brands they will buy beforehand; *partial planners* know they need certain products but do not decide on specific brands until they are in the store; and *impulse purchasers* do no advance planning whatsoever.[68] Figure 9–4 was drawn by a consumer who was participating in a study on consumers' shopping experiences and who was asked to sketch a typical impulse purchaser.

POINT-OF-PURCHASE STIMULI

Because so much decision making apparently occurs while the shopper is in the purchasing environment, retailers are beginning to pay more attention to the amount of information in their stores, as well as to the way it is presented. It has been estimated that impulse purchases increase by ten percent when appropriate displays are used. Each year, U.S. companies spend more than $13 billion on **point-of-purchase stimuli (POP).** A point-of-purchase stimulus can be an elaborate product display or demonstration, a coupon-dispensing machine, or even someone giving out free samples of a new cookie in the grocery aisle.

DRAW-A-PICTURE

1. Think about your image of what kind of person an impulse buyer is. In the space provided below, draw a picture of your image of a typical impulse buyer who is about to make an impulse purchase. Be creative and don't worry about your artistic skills! If you feel that some features of your drawing are unclear, don't hesitate to identify them with a written label.

2. After you have completed your drawing, imagine what is going through your character's mind as he or she is about to make his or her impulse purchase. Then write down your shopper's thoughts in a speech balloon (like you might see in a cartoon strip) that connects to your character's head.

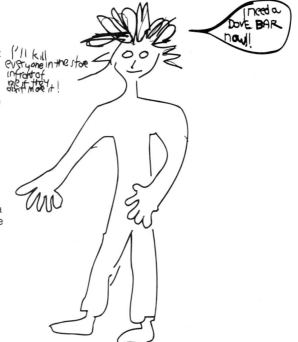

FIGURE 9–4 ▼ One Consumer's Image of an Impulse Buyer   Source: Dennis Rook, "Is Impulse Buying (Yet) a Useful Marketing Concept?" (unpublished manuscript, University of Southern California, Los Angeles, 1990): Fig. 7-A.

MARKETING PITFALL

Cents-off coupons are widely used by manufacturers and retailers to induce consumers to switch brands. While coupons are an important form of sales promotion, evidence regarding their effectiveness at luring *new* customers is mixed. Households that already use the brand offering a coupon are more likely to redeem the coupon, and most customers revert to their original brand after the promotion has expired. As a result, the company that hopes to attract brand switchers by luring them with coupon offers may instead find itself "preaching to the converted."[69]

In-store advertising is becoming very sophisticated, as marketers come to appreciate the influence of the shopping environment in steering consumers toward promoted items. Even Muzak, the company that provides bland background music to stores (see Chapter 2), is getting into the act. Muzak is now using the receivers it has already placed in about 200,000 stores in the United States to broadcast advertising pitches that can be tailored to a store's location and needs. The company claims that its audio ads have resulted in sales increases of almost 30 percent in some product categories, such as toothpaste and cold medicines.[70]

Displays. In-store displays are yet another commonly used device to attract attention in the store environment. While most displays consist of simple racks that dispense the product and/or related coupons, some highlight the value of regarding retailing as theater by supplying the "audience" with elaborate performances and scenery. Some of the more dramatic POP displays have included the following:[71]

- *Timex.* A still-ticking watch sits in the bottom of a filled aquarium.
- *Kellogg's Corn Flakes.* A button with a picture of Cornelius the Rooster is placed within the reach of children near Corn Flakes. When a child presses the button, he or she hears the rooster "cock-a-doodle-do."
- *Elizabeth Arden.* The company introduced "Elizabeth," a computer and video makeover system, who allows customers to test out their images with different shades of makeup, without having to actually apply the products first.
- *Tower Records.* A music sampler allows customers to hear records before buying them and to custom-design their own recordings by mixing and matching singles from assorted artists.
- *Trifari.* This company offers paper "punch-out" versions of its jewelry so that customers can try on the pieces at home.
- *Charmin.* Building on the familiar theme "Please don't squeeze the Charmin," the company deploys the Charmin Squeeze Squad. Employees hide behind stacks of the toilet tissue and jump out and blow horns at any "squeezers" they catch in the aisles.
- *The Farnam Company.* As somber music plays in the background, a huge plastic rat draped in a black shroud lies next to a tombstone to promote the company's Just One Bite rat poison.

Place-Based Media. Advertisers are also being more aggressive about hitting consumers with their messages, wherever they may be. *Place-based media* is a growing, specialized approach featuring media that target consumers based on locations in which messages are delivered. These places can be anything from airports, doctors' offices or college campuses to health clubs. Turner Broadcasting System has begun such ventures as Checkout Channel for grocery stores and Airport Channel, and it has even tested McDTV for McDonald's restaurants.[72] Even MTV is getting into the act: Its new Music Report, to be shown in record stores, is a two-hour "video capsule" featuring video spots and ads for music retailers and corporate sponsors. As an MTV executive observed, "They're already out there at the retail environment. They're ready to spend money."[73]

A company called Privy Promotions is even selling ad space on restroom walls in stadiums. For $2,000, the company will mount a framed ad for a year in a restroom stall, above a sink, or ". . . wherever it looks nice and appropriate," according to Privy's president. He claims ". . . it's a decided opportunity for an advertiser to reach a captive audience. . . ."[74]

Much of the growth in point-of-purchase activity has been in new electronic technologies.[75] Some stores feature talking posters that contain human-body sensors and that speak up when a shopper approaches. The Point-of-Purchase Radio Corporation offers in-store radio networks that are now used by about 60 grocery chains.[76] Some new shopping carts have a small screen, which is keyed to the specific areas of the store through which the cart is wheeled, that displays advertising.[77] In-store video displays allow advertisers to reinforce major media campaigns at the point of purchase.[78]

Some of the most interesting innovations can be found in state-of-the-art vending machines, which now dispense everything from Hormel's microwaveable chili and beef stew and Ore-Ida french fries to software. French consumers can purchase Levi's jeans from a machine called "Libre Service," which offers the pants in ten different sizes. The customer uses a seatbelt to find his or her size, and the jeans sell for about $10 less than the same versions sold in more conventional stores. Because of their frenetic lifestyles, the Japanese are particularly avid users of vending machines. These machines dispense virtually all of life's necessities, plus many luxuries people in other countries would not consider obtaining from a machine. The list includes jewelry, fresh flowers, frozen beef, pornography, business cards, underwear, and even the names of possible dates.[79]

The Salesperson

One of the most important in-store factors is the salesperson, who attempts to influence the buying behavior of the customer.[80] This influence can be understood in terms of **exchange theory,** which stresses that every interaction involves an exchange of value. Each participant gives something to the other and hopes to receive something in return.[81]

RESOURCE EXCHANGE

What "value" does the customer look for in a sales interaction? There are a variety of resources a salesperson might offer. He or she, for example, might offer expertise about the product to make the shopper's choice easier. Alternatively, the customer may be reassured because the salesperson is an admired or likable person whose tastes are similar and who is seen as someone to be trusted.[82] Mark's car purchase, for example, was strongly influenced by the age and sex of Melanie, the salesperson with whom he negotiated. In fact, a long stream of research attests to the impact of a salesperson's appearance on sales effectiveness. In sales, as in much of life, attractive people appear to hold the upper hand.[83]

THE SALES INTERACTION

A buyer/seller situation is like many other dyadic encounters (those within two-person groups); it is a relationship where some agreement must be reached about the roles of each participant, that is, a process of *identity negotiation* occurs.[84] For example, if Melanie immediately establishes herself as an all-knowing expert (and Mark accepts this position), she is likely to have more influence over him through the course of the relationship. Some of the factors that help to determine a salesperson's role (and relative effectiveness) are his or her age, appearance, educational level, and motivation to sell.[85]

In addition, more effective salespersons usually know their customers' traits and preferences better than do ineffective salespersons, since this knowledge allows them to adapt their approach to meet the needs of specific customers.[86] The ability to be adaptable is especially vital when customers and salespeople differ in terms of their *interaction styles*.[87] Consumers, for example, vary in the degree of assertiveness they bring to interactions. At one extreme, nonassertive people believe that complaining is not socially acceptable and may be intimidated in sales situations. Assertive people are more likely to stand up for themselves in firm but nonthreatening ways, while aggressives may resort to rudeness and threats if they do not get their way.[88]

RELATIONSHIP MARKETING

The strategic perspective that stresses the long-term, human side of buyer/seller interactions is called **relationship marketing.** It focuses on the importance of developing long-lasting relational exchanges by building commitment and trust with the customer.[89] This view recognizes that "... the sale merely consummates the courtship. Then the marriage begins. How good the marriage is depends on how well the relationship is managed by the seller."[90] Like romantic involvements, long-term sales relationships typically go through the following five phases.[91]

1. *Awareness.*   The buyer enters the market, perhaps becoming aware of local brands.

2. *Exploration.*   The buyer undergoes search and trial. A minimal investment is made in the relationship. Norms and expectations begin to develop.

3. *Expansion.*   The buyer and seller start to become more interdependent as the relationship becomes solidified.

4. *Commitment.*   A pledge is made (it may be done implicitly) to continue the relationship (e.g., a customer may come to refer to someone as "my hairdresser").

5. *Dissolution.*   The relationship will dissolve unless steps are taken to keep it together. One way for the seller to prevent dissolution is to construct *exit barriers,* things that make it difficult for the buyer to separate. Examples of exit barriers include delayed rebates (customers must accumulate proof-of-purchase seals over time), frequent-flier programs (which make it less tempting to switch airlines), or rental deposits.

Chemical Bank emphasizes the importance of relationship marketing for long-term growth. Fortune 5/2/94. Photo courtesy of Chemical Banking Corporation and Dennis Blachut, Photographer.

POSTPURCHASE SATISFACTION

Consumer satisfaction/dissatisfaction (CS/D) is determined by the overall feelings, or attitude, a person has about a product after it has been purchased. Consumers are engaged in a constant process of evaluating the things they buy as these products are integrated into their daily consumption activities.[92] And, customer satisfaction has a real impact on the bottom line: A recent study conducted among a large sample of Swedish consumers found that product quality affects customer satisfaction, which, in turn, results in increased profitability among firms who provide quality products.[93] Quality is more than a marketing buzzword.

This ad for Chrysler emphasizes the importance many marketers place on earning total customer satisfaction in the 1990s. Newsweek 5/2/94. Photo courtesy of Chrysler Corporation.

Just what do consumers look for in products? That's easy: They want quality and value. Especially because of foreign competition, claims of product quality have become strategically crucial to maintaining a competitive advantage.[94] Consumers use a number of cues to infer quality, including brand name, price, and even their own estimates of how much money has been put into a new product's advertising campaign.[95] These cues and others, such as product warranties and follow-up letters from the company, are often used by consumers to relieve perceived risk and assure themselves that they have made smart purchase decisions.[96]

A Shift in Quality Cues

However, the weighting assigned to different cues is changing as consumers' priorities are being transformed in the 1990s. Many people are part of a trend that the Grey Advertising agency has called "downshifting." They are reining in spending and trying to maximize the value of every dollar. The net result is that price has become a bigger concern; consumers are no longer willing to pay a premium for a brand name if they don't see a tangible difference between a well-known item and other product alternatives. A study done by Grey found that Americans' definition of value has changed from "best in class" to "best in budget range." Two factors are most likely at the heart of this trend: They are (1) a sluggish economy in the early 1990s that has dampened people's expectations that their financial well-being will continue to improve and (2) an increase in consumers viewing many products, such as cereal, diapers, or cigarettes, as commodities with very few differences among brands.[97]

While everyone wants quality, it is not clear exactly what quality means. Certainly, many manufacturers claim to provide it. The Ford Motor Company ad shown here emphasizes "Quality is job 1." Similar claims that have been made at one time or another by car manufacturers include the following:[98]

> Lincoln-Mercury: ". . . the highest quality cars of any major American car company"
> Chrysler: ". . . quality engineered to be the best"
> GMC trucks: ". . . quality built yet economical"
> Oldsmobile: ". . . fulfilling the quality needs of American drivers"
> Audi: ". . . quality backed by our outstanding new warranty"

What Is Quality?

In the book *Zen and the Art of Motorcycle Maintenance,* a cult hero of college students in an earlier generation literally went crazy trying to figure out the meaning of quality.[99] Marketers appear to use the word quality as a catchall for "good." Because of its wide and imprecise usage, the attribute of "quality" threatens to become a meaningless claim. If everyone has it, what good is it?

ISO 9000

One way to define quality is to establish uniform standards to which products from around the world must conform. This is the intent of the International Standards

This ad for Ford relies on a common claim about "quality." Courtesy of Ford Motor Company.

Organization, a Geneva-based organization that does just that. A set of quality criteria were initially developed in 1987 to regulate product quality. The broad set of guidelines is known as **ISO 9000.** The guidelines cover issues related to the manufacture and installation of products, as well as postsale servicing. A version of ISO 9000 has also been developed for American companies, and any firms wishing to sell their products in Europe are at a great disadvantage if they do not comply.[100]

THE IMPORTANCE OF EXPECTATIONS

Global standards for quality help to ensure that products work as promised, but consumers' evaluations of those products are a bit more complex. Satisfaction or dissatisfaction is more than a reaction to the actual performance quality of a product or service. It is influenced by prior expectations regarding the level of quality. According to the **expectancy disconfirmation model,** consumers form beliefs about product performance based upon prior experience with the product and/or upon communications about the product that imply a certain level of quality.[101] When something performs the way we thought it would, we may not think much about it. If, on the other hand, something fails to live up to expectations, a negative affect may result. And, if performance happens to exceed our expectations, we are satisfied and pleased.

To understand this perspective, think about different types of restaurants. People expect to be provided with sparkling clear glassware at fancy restaurants, and they might become upset if they discover grimy glasses. On the other hand, we may not be surprised to find fingerprints on our beer mugs at a local greasy spoon; we may even shrug it off because it contributes to the place's "charm." An important lesson emerges for marketers from this perspective: Don't overpromise.[102]

QUALITY AND PRODUCT FAILURES

The power of quality claims is most evident when they are not fulfilled, as when a company's product fails in some way. Here, consumers' expectations are dashed, and dissatisfaction results. In these situations, marketers immediately take steps to reassure customers. When the company confronts the problem truthfully, consumers often are willing to forgive and forget, as was the case for Tylenol (product tampering), Chrysler (disconnecting odometers on executives' cars and reselling them as new), or Perrier (traces of benzene found in the water). When the company appears to be dragging its heels or covering up, on the other hand, consumer resentment will grow, as occurred during Union Carbide's chemical disaster in India and with Exxon following the massive Alaskan oil spill caused by its tanker, the *Exxon Valdez*.

Acting on Dissatisfaction

If a person is not happy with a product or service, what can be done? Essentially, a consumer has three different courses of action that can be taken (note that more than one can be taken).[103]

1. *Voice response.* The consumer can appeal directly to the retailer for redress (e.g., a refund).

2. *Private response.* The consumer can express dissatisfaction about the store or product to friends and/or can boycott the store. As will be discussed in Chapter 11, negative word of mouth (WOM) can be very damaging to a store's reputation.

3. *Third-party response.* The consumer can take legal action against the merchant, register a complaint with the Better Business Bureau, or perhaps write a letter to a newspaper.

A number of factors influence which route is eventually taken. The consumer may, in general, be an assertive or a meek person. Action is more likely to be taken for expensive products, such as household durables, cars, and clothing, than for inexpensive products.[104] Also, if the consumer does not believe that the store will respond well to a complaint, the person will be more likely to simply switch brands than fight.[105] Ironically, marketers should actually *encourage* consumers to complain to them: People are more likely to spread the word about unresolved negative experiences to their friends than they are to boast about positive occurrences.[106]

In this quality-conscious era, it is essential for companies to stand behind their products—even if it means destroying allegedly defective ones. That is exactly what the Nissan Motor Co. did with over 22,000 of its 1987–90 C22 vans. After announcing three safety recalls to fix problems with some of the vans, the company decided it would be easier in some cases to buy them back from their owners and simply crush them. Although some owners were not thrilled with the arrangement, others appreciate the company's attention to quality. As one van owner observed, "Anybody who would . . . invest that kind of money to keep good will, they've got me forever," That is exactly the type of positive reaction Nissan is counting on. Quoted in Neal Templin, "Nissan Recalls—and Destroys—Some Minivans," The Wall Street Journal (December 9, 1993): B1 (2). Picture courtesy of Nissan North Amrica, Inc. Reproduced by permission.

PRODUCT DISPOSAL

Because people often do form strong attachments to products, the decision to dispose of something may be a painful one. One function performed by possessions is to serve as anchors for our identities: Our past lives on in our things.[107] This attachment is exemplified by the Japanese, who ritually "retire" worn-out sewing needles, chopsticks, and even computer chips by burning them as thanks for good service.[108]

Although some people have more trouble than others in discarding things, even a "pack rat" does not keep everything. Consumers must often dispose of things, either because they have fulfilled their designated functions or possibly because they no longer fit with consumers' views of themselves. Concern about the environment coupled with a need for convenience has made ease of product disposal a key attribute in categories from razors to diapers.

Disposal Options

When a consumer decides that a product is no longer of use, several choices are available. The person can either (1) keep the item, (2) temporarily dispose of it, or (3) permanently dispose of it. In many cases, a new product is acquired even though the old one still functions. Some reasons for this replacement include a desire for new features, a change in the person's environment (e.g., a refrigerator is the wrong color for a freshly painted kitchen), or a change in the person's role or self-image.[109] Figure 9–5 provides an overview of consumers' disposal options.

The issue of product disposition is doubly vital because of its enormous public policy implications. We live in a throwaway society, which creates problems for the environment and also results in a great deal of unfortunate waste. Training consumers to recycle has become a priority in many countries. Japan recycles about 40 percent of its garbage, and this relatively high rate of compliance is partly due to the social value the Japanese place on recycling. Citizens are encouraged by garbage trucks that periodically rumble through the streets playing classical music or children's songs.[110]

A recent study examined the relevant goals consumers have in recycling. It used a means-end chain analysis of the type described in Chapter 4 to identify how specific instrumental goals are linked to more abstract terminal values. The most important lower-order goals identified were "avoid filling up landfills," "reduce waste," "reuse materials," and "save the environment." These were linked to the terminal values of "promote health/avoid sickness," "achieve life-sustaining ends," and "provide for future generations." By applying such techniques to study recycling and other product disposal behaviors, social marketers will find it easier to design advertising copy and other messages that tap into the underlying values that will motivate people to increase environmentally responsible behavior.[111]

Lateral Cycling: Junk Versus "Junque"

Interesting consumer processes occur during **lateral cycling,** where already purchased objects are sold to others or exchanged for still other things. Many purchases are made secondhand, rather than new. The reuse of other people's things is so important in our throwaway society because, as one researcher put it, ". . . there is no longer an 'away' to throw things to."[112]

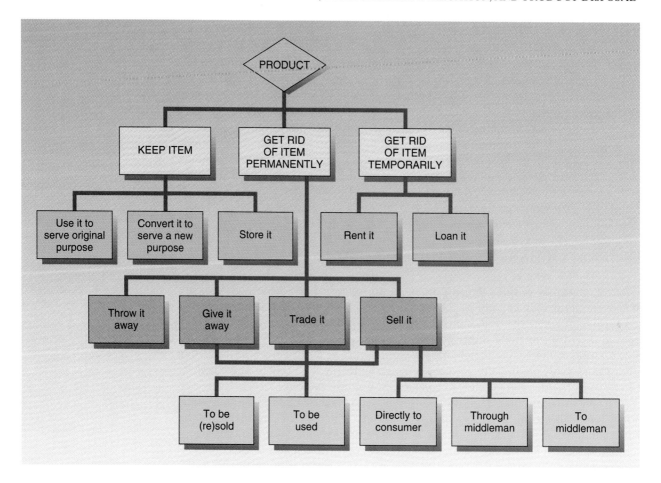

FIGURE 9–5 ▼ **Consumers' Disposal Options** Source: Jacob Jacoby, Carol K. Berning, and Thomas F. Dietvorst, "What About Disposition?" *Journal of Marketing* 41 (April 1977): 23. By permission of American Marketing Association.

✳ *M*ARKETING OPPORTUNITY

Some enterprising entrepreneurs have found profitable ways to encourage recycling by creating fashion items out of recycled materials. Two young jewelry designers in New York created a fad by making necklaces out of old bottle caps. They even pay homeless people to collect the caps. A Pittsburgh-based company called Little Earth Productions Incorporated makes all of its products from recycled materials. They sell backpacks decorated with old license plates, a shoulder bag made from rubber and hubcaps, and even purses crafted from discarded tuna cans. In addition to selling their unusual items in American boutiques, the company has started to expand overseas. It discovered that Japanese consumers liked the concept but felt the bags were too bulky, so a line of smaller articles was designed for the Japanese market. [113]

This Dutch Volkswagen ad focuses on recycling. The copy says, "And when you've had enough of it, we'll clear it away nicely." DDB Needham Worldwide, Amsterdam Lurzer's Achiv 1994. Photo courtesy of Volkswagen and DDB Needham Worldwide BV Amsterdam.

Flea markets, garage sales, classified advertisements, bartering for services, hand-me-downs, and the black market all represent important alternative marketing systems that operate in addition to the formal marketplace. For example, the number of used-merchandise retail establishments has grown at about ten times the rate of other stores.[114] While traditional marketers have not paid much attention to used-product sellers, factors such as concern about the environment, demands for quality, and cost and fashion consciousness are conspiring to make these "secondary" markets more important.[115] Interest in antiques, period accessories, and specialty magazines catering to this niche is increasing. Other growth areas include student markets for used computers and textbooks, as well as ski swaps, where millions of dollars of used ski equipment are exchanged.

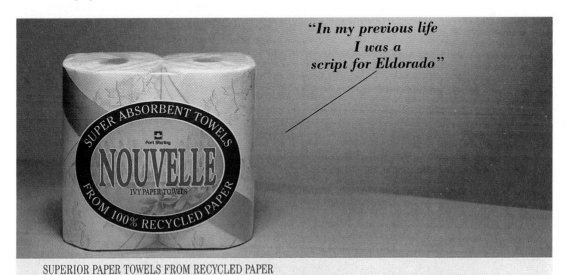

This British ad for paper towels takes a humorous route to emphasize that the paper towels are made from recycled paper. Lurzer's Archiv, 1994, 91. Photo courtesy of BDH, Manchester, UK. Creative Team; Wayne Hanson, Graham Daldry.

Original Drawing

FIGURE 10–2 ▼ **The Transmission of Misinformation: These drawings provide a classic example of the distortions that can occur as information is transmitted from person to person. As each participant reproduces the figure, it gradually changes from an owl to a cat.**   Source: Kenneth J. Gergen and Mary Gergen, *Social Psychology* (New York: Harcourt Brace Jovanovich, 1981): 365, Fig. 10–3; adapted from F. C. Bartlett, *Remembering* (Cambridge, England: Cambridge University Press, 1932).

ences. While rumors sometimes die out by themselves, in other instances a company may take direct action to counteract them. A French margarine was rumored to contain contaminants, and the company addressed this in its advertising by referring to the story as "The rumor that costs you dearly."[68]

Several marketers in Indonesia, including Nestlé, were hurt by rumors that their foods contain pork, which is prohibited to the 160 million Muslim consumers in that country. Islamic preachers, or *mullahs,* responded to these rumors by warning consumers not to buy products that might be tainted with pork fat. Nestlé spent more than $250,000 on an ad campaign to counteract the rumors.[69]

CONSUMER BOYCOTTS

Sometimes a negative experience can trigger an organized and devastating response, as when a consumer group organizes a *boycott* of a company's products. About 100 boycott campaigns (including threats to boycott if a company does not change some policy) are currently in effect. These efforts can include protests against everything from the use of products from a politically undesirable country (as when Procter & Gamble used Salvadoran beans for its Folgers coffee) to the inclusion of obscene or inflammatory lyrics in songs (as when law enforcement organizations threatened to boycott Time Warner after it distributed a rap song by Ice-T entitled "Cop Killer").

Boycotts are not always effective. Studies show that only 18 percent of Americans participate in them. However, those who do are disproportionately upscale and well educated, so they are a group companies especially don't want to alienate. One increasingly popular solution used by marketers is setting up a joint task force with a boycotting organization to try to iron out the problem. McDonald's recently used this approach with the Environmental Defense Fund, which was concerned about its use of polystyrene containers and bleached paper. The company agreed to test a composting program and to switch to plain brown bags.[70]

OPINION LEADERSHIP

Although consumers get information from personal sources, they do not tend to ask just *anyone* for advice about purchases. Everyone knows people who are knowledgeable about products and whose advice is taken seriously by others. These individuals are **opinion leaders.** An opinion leader is a person who is frequently able to influence others' attitudes or behaviors.[71]

If you decide to buy a new stereo, you will most likely seek advice from a friend who knows a lot about sound systems. This friend may own a sophisticated system, or he or she may subscribe to specialized magazines, such as *Stereo Review,* and spend free time browsing through electronics stores. On the other hand, you may have another friend who has a reputation for being stylish and who spends *his* free time reading *Gentlemen's Quarterly* and shopping at trendy boutiques. While you might not bring up your stereo problem with him, you may take him with you to shop for a new fall wardrobe.

This ad for MTV focuses on the importance of young opinion leaders in shaping their friends' preferences. Courtesy of Viacom, International.

Opinion leadership is an important influence on a brand's popularity in many categories. One prominent example is the role it plays in athletic shoe marketing. Athletic shoes, despite price tags of $100 and more, are very much a fashion statement, a phenomenon largely fueled by inner-city kids. Many of the sneaker styles originate in the inner city and then spread outward by word of mouth. As one marketer noted, "The urban kid stands for hard-core experience. . . . That, to a youth in the suburbs, represents authenticity."

Manufacturers pay close attention to these inner-city trendsetters and try to woo them to "endorse" their styles. Nike flew over 20 owners of sporting goods stores in urban areas to Chicago to find out how to influence inner-city kids. Converse spent a year talking to groups of kids in cities before rolling out its Bold line, and Avia tests its models on inner-city focus groups before "going national." Reebok does its part by repaving inner-city basketball courts to curry favor with young opinion leaders.

In addition to paying a few major athletes to endorse shoes, sneaker companies pay many high school and college coaches to outfit team players with their footwear, since this provides exposure and credibility when other kids see their role models wearing certain types of shoes. For example, Duke University's basketball coach reportedly signed an agreement under which he will receive over $7 million over a 15-year period from Nike in return for making the company's gear available to his players.[72]

The Nature of Opinion Leadership

Opinion leaders are valuable information sources for a number of reasons.

1. They are technically competent and thus are convincing because they possess expert power.[73]

2. They have prescreened, evaluated, and synthesized product information in an unbiased way, so they possess knowledge power.[74] Unlike commercial endorsers, opinion leaders do not actually represent the interests of one company. They are more credible because they have no "axe to grind."

3. They tend to be socially active and highly interconnected in their communities.[75] They are likely to hold office in community groups and clubs and to be active outside of the home. As a result, opinion leaders often have legitimate power by virtue of their social standing.

4. They tend to be similar to the consumer in terms of their values and beliefs, so they possess referent power. Note that while opinion leaders are set apart by their interest or expertise in a product category, they are more convincing to the extent that they are *homophilous* rather than *heterophilous*. *Homophily* refers to the degree that a pair of individuals is similar in terms of education, social status, and beliefs.[76] Effective opinion leaders tend to be slightly higher than those they influence, in terms of status and educational attainment, but not so high as to be in a different social class.

5. Opinion leaders often are among the first to buy new products, so they absorb much of the risk. This experience reduces uncertainty for others who are not as courageous. And, while company-sponsored communications tend to focus exclusively on the positive aspects of a product, this hands-on experience

makes opinion leaders more likely to impart *both* positive and negative information about product performance.

THE EXTENT OF AN OPINION LEADER'S INFLUENCE

When marketers and social scientists initially developed the concept of the opinion leader, it was assumed that certain influential people in a community would exert an overall impact on group members' attitudes. Later work, however, began to question the assumption that there is such a thing as a *generalized opinion leader,* somebody whose recommendations are sought for all types of purchases. Very few people are capable of being expert in a number of fields. Sociologists distinguish between those who are *monomorphic,* or experts in a limited field, and those who are *polymorphic,* or experts in several fields.[77] Even the opinion leaders who are polymorphic tend to concentrate on one broad domain, such as electronics or fashion.

Research on opinion leadership generally indicates that while opinion leaders do exist for multiple product categories, expertise tends to overlap across similar categories. It is rare to find a generalized opinion leader. An opinion leader for home appliances is likely to serve a similar function for home cleaners, but not for cosmetics. In contrast, a *fashion opinion leader,* whose primary influence is on clothing choices, may also be consulted for recommendations on cosmetics purchases, but not necessarily on microwave ovens.[78]

OPINION LEADERS VERSUS OTHER CONSUMER TYPES

Early conceptions of the role of the opinion leader also assumed a static process: The opinion leader absorbs information from the mass media and, in turn, transmits these data to opinion receivers. This view has turned out to be overly simplified; it confuses the functions of several different types of consumers.

Innovative Communicators.   Opinion leaders may or may not be purchasers of the products they recommend. Early purchasers are known as *innovators.* Opinion leaders who are also early purchasers have been termed *innovative communicators.* One study identified a number of characteristics of college men who were innovative communicators for fashion products. These men were among the first to buy new fashions, and their fashion opinions were incorporated by other students in their own clothing decisions. Other characteristics of the men included the following:[79]

- They were socially active.
- They were appearance-conscious and narcissistic (i.e., they were quite fond of themselves and self-centered).
- They were involved in rock culture.
- They were heavy magazine readers, including *Playboy* and *Sports Illustrated.*
- They were likely to own more clothing, and a broader range of styles, than other students.
- Their intellectual interests were relatively limited.

Opinion Seekers.   Opinion leaders also are likely to be *opinion seekers.* They are generally more involved in a product category and actively search for information. As a result, they are more likely to talk about products with others and to solicit others' opinions, as well. Contrary to the static view of opinion leadership, most product-related conversation does not take place in a "lecture" format, wherein one person does all of the talking. A lot of product-related conversation is prompted by the situation and occurs in the context of a casual interaction rather than as formal instruction.[80] One study, which found that opinion seeking is especially high for food products, revealed that two-thirds of opinion seekers also view themselves as opinion leaders.[81] This updated view of interpersonal product communication is contrasted with the traditional view in Figure 10–3.

Market Mavens.   Consumers who are expert in a product category may not actively communicate with others, while other consumers may have a more general interest in being involved in product discussions. A consumer category called the **market maven** has been proposed to describe people who are actively involved in transmitting marketplace information of all types. Market mavens are not necessarily interested in certain products and may not necessarily be early purchasers of products. They come closer to the function of a generalized opinion leader because they tend to have a solid overall knowledge of how and where to procure products.[82] A scale that has been used to identify market mavens appears in Figure 10–4.

Surrogate Consumers.   In addition to everyday consumers who are influential in affecting others' purchase decisions, a class of marketing intermediary called the **surrogate consumer** is an active player in many categories. A surrogate consumer is a person who is hired to provide input into purchase decisions. Unlike the opinion leader or market maven, the surrogate is usually compensated for this involvement.

Interior decorators, stockbrokers, professional shoppers, or college consultants can all be thought of as surrogate consumers. Whether or not they actually make the purchase on behalf of the consumer, surrogates' recommendations can be enormously influential. The consumer in essence relinquishes control over several or all decision-making functions, such as information search, evaluation of alternatives, or

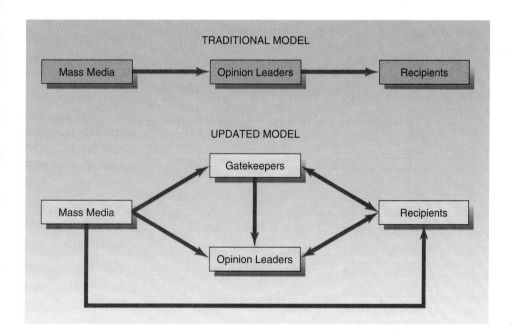

FIGURE 10–3   ▼   **Perspectives on the Communications Process**

1. I like introducing new brands and products to my friends.

2. I like helping people by providing them with information about many kinds of products.

3. People ask me for Information about products, places to shop, or sales.

4. If someone asked me where to get the best buy on several types of products, I could tell him or her where to shop.

5. My friends think of me as a good source of information when it comes to new products or sales.

6. Think about a person who has information about a variety of products and likes to share this information with others. This person knows about new products, sales, stores, and so on, but does not necessarily feel he or she is an expert on one particular product. How well would you say this description fits you?

FIGURE 10–4 ▼ Scale Items Used to Identify Market Mavens Source: Adapted from Lawrence Feick and Linda Price, "The Market Maven: A Diffuser of Marketplace Information," *Journal of Marketing* 51 (January 1987): 83–7.

the actual purchase. For example, a client may commission an interior decorator to redo her house, while a broker may be entrusted to make crucial buy/sell decisions on behalf of investors. The involvement of surrogates in a wide range of purchase decisions tends to be overlooked by many marketers, who may be mistargeting their communications to end-consumers instead of to the surrogates who are actually sifting through product information.[83]

Identifying Opinion Leaders

Because opinion leaders are so central to consumer decision making, marketers are quite interested in identifying influential people for a product category. In fact, many ads are intended to reach these influentials rather than the average consumer, especially if the ads contain a lot of technical information. The average television purchaser probably would not be excited by an ad for a Pioneer projection television that claims to have a lens with a "maximum bore of 160 mm" and a "new high-voltage stabilizing circuit." On the other hand, an electronics buff might be quite impressed by this information and, in turn, take it into consideration when recommending a projection television to a more naive friend.

PROFESSIONAL OPINION LEADERS

Perhaps the easiest way to find opinion leaders is to target people who are paid to give expert opinions. *Professional opinion leaders* are people like doctors or scientists who obtain specialized information from technical journals and other practitioners. One study that examined some choices of materials used by prosthodontists (crown- and bridge-restoration specialists) traced the colleagues who tended to be contacted for advice and found a small set of peers who were influential in determining choices around the country.[84]

Marketers who are trying to gain consumer acceptance for their products sometimes find it easier to try to win over professional opinion leaders, who (they hope) will, in turn, recommend their products to customers. A case in point is the recent effort by Roc S.A., maker of Europe's leading brand of hypoallergenic lotions, to break into the $4 billion American market for skin-care products. Instead of competing head-to-head with the lavish consumer advertising of Revlon or Estée Lauder, the French company decided to first gain medical acceptance by winning over pharmacists and dermatologists. In 1994, the company began advertising in medical journals, and the product was distributed to dermatologists and to drugstores patronized by patients of skin doctors. A toll-free number was established to provide interested consumers with the names of pharmacies carrying the line.[85]

Of course, this approach can backfire if it is carried to an extreme and compromises the credibility of professional opinion leaders. The Upjohn Company recently got in trouble for paying pharmacists to convince patients to switch prescriptions from a generic diabetes drug to the Upjohn brand. The company paid $8 every time a patient switched, and pharmacists also were reimbursed for calling doctors and patients to suggest the substitution. Upjohn claims it was merely compensating the opinion leaders for the time they spent counseling diabetes patients. In an agreement reached with eight states over the plan, Upjohn now advises patients that there could be medical risks in switching from one drug to another. A similar agreement was reached with Miles Inc., which had also been paying pharmacists (this time, $35) for each new prescription they wrote for a drug used to lower patients' blood pressure.[86]

CONSUMER OPINION LEADERS

Unfortunately, since most opinion leaders are everyday consumers and are not formally included in marketing efforts, they are harder to find. A celebrity or an influential industry executive is, by definition, easy to locate. He or she has national or at least regional visibility or may be listed in published directories. In contrast, most opinion leaders tend to operate at the local level and may influence five to ten consumers rather than an entire market segment. In some cases, companies have been known to identify influentials and involve them directly in their marketing efforts, hoping to create a "ripple effect" as these consumers sing the company's praises to their friends. Many department stores, for example, have "fashion panels," usually composed of adolescent girls, who provide input into fashion trends, participate in fashion shows, and so on.

Because of the difficulties involved in identifying specific opinion leaders in a large market, most attempts to do so instead focus on exploratory studies in which the characteristics of representative opinion leaders can be identified and then generalized to the larger market. This knowledge helps marketers target their product-related information to appropriate settings and media. For example, one attempt to identify financial opinion leaders found that these consumers were more likely to be involved in managing their own finances and tended to use a computer to do so. They also were more likely to follow their investments on a daily basis and to read books and watch television shows devoted to financial issues.[87]

THE SELF-DESIGNATING METHOD

The most commonly used technique to identify opinion leaders is simply to ask individual consumers whether they consider themselves to be opinion leaders. This is called the *self-designating method.*

There are problems with self-designation. While respondents who report a greater degree of interest in a product category are more likely to be opinion leaders, the results of surveys intended to identify self-designated opinion leaders must be viewed with some skepticism. Some people have a tendency to inflate their own importance and influence, while others who really are influential might not admit to this quality.[88] Just because we transmit advice about products does not mean other people *take* that advice. For someone to be considered a bona fide opinion leader, his or her advice must actually be heard and heeded by opinion seekers. An alternative to self-designation is to select certain group members (*key informants*) who, in turn, are asked to identify opinion leaders. The success of this approach hinges on locating those who have accurate knowledge of the group and on minimizing their response biases (e.g., the tendency to inflate one's own influence on the choices of others).

While the self-designating method is not as reliable as a more systematic analysis (where individual claims of influence can be verified by asking others whether the person is really influential), it does have the advantage of being easy to administer to a large group of potential opinion leaders. In some cases, not all members of a community are surveyed. An updated version of the original measurement scale developed for self-designation of opinion leaders is shown in Figure 10–5.[89]

SOCIOMETRY

Sociometric methods, which trace communication patterns among group members, allow researchers to systematically map out interactions that take place among group members. By asking participants whom they go to for product information,

---

Please rate yourself on the following scales relating to your interactions with friends and neighbors regarding _____.

1. In general, do you talk to your friends and neighbors about _____:
   very often   never
   5   4   3   2   1

2. When you talk to your friends and neighbors about _____ do you:
   give a great deal of information   give very little information
   5   4   3   2   1

3. During the past six months, how many people have you told about a new _____?
   told a number of people   told no one
   5   4   3   2   1

4. Compared with your circle of friends, how likely are you to be asked about new _____?
   very likely to be asked   not at all likely to be
   a   s   k   e   d
   5   4   3   2   1

5. In discussion of new _____, which of the following happens most?
   you tell your friends about _____   your friends tell you about _____
   5   4   3   2   1

6. Overall in all of your discussions with friends and neighbors are you:
   often used as a source of advice   not used as a source of advice

---

FIGURE 10–5 ▼ A Revised and Updated Version of the Opinion Leadership Scale   Source: Adapted from Terry L. Childers, "Assessment of the Psychometric Properties of an Opinion Leadership Scale," *Journal of Marketing Research* 23 (May 1986): 184–8; and Leisa Reinecke Flynn, Ronald E. Goldsmith, and Jacqueline K. Eastman, "The King and Summers Opinion Leadership Scale: Revision and Refinement," *Journal of Business Research* 31 (1994): 55–64.

those who tend to be sources of product-related information can be identified. While this method is the most precise, it is very hard and expensive to implement, since it involves very close study of interaction patterns in small groups. For this reason, sociometric techniques are best applied in closed, self-contained social settings, such as hospitals, prisons, and army bases, where members are largely isolated from other social networks.

Many professionals and services marketers depend primarily upon word of mouth to generate business. In many cases, consumers recommend a service provider to a friend or co-worker, and, in other cases, other business people make recommendations to their customers. For example, only 0.2 percent of respondents in one study reported choosing physicians based on advertising. Advice from family and friends was the most widely used criterion.[90]

Sociometric analyses can be used to better understand *referral behavior* and to locate strengths and weaknesses in terms of how one's reputation is communicated through a community. *Network analysis* focuses on communication in social systems; it considers the relations among people in a *referral network* and measures the *tie strength* among them. Tie strength refers to the nature of the bond between people. It can range from strong primary (e.g., one's spouse) to weak secondary (e.g., an acquaintance that one rarely sees). A strong tie relationship may be thought of as a primary reference group, in which interactions are frequent and important to the individual.

While strong ties are important, weak ties can perform a *bridging function*. This type of connection allows a consumer access between subgroups. For example, you might have a regular group of friends who serve as a primary reference group (strong ties). If you have an interest in tennis, say, one of these friends might introduce you to a group of people in her dorm who play on the tennis team. As a result, you gain access to their valuable expertise through this bridging function. This referral process demonstrates the strength of weak ties. One study using this method examined similarities in brand choice among members of a college sorority. The

This ad for Chemical Bank emphasizes that many consumer decisions are made on the basis of personal recommendations rather than because of persuasive advertising. Copyright 1990 by Chemical Bank. Reprinted by permission of Chemical Bank, New York.

researchers found evidence that subgroups, or *cliques*, within the sorority were likely to share preferences for various products. In some cases, even choices of "private" (i.e., socially inconspicuous) products were shared, possibly because of structural variables, such as shared bathrooms in the sorority house.[91]

One study analyzed the referral networks of a services marketer (in this case, a piano tuner) to demonstrate how referral patterns can be better understood. The researchers contacted all of the piano tuner's customers and asked them how they found out about him (referral paths). The paths were identified, and the researchers were able to describe where business was being generated (whether through friends, business contacts, etc.) and also to pinpoint opinion leaders in the system (i.e., people who were a referral source for more than one customer).[92] This technique could conceivably be applied by many service providers to identify those customers who are responsible for generating a lot of business.

THE DIFFUSION OF INNOVATIONS

New products and styles termed **innovations** constantly enter the market. These new products or services occur in both consumer and industrial settings. Innovations may take the form of a clothing style (e.g., skirts for men), a new manufacturing technique, or a novel way to deliver a service. If an innovation is successful (most are not), it spreads through the population. First it is bought and/or used by only a few people, and then more and more consumers decide to adopt it, until, in some cases, it seems that almost everyone has bought or tried the innovation. **Diffusion of innovations** refers to the process whereby a new product, service, or idea spreads through a population.

*M*ARKETING PITFALL

The issue of what exactly constitutes a "new" product is quite important to many businesses. It is said that "imitation is the sincerest form of flattery," and decisions regarding how much (if at all) one's product should resemble those of competitors are often a centerpiece of marketing strategy (e.g., packaging of "me-too" or look-alike products). On the other hand, the product cannot be an exact duplicate; patent law is concerned with the precise definition of what is a new product and protecting that invention from illegal imitation.

A **knockoff** is a style that has deliberately been copied and modified, often with the intent to sell to a larger or different market. For example, *haute couture* clothing styles presented by top designers in Paris and elsewhere are commonly "knocked off" by other designers and sold to the mass market. It is difficult to legally protect a design (as opposed to a technological feature), but pressure is building in many industries to do just that. Manufacturers argue that a distinctive curve on a car bumper, say, is as important to the integrity of the car as is a mechanical innovation. Legislation is being considered to protect new designs with a ten-year copyright (clothing would be exempt).[93] This movement highlights the importance of the question "What exactly is an innovation?"

Adopting Innovations

A consumer's adoption of an innovation resembles the decision-making sequence discussed in Chapter 8. The person moves through the stages of awareness, information search, evaluation, trial, and adoption, although the relative importance of each stage may differ depending upon how much is already known about a product, as well as on cultural factors that may affect people's willingness to try new things.[94]

However, even within the same culture, not all people adopt an innovation at the same rate. Some do so quite rapidly, and others never do at all. Consumers can be placed into approximate categories based upon their likelihood of adopting an innovation. The categories of adopters, shown in Figure 10–6, can be related to phases of the product-life-cycle concept used widely by marketing strategists.

As can be seen in Figure 10–6, roughly one-sixth of the population (innovators and early adopters) are very quick to adopt new products, and one-sixth of the people (laggards) are very slow. The other two-thirds are somewhere in the middle, and these majority adopters represent the mainstream public. These consumers are interested in new things, but they do not want them to be too new. In some cases, people deliberately wait to adopt an innovation because they assume that its technological qualities will be improved or that its price will fall after it has been on the market awhile.[95] Keep in mind that the proportion of consumers falling into each category is an estimate; the actual size of each depends upon such factors as the complexity of the product, its cost, and so on.

Even though **innovators** represent only 2.5 percent of the population, marketers are always interested in identifying them. These are the brave souls who are always on the lookout for novel developments and will be the first to try a new offering. Just as generalized opinion leaders do not appear to exist, innovators tend to be category-specific, as well. A person who is an innovator in one area may even be a laggard in another. For example, a gentleman who prides himself as being on the cut-

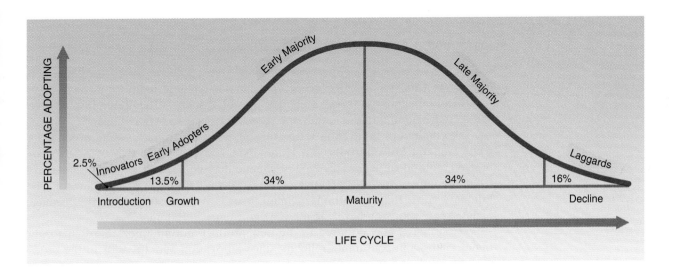

FIGURE 10–6 ▼ **Types of Adopters**

ting edge of fashion may have no conception of new developments in recording technology and may still stubbornly cling to his phonograph albums even while he searches for the latest *avant-garde* clothing styles in obscure boutiques.

Despite this qualification, some generalizations can be offered regarding the profile of innovators.[96] Not surprisingly, for example, they tend to have more favorable attitudes toward taking risks. They also are likely to have higher educational and income levels and to be socially active.

Early adopters share many of the same characteristics as innovators, but an important difference is their degree of concern for social acceptance, especially with regard to expressive products, such as clothing, cosmetics, and so on. Generally speaking, an early adopter is receptive to new styles because he or she is involved in the product category and also places high value on being in fashion. What appears on the surface to be a fairly high-risk adoption (e.g., wearing a skirt three inches above the knee when most people are wearing them below the knee) is actually not *that* risky. The style change has already been "field-tested" by innovators, who truly took the fashion risk. Early adopters are likely to be found in "fashion-forward" stores featuring the latest "hot" designers. In contrast, true innovators are more likely to be found in small boutiques featuring as-yet-unknown designers.

Types of Innovations

Innovations can occur on a symbolic level or a technological level. A **symbolic innovation** communicates a new social meaning (e.g., a new hairstyle or car design), while a **technological innovation** involves some functional change (e.g., central air-conditioning or car airbags).[97] Whether symbolic or functional, new products, services, and ideas have characteristics that determine the degree to which they will probably diffuse. As a general rule, innovations that are more novel are least likely to diffuse, because things that are fairly similar to what is already available require fewer changes in behavior to use. On the other hand, an innovation that radically alters a person's lifestyle requires the person to modify his or her way of doing things and thus requires more effort to adapt to the change.

BEHAVIORAL DEMANDS OF INNOVATIONS

Innovations can be categorized in terms of the degree to which they demand changes in behavior from adopters. Three major types of innovations have been identified, though these three categories are not absolutes. They refer, in a relative sense, to the amount of disruption or change they bring to people's lives.

A **continuous innovation** refers to a modification of an existing product, as when General Mills introduced a Honey Nut version of Cheerios or Levi's promoted shrink-to-fit jeans. This type of change may be used to set one brand apart from its competitors. Most product innovations are of this type; that is, they are evolutionary rather than revolutionary. Small changes are made to position the product, add line extensions, or merely to alleviate consumer boredom.

Consumers may be lured to the new product, but adoption represents only minor changes in consumption habits, since innovation perhaps adds to the product's convenience or to the range of choices available. A typewriter company, for example, many years ago modified the shape of its product to make it more "user friendly" to secretaries. One simple change was the curving of the tops of the keys, a convention that is carried over on today's computer keyboards. The reason for the change was that secretaries had complained about the difficulty of typing with long fingernails on the flat surfaces.

A **dynamically continuous innovation** is a more pronounced change in an existing product, as represented by self-focusing 35 mm cameras or Touch-Tone telephones. These innovations have a modest impact on the way people do things, creating some behavioral changes. When introduced, the IBM Selectric typewriter, which uses a typing ball rather than individual keys, permitted secretaries to instantly change the typeface of manuscripts by replacing one Selectric ball with another.

A **discontinuous innovation** creates major changes in the way we live. Major inventions, such as the airplane, the car, the computer, and television have radically changed modern lifestyles. The personal computer has, in many cases, supplanted the typewriter, and it has created the phenomenon of "telecommuters" by allowing many consumers to work out of their homes. Of course, the cycle continues, as new continuous innovations (e.g., new versions of software) are constantly being made for computers; dynamically continuous innovations, such as the keyboard "mouse,"

The personal computer is an innovation that has significantly changed the way we live. These photographs are reproduced courtesy of International Business Machines Corporation.

compete for adoption; and discontinuous innovations like wristwatch personal computers loom on the horizon.

PREREQUISITES FOR SUCCESSFUL ADOPTION

Regardless of how much behavioral change is demanded by an innovation, several factors are desirable for a new product to succeed.[98]

- **Compatibility.**   The innovation should be compatible with consumers' lifestyles. As one illustration, a manufacturer of personal-care products tried unsuccessfully several years ago to introduce a cream hair remover for men as a substitute for razors and shaving cream. This formulation was similar to that used widely by women to remove hair from their legs. Although the product was simple and convenient to use, it failed because men were not interested in a product they perceived to be too feminine and thus threatening to their masculine self-concepts.

- **Trialability.**   Since an unknown is accompanied by high perceived risk, people are more likely to adopt an innovation if they can experiment with it prior to making a commitment. To reduce this risk, companies often choose the expensive strategy of distributing free "trial-size" samples of new products.

- **Complexity.**   The product should be low in complexity. A product that is easier to understand and use will be chosen over a competitor. This strategy requires less effort from the consumer, and it also lowers perceived risk. Manufacturers of videocassette recorders, for example, have put a lot of effort into simplifying VCR usage (e.g., on-screen programming) to encourage adoption.

- **Observability.**   Innovations that are easily observable are more likely to spread, since this quality makes it more likely that other potential adopters will become aware of its existence. The rapid proliferation of fanny packs (pouches worn around the waist in lieu of wallets or purses) was due to their high visibility. It was easy for others to see the convenience offered by this alternative.

- **Relative Advantage.**   Most importantly, the product should offer relative advantage over other alternatives. The consumer must believe that its use will provide a benefit other products cannot offer. Two popular new products demonstrate the importance of possessing a perceived relative advantage vis-à-vis existing products: Energizer Green Power Batteries are promoted as being better for the environment because they contain less mercury, and the Bugchaser is a wristband containing insect repellent. Mothers with young children have liked it because it is nontoxic and nonstaining. In contrast, the Crazy Blue Air Freshener, which was added to windshield wiper fluid and emitted a fragrance when the wipers were turned on, fizzled: People didn't see the need for the product and felt there were simpler ways to freshen their cars if they cared to.

- Consumers belong to or admire many different groups and are often influenced in their purchase decisions by a desire to be accepted by others.

- Individuals have influence in a group to the extent that they possess *social power;* types of power include information power, referent power, legitimate power, expert power, reward power, and coercive power.

- We conform to the desires of others for one of two basic reasons. People who model their behavior after others because they take others' behavior as evidence of the correct way to act are conforming because of *informational social influence.* Those who conform to satisfy the expectations of others and/or to be accepted by the group are affected by *normative social influence.*

- Group members often do things they would not do as individuals because their identities become merged with the group; they become *deindividuated.*

- Individuals or groups whose opinions or behavior are particularly important to consumers are *reference groups.* Both formal and informal groups influence the individual's purchase decisions, although the impact of reference-group influence is affected by such factors as the conspicuousness of the product and the relevance of the reference group for a particular purchase.

- *Opinion leaders* who are knowledgeable about a product and whose opinions are highly regarded tend to influence others' choices. Specific opinion leaders are somewhat hard to identify, but marketers who know their general characteristics can try to target them in their media and promotional strategies.

- Other influencers are *market mavens,* who have a general interest in marketplace activities, and *surrogate consumers,* who are compensated for their advice about purchases.

- Much of what we know about products comes about through *word-of-mouth communication (WOM)* rather than formal advertising. Product-related information tends to be exchanged in casual conversations.

- While word-of-mouth often is helpful for making consumers aware of products, it can also hurt companies when damaging product rumors or negative word-of-mouth occurs.

- *Sociometric methods* are used to trace referral patterns. This information can be used to identify opinion leaders and other influential consumers.

- The *diffusion of innovations* refers to the process whereby a new product, service, or idea spreads through a population. A consumer's decision to adopt a new item depends on his or her personal characteristics (i.e., if he or she is inclined to try new things) and on characteristics of the item. Products stand a better chance of being adopted if they demand relatively little change in behavior from consumers and are compatible with current practices. They are also more likely to diffuse if they can be tried prior to purchase, if they are not complex, if their use is visible to others, and, most importantly, if they provide a relative advantage vis-à-vis existing products.

KEY TERMS

Affinity marketing p. 346

Comparative influence p. 341

Compatibility p. 370

Complexity p. 370

Conformity p. 348

Continuous innovation p. 368

Decision polarization p. 352

Deindividuation p. 351

Diffusion of innovations p. 366

Discontinuous innovation p. 369

Dynamically continuous innovation p. 369

Early adopters p. 368

Information power p. 345

Informational social influence p. 349

Innovations p. 366

Innovators p. 367

Knockoff p. 366

Market maven p. 361

Normative influence p. 341

Normative social influence p. 349

Norms p. 348

Observability p. 370

Opinion leaders p. 358

Reactance p. 353

Reference group p. 340

Referent power p. 345

Relative advantage p. 370

Social comparison theory p. 349

Social power p. 344

Sociometric methods p. 364

Surrogate consumer p. 361

Symbolic innovation p. 368

Technological innovation p. 368

Trialability p. 370

Word-of-mouth communication (WOM) p. 354

CONSUMER BEHAVIOR CHALLENGE

1. Compare and contrast the five bases of power described in the text. Which are most likely to be relevant for marketing efforts?

2. Why is referent power an especially potent force for marketing appeals? What are factors that help to predict whether reference groups will or will not be a powerful influence on a person's purchase decisions?

3. Evaluate the strategic soundness of the concept of affinity marketing. For what type of linkages is this strategy most likely to be a success?

4. Discuss some factors that determine the amount of conformity likely to be observed among consumers.

5. Under what conditions are we more likely to engage in social comparison with dissimilar others versus similar others? How might this dimension be used in the design of marketing appeals?

6. Discuss some reasons for the effectiveness of home-shopping parties as a selling tool. What factors might reduce the power of this strategy?

7. Discuss some factors that influence whether or not membership groups will have a significant influence on a person's behavior.

8. Why is word-of-mouth communication often more persuasive than advertising?

9. Is there such a thing as a generalized opinion leader? What is likely to determine if an opinion leader will be influential with regard to a specific product category?

10. The adoption of a certain brand of shoe or apparel by athletes can be a powerful influence on students and other fans. Should high school and college coaches be paid to determine what brand of athletic equipment their players will wear?

11. The power of unspoken social norms often becomes obvious only when these norms are violated. To witness this result firsthand, try one of the following: stand facing the back wall in an elevator; serve dessert before the main course; offer to pay cash for dinner at a friend's home; wear pajamas to class; or tell someone *not* to have a nice day.

12. Identify a set of avoidance groups for your peers. Can you identify any consumption decisions that are made with these groups in mind?

13. Identify fashion opinion leaders on your campus. Do they fit the profile discussed in the chapter?

14. Conduct a sociometric analysis within your dormitory or neighborhood. For a product category such as music or cars, ask each individual to identify other individuals with whom they share information. Systematically trace all of these avenues of communication, and identify opinion leaders by locating individuals who are repeatedly named as providing helpful information.

15. The chapter discusses a situation where professional actors are paid to order a certain drink in a bar to stimulate word-of-mouth. Some marketing executives defend this practice. As one commented, "Twenty years ago, the way you expanded sales at a bar was to give the bartender a hundred bucks. This is moving the power from behind the bar to in front of the bar." On the other hand, some critics of the strategy view this as unethical behavior. One commented, "People have the right to know when they're being advertised to."[100] What do you think?

16. Innovators are a small minority of consumers, yet marketers are very interested in identifying and reaching them. Why? How might you go about locating innovators?

17. Provide an example of a discontinuous innovation currently vying for adoption. What are the factors working for and against its eventual success in the marketplace?

Freshly brewed coffee for ten.

For one.

Aroma-fresh pouch.

Contains ground roast coffee in its own filter.

Folgers Coffee Singles
THE ULTIMATE ONE CUP COFFEE MACHINE.

Folger's Coffee has addressed an important need by allowing single people to brew one cup of coffee at a time. Courtesy of Procter & Gamble.

Procter & Gamble introduced Folger's Singles—single-serving coffee bags for people who live alone and don't need a full pot.[40]

Single men and women are quite different markets. More than half of single men are under the age of 35, while more than half of single women are over 65. Despite single males' greater incomes, single women dominate many markets because of their spending patterns. Single women are more likely to own a home, and they spend more on housing-related items and furniture. Single men, in contrast, spend more overall in restaurants and on cars. However, these spending patterns are also significantly affected by age: Middle-aged single women, for example, actually spend more than their male counterparts on cars.[41]

WHO'S LIVING AT HOME?

In many cases, the nuclear family is being transformed to resemble the old-fashioned extended family. Many adults are being forced to care for parents as well as children. In fact, Americans, on average, spend 17 years caring for children but 18 years assisting aged parents.[42] Middle-aged people have been termed "the sandwich generation," because they must attend to those above and below them in age.

In addition to dealing with live-in parents, many adults are surprised to find that their children are living with them longer or are moving back in, well after the "lease" has expired.[43] These returnees have been termed **boomerang kids** by demographers (you "throw them away" and they keep coming back!). The number of children between 18 and 34 living at home has grown by one-third in the last 15 years. If this trend continues, it will affect a variety of markets as boomerang kids spend less on housing and staples and more on discretionary purchases, such as entertainment.

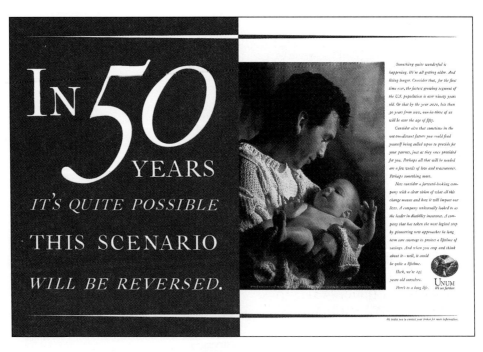

There is a famous saying, "The child is father to the man." This insurance ad reminds us that children, especially those who belong to "the sandwich generation," are often eventually put in the position of caring for their parents. Courtesy of UNUM.

ALTERNATE FAMILY STRUCTURES

Recall that the U.S. Census Bureau regards any occupied housing unit as a household, regardless of the relationships among people living there. Thus, one person living alone, three roommates, or two lovers, all constitute households. The latter arrangement is somewhat euphemistically referred to as *POSSLQ,* which stands for persons of opposite sex sharing living quarters.

Motorola recognizes the new, mobile lifestyles of many modern families. The company has positioned its paging products to meet the needs of on-the-go parents. Courtesy of Motorola Paging Products Group.

This ad for Family Circle *magazine humorously emphasizes that some traditional family values persist among young people of the 1990s. © 1992, The Family Circle, Inc.*

Less traditional households will rapidly increase in this decade if trends persist. For example, nonmarried households headed by men with children under the age of 18 increased by a third between 1981 and 1990.[44] Almost 10 million American children live in homes with a stepparent or with other kids who are not full brothers or sisters, and 24 percent of all children live in one-parent families.[45] The U.S. Census Bureau forecasts a decline in the number of family households with children and an increase in the number of people living alone in the 1990s. By the year 2000, families will decline 71 percent, married couples will shrink by 3 percent, and families with children will decrease from 25 percent to 20 percent of all families.[46]

This has necessitated changes in family classifications. Families worldwide are becoming smaller and less traditional. Although Scandinavian countries are pacesetters in developing nontraditional forms of family living, the United States has the highest incidence of divorce and single-parent households of any country.[47] To account for the rapid changes in the way families are structured, the U.S. Census included three new categories of family members for its 1990 survey: (1) natural-born or adopted child, (2) foster child, and (3) unmarried partners. The first two classifications are intended to distinguish stepchildren from other children, and the latter category identifies cohabiting couples, such as unmarried heterosexuals and homosexual or lesbian couples.[48]

Effects of Family Structure on Consumption

A family's needs and expenditures are affected by such factors as the number of people (children and adults) in the family, the ages of family members, and whether one, two, or more adults are employed outside of the home.

Two important factors that determine how a couple spends time and money are whether they have children and whether the woman works. Couples with children generally have higher expenses, such as for food and utility bills.[49] In addition, a recently married couple makes very different expenditures than one with young

*M*ARKETING OPPORTUNITY

Many people are extremely attached to pets, to the point where companion animals might be considered part of the family. Forty-two percent of American households own at least one pet.[50] Americans spend $20 billion a year on their pets (more than they spend on movies and home videos combined).[51] This passion for pets is not confined to the United States; in France, there are twice as many dogs and cats as children.[52]

The inclusion of pets as family members creates many marketing opportunities, ranging from bejeweled leashes to professional dog walkers. Listed below are samples of some recent attempts to cater to people's pet attachments.[53]

● Macy's department store opened a Petigree shop for dogs and cats. Says one employee, "You can put your dog in a pink satin party dress or a 1920s flapper dress with fringe." Other items include a wedding dress for dogs (for $100, and the veil is extra), a $48 black dinner jacket, and a $30 trench coat.

● A veterinarian in Maryland offers holistic medicine for pets. He features natural foods, acupuncture, and chiropractic massages. The doctor also sells the Rodeo Drive Fragrance Collection, a set of spray colognes for dogs.

● A 25-minute video, titled *Doggie Adventure,* was produced for dogs. Shot with a camera balanced two feet off the ground, it takes viewers on a romp from a dog's perspective.

● Kennelwood Village, a day-care center for dogs in St. Louis, features a swimming pool (with a lifeguard on duty), tetherball tournaments, and whirlpool therapy for arthritic canines.

● In Britain, pet insurance is a $150 million industry. In a pet-crazed country where some restaurants feed animals but not children, more than a million pets are covered. Similarly, about 85 percent of Swedish dogs carry health and life insurance.

children, which, in turn, is quite different from a couple with children in college, and so on. Families with working mothers also must often make allowances for such expenses as day care and a work wardrobe for the woman.

Recognizing that family needs and expenditures change over time, the concept of the **family life cycle (FLC)** has been widely used by marketers. The FLC combines trends in income and family composition with the changes in demands placed upon this income. As we age, our preferences for products and activities tend to change. In many cases, our income levels tend to rise (at least until retirement), so that we can afford more, as well. In addition, many purchases that must be made at an early age do not have to be repeated very often. For example, we tend to accumulate durable goods, such as large appliances, and only replace them as necessary.

This focus on longitudinal changes in priorities is particularly valuable in predicting demand for specific product categories over time. For example, the money spent by a couple with no children on dinners out and vacations will probably be diverted for quite different purchases after the birth of a child. While a number of models have been proposed to describe family life cycle stages, their usefulness has

Social life. Sex life. Sleeping habits. Laundry powder.
Having a baby changes everything. Almost.

Sunlight actually rinses cleaner than Ivory Snow (no soapy residue is left behind), making it perfect for your entire family's wash. So even if the rest of your life has been turned upside down, when it comes to laundry, all you'll have to change are diapers.

Soft on babies. Tough on stains.

This ad for Unilever Canada's Sunlight detergent reminds new parents how much their lives will change with the arrival of a baby. Courtesy of Unilever Canada and MacLaren Lintas, Inc.

been limited because, in many cases, they have failed to take into account such important social trends as the changing role of women, the acceleration of alternative lifestyles, childless and delayed-child marriages, and single-parent households.

Four variables are necessary to adequately describe these trends: Age of the adult head-of-household, marital status, the presence or absence of children in the home, and the children's ages. In addition, our definition of marital status (at least for analysis purposes) must be relaxed to include any couple living together who are in a long-term relationship. Thus, while roommates might not be considered "married," a man and woman who have established a household would be, as would two homosexual men who have a similar understanding.

When these changes are considered, this approach allows us to identify categories that include many more types of family situations.[54] These categories are listed in Table 11–2. For example, a distinction is made between the consumption needs of people in the Full Nest I category (wherein the youngest child is less than six); the Full Nest II category (wherein the youngest child is older than six); the Full Nest III category (wherein the youngest child is older than six and the parents are middle-aged); and the Delayed Full Nest (wherein the parents are middle-aged but the youngest child is younger than six).

As might be expected, consumers classified into these categories show marked differences in consumption patterns. Young bachelors and newlyweds have the most "modern" sex-role attitudes and are the most likely to engage in exercise; to go out

This ad for Ethan Allen furniture borrows two categories—full house and empty nest—from the family-life-cycle concept to illustrate that its products meet people's diverse needs as they progress through life. Courtesy of Ethan Allen, Inc.

to bars, concerts, movies, and restaurants; to go out dancing; and to consume more alcohol. Families with young children are more likely to consume health foods, such as fruit, juice, and yogurt, while those made up of single parents and older children buy more junk foods. The dollar value of homes, cars, and other durables is lowest for bachelors and single parents but increases as people go through the full-nest and childless-couple stages. Perhaps reflecting the bounty of wedding gifts, newlyweds are the most likely to own such appliances as toaster ovens and electric coffee grinders. Babysitter and day-care usage is, of course, highest among single-parent

Ikea recently made history by daring to create what is believed to be the first main-stream TV ad to feature a gay relationship. Courtesy of IKEA US, Inc.

TABLE 11-2 ▼ The Family Life Cycle: An Updated View

	AGE OF HEAD OF HOUSEHOLD		
	UNDER 35	35–64	OVER 64
One adult in household	Bachelor I	Bachelor II	Bachelor III
Two adults in household	Young couple	Childless couple	Older couple
Two adults plus children in household	Full nest I Full nest II	Delayed full nest Full nest III	

Source: Adapted from Mary C. Gilly and Ben M. Enis, "Recycling the Family Life Cycle: A Proposal for Redefinition," in *Advances in Consumer Research* 9, ed. Andrew A. Mitchell, Ann Arbor, MI: Association for Consumer Research, 1982): 274, Fig. 1.

and full-nest households, while home-maintenance services (e.g., lawn mowing) are most likely to be employed by older couples and bachelors.

The increase in the number of categories creates many opportunities for enterprising marketers. For example, divorced people undergo a process of transition to a new social role. This change is often accompanied by the disposition of possessions linked to the former role and the need to acquire a set of possessions that help to express the person's new identity as he or she experiments with new lifestyles.[55]

THE INTIMATE CORPORATION: FAMILY DECISION MAKING

The decision process within a household unit in some way resembles a business conference. Certain matters are put on the table for discussion, different members may have different priorities and agendas, and there may be power struggles that rival any tale of corporate intrigue. In just about every living situation, whether a conventional family, students sharing a sorority house or apartment, or some other nontraditional arrangement, group members seem to take on different roles just as purchasing agents, engineers, account executives, and others do within a company.

Household Decisions

Two basic types of decisions are made by families.[56] In a **consensual purchase decision,** the group agrees on the desired purchase and differs only in terms of how it will be achieved. In these circumstances, the family will most likely engage in problem solving and consider alternatives until the means for satisfying the group's goal is found. For example, a household considering adding a dog to the family but concerned about who will take care of it might decide to get a dog and draw up a chart assigning individuals to specific duties.

Unfortunately, life is not always so easy. In an **accommodative purchase decision,** group members have different preferences or priorities and cannot agree on a purchase that will satisfy the minimum expectations of all involved. It is here that bargaining, coercion, compromise, and the wielding of power are all likely to be used to achieve the primary goal of agreement on the purchase itself. Family decisions often are characterized by an accommodative rather than a consensual decision.

Conflict occurs when there is not complete correspondence in family members' needs and preferences. While money is the most common source of conflict between marriage partners, television choices come in a close second![57] Some specific factors determining the degree of family-decision conflict include the following:[58]

- *Interpersonal need.* This factor depends on a person's level of investment in the group. A child in a family situation may care more about what his or her family buys for the house than will a college student who is temporarily living in a dorm.

- *Product involvement and utility.* This involves the degree to which the product in question will be used or will satisfy a need. A family member who is an avid coffee drinker will obviously be more interested in the purchase of a new coffeemaker to replace a malfunctioning one than a similar expenditure for some other item.

- *Responsibility.* Responsibility for procurement, maintenance, payment, and so on influences the degree of family conflict. People are more likely to have disagreements about a decision if it entails long-term consequences and commitments. For example, a family decision about getting a dog may involve conflict regarding who will be responsible for walking it and feeding it.

- *Power.* The degree to which one family member exerts influence over the others in making decisions is a factor. In traditional families, the husband tends to have more power than the wife, who, in turn, has more than the oldest child, and so on. In family decisions, conflict can arise when one person continually uses the power he or she has within the group to satisfy his or her priorities. For example, if L.J. believed that his life would end if he did not have a heavy metal birthday party, he might be more willing to resort to extreme tactics to influence his parents, perhaps by throwing a tantrum or refusing to participate in family chores.

In general, decisions will involve conflict among family members to the extent that they are somehow important or novel and/or if individuals have strong opinions about good and bad alternatives. The degree to which these factors generate conflict determines the type of decision the family will make.[59]

Sex Roles and Decision-Making Responsibilities

Traditionally, some buying decisions, termed **autocratic decisions,** were usually made by one or the other spouse. Men, for instance, often had sole responsibility for selecting a car, while most decorating choices fell to women. Other decisions, such as vacation destinations, were made jointly; these are known as **syncratic decisions.**

IDENTIFYING THE DECISION MAKER

The nature of consumer decision making within a particular product category is an important issue for marketers, so that they know whom to target and whether or not they need to reach both spouses to influence a decision. For example, when market research in the 1950s indicated that women were playing a larger role in household purchasing decisions, lawn mower manufacturers began to emphasize the rotary mower over other power mowers. Rotary mowers, which conceal the cutting blades and engine, were often depicted being used by young women and smiling grandmothers to downplay fears of injuries.[60]

Researchers have paid special attention to which spouse plays the role of what has been called the **family financial officer (FFO),** who keeps track of the family's bills and decides how any surplus funds will be spent. Among newlyweds, this role tends to be played jointly, and then, over time, one spouse or the other tends to take over these responsibilities.[61]

In traditional families (and especially those with members having low educational levels), women are primarily responsible for family financial management—that is, the man makes it, and the woman spends it.[62] Each spouse "specializes" in certain activities.[63] The pattern is different among families in which spouses adhere to more modern sex-role norms. These couples believe that there should be more shared participation in family-maintenance activities. In these cases, husbands assume more responsibility for laundering, housecleaning, grocery shopping, and so on, while the wife shares in such traditionally "male" tasks as home maintenance and garbage removal.[64] Of course, cultural background is an important determinant of the dominance of the husband or wife in certain activities. For example, husbands tend to be more dominant in decision making among couples with a strong Hispanic-American ethnic identification.[65]

Four factors appear to determine the degree to which decisions will be made jointly or by one or the other spouse.[66]

1. *Sex-role stereotypes.* Couples who believe in traditional sex-role stereotypes tend to make individual decisions for sex-typed products (i.e., those considered to be "masculine" or "feminine").

2. *Spousal resources.* The spouse who contributes more resources to the family has the greater influence.

MULTICULTURAL DIMENSIONS

Japan's rapid modernization is causing some radical changes in its family structure—not all of them good. Although traditional sex roles are quite robust in Japan, recently women are starting to rebel against the inevitability of getting married at a young age and staying home with babies. The number of unmarried people older than 30 has doubled in the last 20 years.

Women report that they are getting fed up with playing housekeeper to men who lounge around the house when they are not at work. Many have instead chosen to live with their families, save their money, and travel. Some married women are also starting to complain about their husbands, who have been described as "absentee fathers." Japanese fathers spend so much time working that more than a quarter of children surveyed said their dads never take them for walks or play games with them. Due to long work hours, a typical Japanese father has only 36 minutes a day available to spend with his kids. About 60 percent of Japanese men typically do not eat breakfast at home, and about 30 percent regularly miss dinner.

To counteract these trends, Japan's Education Ministry is going into companies to conduct seminars on the art of being a family man. And in a more controversial move, the Japanese government is offering a "reward" of 5,000 yen per month (about $38) for couples who have a second child and twice that amount for a third child. Many Japanese women are angered and insulted by this policy, claiming that the government is treating them like machines.[67]

3. *Experience.* Individual decisions are made more frequently when the couple has gained experience as a decision-making unit.

4. *Socioeconomic status.* Joint decisions are made more by middle-class families than in either higher- or lower-class families.

With many women now working outside of the home, men are participating more in housekeeping activities. In one-fifth of American homes, men do most of the shopping, and nearly one-fifth of men do at least seven loads of laundry a week.[68] Still, women continue to do the lion's share of household chores. Ironically, this even appears to be true when the woman's outside income actually exceeds that of her husband![69] Overall, the degree to which a couple adheres to traditional sex-role norms determines how much their allocation of responsibilities will fall along familiar lines and how their consumer-decision-making responsibilities will be allocated.

Despite recent changes in decision-making responsibilities, women still are primarily responsible for the continuation of the family's **kin-network system:** They perform the rituals intended to maintain ties among family members, both immediate and extended. This function includes such activities as coordinating visits among relatives, calling and writing family members, sending greeting cards, making social engagements, and so on.[70] This organizing role means that women often make important decisions about their families' leisure activities and are more likely to decide with whom their families will socialize.

HEURISTICS IN JOINT DECISION MAKING

The **synoptic ideal** calls for the husband and wife to take a common view and act as joint decision makers. According to this ideal, they would very thoughtfully weigh alternatives, assign one another well-defined roles, and calmly make mutually beneficial consumer decisions. That couple would act rationally and analytically and would use as much information as possible to maximize joint utility. In reality, however, spousal decision making is often characterized by the use of influence or methods that are likely to reduce conflict. A couple "reaches" rather than "makes" a decision. This process has been described as "muddling through."[71]

One common technique for simplifying the decision-making process is the use of *heuristics* (see Chapter 8). Some decision-making patterns frequently observed when a couple makes decisions in buying a new house illustrate the use of heuristics.

1. The couple's areas of common preference are based upon salient, objective dimensions rather than more subtle, hard-to-define cues. For example, a couple may easily agree on the number of bedrooms they need in the new home but will have more difficulty achieving a common view of how the home should look.

2. The couple agrees on a system of task specialization, wherein each is responsible for certain duties or decision areas and does not interfere in the other's "turf." For many couples, these assignments are likely to be influenced by their perceived sex roles. For example, the wife may scout out houses in advance that meet the couple's requirements, while the husband determines whether the couple can obtain a mortgage.

3. Concessions are based on the intensity of each spouse's preferences. One spouse will yield to the influence of the other in many cases simply because his or her level of preference for a certain attribute is not particularly intense,

whereas in other situations he or she will be willing to exert effort to obtain a favorable decision.[72] In cases where intense preferences for different attributes exist, rather than attempt to influence each other, spouses will "trade off" a less-intense preference for a more strongly felt one. For example, a husband who is somewhat indifferent about kitchen design may give in to his wife but expect that, in turn, he will be allowed to design his own garage workshop.

CHILDREN AS DECISION MAKERS: CONSUMERS-IN-TRAINING

Anyone who has had the "delightful" experience of grocery shopping with one or more children in tow knows that kids often have a say in what their parents buy, especially for such products as cereal.[73] It has been estimated that children between the ages of 4 and 12 collectively spend or influence their parents to spend about $140 billion a year.[74] Table 11–3 documents kids' influence in ten different product categories.

Parental yielding occurs when a parental decision maker is influenced by a child's request and "surrenders." The strategies kids use to request purchases were documented in a recent study. While most children simply asked for things, some other common tactics included saying they had seen it on television, saying that a sibling or friend has it, or bargaining by offering to do chores. Other actions were less innocuous; they included directly placing the object in the cart and continuous pleading.[75]

Children often play important roles in family consumer decision making, and they are gaining responsibility as consumers in their own right. They continue to support the toy and candy industries, of course, but now they also buy and/or influence the purchase of many other products, as well. For better or for worse, the new generation is, as the bumper sticker proclaims, "Born to Shop." Shopping now ranks

TABLE 11–3 ▼ Kids' Influence on Household Purchases

TOP 10 SELECTED PRODUCTS	INDUSTRY SALES ($ BILLIONS)	INFLUENCE FACTOR (%)	SALES INFLUENCE ($ BILLIONS)
Fruit snacks	0.30	80	0.24
Frozen novelties	1.40	75	1.05
Kids' beauty aids	1.20	70	0.84
Kids' fragrances	0.30	70	0.21
Toys	13.40	70	9.38
Canned pasta	0.57	60	0.34
Kids' clothing	18.40	60	11.04
Video games	3.50	60	2.10
Hot cereals	0.74	50	0.37
Kids' shoes	2.00	50	1.00

Source: "Charting the Children's Market," *Adweek* (February 10, 1992): 42. Reprinted with permission of James J. McNeal, Texas A&M University, College Station, Texas.

Recognizing that kids influence food purchases, Oscar Mayer attempts to create a positive image for its lunch meats in this poster for use in school cafeterias. Courtesy of Oscar Mayer Foods Corporation. The Oscar Mayer rhomboid, Lunch Is What You Make of It, and Lunchables are trademarks of Oscar Mayer Foods Corporation, Madison, Wisconsin.

among the top seven interests and activities of America's children.[76] Over 80 percent of young respondents in one survey said their primary wish was to have more money to buy things.[77] In this section, we'll consider how kids learn to make these choices.

Consumer Socialization

Children do not spring from the womb with consumer skills already in memory. **Consumer socialization** has been defined as the process ". . . by which young people acquire skills, knowledge, and attitudes relevant to their functioning in the marketplace."[78] Where does this knowledge come from? Friends and teachers certainly participate in this process. For instance, children talk to one another about consumer products, and this tendency increases with age.[79] Especially for young children, though, the two primary socialization sources are the family and the media.

INFLUENCE OF PARENTS

Parents' influences in consumer socialization are both direct and indirect. They deliberately try to instill their own values about consumption in their children ("you're going to learn the value of a dollar"). Parents also determine the degree to which their children will be exposed to other information sources, such as television, salespeople, and peers.[80] And, grown-ups serve as significant models for observational learning (see Chapter 3). Children learn about consumption by watching their parents' behavior and imitating it. This modeling is facilitated by marketers who package adult products in child versions.

The process of consumer socialization begins with infants, who accompany their parents to stores where they are initially exposed to marketing stimuli. Within the first two years, children begin to make requests for desired objects. As kids learn to walk, they also begin to make their own selections when they are in stores. By around the age of five, most kids are making purchases with the help of parents and grandparents, and, by eight, most are making independent purchases and have become full-fledged consumers.[81] The sequence of steps involved in turning kids into consumers is summarized in Figure 11–1.

Three dimensions combine to produce different "segments" of parental styles. Parents characterized by certain styles have been found to socialize their children differently.[82] For example, "authoritarian parents," who are hostile, restrictive, and emotionally uninvolved, do not have warm relationships with their children, are active in filtering the types of media to which their children are exposed, and tend to have negative views about advertising. "Neglecting parents" also do not have warm relationships, but they are more detached from their children and do not exercise much control over what their children do. In contrast, "indulgent parents" communicate more with their children about consumption-related matters and are less restrictive. They believe that children should be allowed to learn about the marketplace without much interference.

INFLUENCE OF TELEVISION

It's no secret that kids watch a lot of television. As a result, they are constantly bombarded with messages about consumption, contained both in commercials and in the

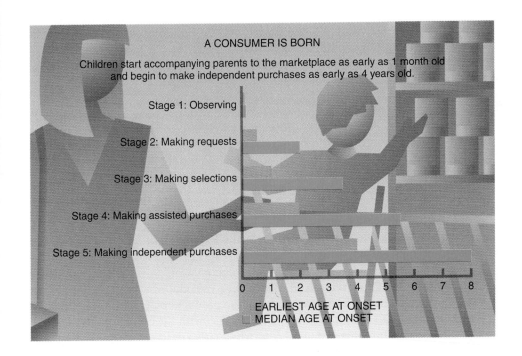

FIGURE 11–1 ▼ Five Stages of Consumer Development by Earliest Age at Onset and Median Age at Onset Source: Adapted from McNeal and Yeh, *American Demographics* (June 1993): 36. Reprinted by permission of American Demographics, Inc.

shows themselves. The media teaches people about a culture's values and myths. The more a child is exposed to television, whether the show is *Friends* or *Teenage Mutant Ninja Turtles,* the more he or she will accept the images depicted there as real.[83]

In addition to the large volume of programming targeted directly to children, kids also are exposed to idealized images of what it is like to be an adult. Since children over the age of six do about a quarter of their television viewing during prime time, they are affected by programs and commercials targeted to adults. For example, young girls exposed to adult lipstick commercials learn to associate lipstick with beauty.[84]

Sex-Role Socialization

Children pick up on the concept of gender identity (see Chapter 7) at an earlier age than was previously believed—perhaps as young as age one or two. By the age of three, most children categorize driving a truck as masculine and cooking and cleaning as feminine.[85] Even cartoon characters who are portrayed as helpless are most likely to wear frilly or ruffled dresses.[86] Toy companies perpetuate these stereotypes by promoting gender-linked toys with commercials that reinforce sex-role expectations through their casting, emotional tone, and copy.[87]

One function of child's play is to rehearse for adulthood. Children act out different roles they might assume later in life and learn about the expectations others have of them. The toy industry provides the props children use to perform these roles.[88] Depending on which side of the debate you're on, these toys either reflect or teach children about what society expects of males versus females. While preschool boys and girls do not exhibit many differences in toy preferences, after the age of five they part company: Girls tend to stick with dolls, while boys gravitate toward "action figures" and high-tech diversions. Industry critics charge that this is because the toy industry is dominated by males, while toy company executives counter that they are simply responding to kids' natural preferences.[89]

Often "traditional" sex roles are stressed in children's products; the same item may be designed and positioned differently for boys and girls. Huffy, for example, manufactures bicycles for both boys and girls. The boys' versions have names like "Sigma" and "Vortex," and they are described as having ". . . maxed-out features that'll pump your pulse." The girls' version of the same bike is more sedate. It is called "Sweet Style," and it comes in pink or purple. As a company executive described it in contrast to the boys' bikes, the girls' model ". . . is a fashion bike. It's not built for racing or jumping—just the look."[90]

Some companies have tried to level the playing field by doing research to understand differences in how boys and girls play. Lego Systems sells about 90 percent of its construction kits to boys, but the company would love to increase its sales by selling more sets to girls, as well. When Lego introduced a special Lego set with parts that would allow girls to make jewelry, the product bombed. Still, there is hope: When Lego executives watched boys and girls play with Lego bricks in focus groups, they noticed that boys tend to build cars, while girls are likely to build living areas. This observation led to the introduction in 1992 of Paradisa, a Lego set with such colors as lavender and pink that is designed for building "socially oriented structures," such as homes, swimming pools, and stables. Sales to girls have picked up, although the company's sales to boys are still nine times larger than its sales to girls.[91]

Cognitive Development

The ability of children to make mature, "adult" consumer decisions obviously increases with age (not that grown-ups always make mature decisions). Kids can be segmented by age in terms of their **stage of cognitive development,** or ability to comprehend concepts of increasing complexity. Some recent evidence indicates that young children are able to learn consumption-related information surprisingly well, depending on the format in which the information is presented (e.g., learning is enhanced if a videotaped vignette is presented to small children repeatedly).[92]

PIAGETIAN STAGES OF DEVELOPMENT

The foremost proponent of the idea that children pass through distinct stages of cognitive development was the Swiss psychologist Jean Piaget, who believed that each stage is characterized by a certain cognitive structure the child uses to handle information.[93] In one classic demonstration of cognitive development, Piaget poured the contents of a short, squat glass of lemonade into a taller, thinner glass. Five-year-olds, who still believed that the shape of the glass determined its contents, thought this glass held more liquid than the first glass. They are in what Piaget termed a *preoperational stage of development.* In contrast, six-year-olds tended to be unsure, but seven-year-olds knew the amount of lemonade had not changed.

AN ALTERNATIVE TO PIAGET

Many developmental specialists no longer believe that children necessarily pass through these fixed stages at the same time. An alternative approach regards children as differing in information-processing capability, or ability to store and retrieve information from memory (see Chapter 3). The following three segments have been identified by this approach.[94]

1. *Limited.*　Below the age of 6, children do not employ storage-and-retrieval strategies.
2. *Cued.*　Children between the ages of 6 and 12 employ these strategies but only when prompted.
3. *Strategic.*　Children 12 and older spontaneously employ storage-and-retrieval strategies.

This sequence of development underscores the notion that children do not think like adults and they cannot be expected to use information the same way. It also reminds us that they do not necessarily form the same conclusions as adults do when presented with product information. For example, kids are not as likely to realize that something they see on television is not "real," and as a result they are more vulnerable to persuasive messages.

Marketing Research and Children

Despite their buying power, relatively little real data on children's preferences or influences on spending patterns are available. Compared to adults, kids are difficult subjects for market researchers. They tend to be undependable reporters of their own behavior, they have poor recall, and they often do not understand abstract questions.[95] This problem is compounded in Europe, where some countries restrict marketers' ability to interview children.

Still, market research can pay off, and many companies, as well as a number of specialized firms, have been successful in researching some aspects of this segment.[96] After interviewing elementary school kids, Campbell Soup Co. discovered that kids like soup but are afraid to admit it, because they associate it with "nerds." The company decided to reintroduce the Campbell Kids in its advertising after a prolonged absence, but they are now slimmed down and more athletic to reflect an updated, "unnerdy" image.[97]

PRODUCT TESTING

A particularly helpful type of research with children is product testing. Young subjects can provide a valuable perspective on what products will succeed with other kids. One candy company has a Candy Tasters Club, composed of 1,200 kids aged 6 to 16, that evaluates its product ideas. For example, the group nixed the idea of a Batman lollipop, claiming that the superhero was too macho to be a sucker.[98] The Fisher-Price Company maintains a nursery known as the Playlab. Children are chosen from a waiting list of 4,000 to play with new toys, while staff members watch from behind a one-way mirror.[99]

Other techniques include ethnographic research, where researchers hang around with kids or videotape them as they shop. The most successful interviewers are those who try not to be "adultcentric" (i.e., as an adult authority figure who assumes that children's beliefs are just unreal fantasies); they act as friends to the children and are willing to use a variety of projective techniques and props to get children to express themselves in their own terms.[100]

MESSAGE COMPREHENSION

Since children differ in their abilities to process product-related information, many serious ethical issues are raised when advertisers try to appeal directly to them.[101] Kids tend to accept what they see on television as real, and they do not necessarily understand the persuasive intent of commercials—that is, that they are paid advertisements. Preschool children may not have the ability to make any distinctions between programming and commercials.

Kids' cognitive defenses are not yet sufficiently developed to filter out commercial appeals, so, in a sense, altering their brand preferences may be likened to "shooting fish in a barrel," as one critic put it.[102] Although some ads include a disclaimer, which is a disclosure intended to clarify a potentially misleading or deceptive statement, the evidence suggests that young children do not adequately understand these, either.[103]

Children's levels of understanding are especially hard to assess, since preschoolers are not very good at verbal responses. One way around this problem is to show children pictures of kids in different scenarios and ask them to point to which sketch corresponds to what a commercial is trying to get them to do.

The problem with children's processing of commercials has been exacerbated by television programming that essentially showcases toys (e.g., Jem, G.I. Joe, Transformers). This format (much like that of "infomercials" for adults described in Chapter 6) has been the target of a lot of criticism because it blurs the line between programming and commercials.[104] Parents' groups object to such shows because, as

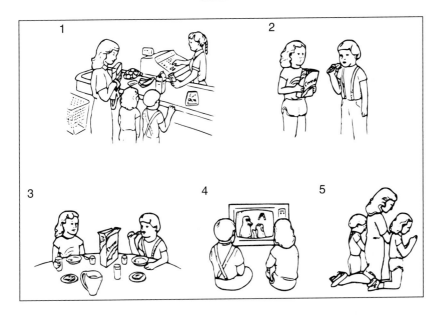

FIGURE 11–2 ▼ Sketches used to Measure Children's Perception of the Intent of Commercials: In the example shown here, a child who points to sketch 1 after seeing a cereal commercial as opposed to, say, sketches 2 or 3 would be said to understand the underlying intent of the commercial. Sketch 1 was in fact selected by only 7.5 percent of four-year-olds but 20 percent of five-year-olds. Source: M. Carole Macklin, "Preschoolers' Understanding of the Informational Function of Television Advertising," *Journal of Consumer Research* 14 (September 1987): 234. Reprinted by permission of The University of Chicago Press.

one mother put it, the ". . . whole show is one big commercial."[105] In the next section, we'll consider some of the serious objections that have been raised when kids are appealed to as consumers.

Advertising to Children: An Ethical Minefield

It has been suggested that children should be better educated as to how advertising works and encouraged to question what they see on television, perhaps through public-service advertising.[106] Of some help is *Penny Power*, a kids' version of *Consumer Reports* aimed at 9- to 14-year-olds. It has been estimated that 20 percent of the advertising complaints received come from children, most of whom read *Penny Power*.[107]

In addition, the Children's Advertising Review Unit (CARU) of the Council of Better Business Bureaus, Inc., maintains industry guidelines in such areas as product claims (e.g., is it clear how the toy actually looks and works?); the use of fantasy elements (e.g., are they clearly "just pretend"?); sales pressure techniques (e.g., do techniques used suggest that the child will be better than others if he or she owns the product); endorsements by program characters; and disclosures and disclaimers (e.g., "you or your parents have to put it together" versus "assembly required").[108]

MARKETING OPPORTUNITY

Benetton, the Italian clothing company, has helped to make multi-racialism fashionable with its long-running "United-Colors-of-Benetton" campaign. The steady increase in the number of mixed marriages is creating opportunities for other marketers who wish to meet the needs of children raised in multicultural families. Because many kids are exposed to others from diverse cultural backgrounds, some marketing executives feel that their racial attitudes will be quite different from those of their parents. As a senior MTV executive observed, "Tolerance and diversity is [sic] absolutely the number-one shared value" among young adults.

These encounters with diverse cultural traditions create the needs for products and services that allow consumers to celebrate multiple heritages. For example, books like *Modern Bride Wedding Celebrations* contain information about wedding traditions for different ethnic groups to allow interracial couples to mix and match. Magazines with titles like *Interrace* and *New People* also are springing up to cater to this segment. They feature advertising for toys, books, and dating services with interracial themes. Still, there is a void in the market for such products as interracial wedding cake decorations, books, dolls, and other items that combine the traditions of different subcultures.[19]

was only 63 percent of that of whites, the proportions of monies allocated to different categories do not vary all that much. Both African-Americans and whites spent about two-thirds of their incomes on housing, transportation, and food.[20]

African-American/White Consumption Differences

Nonetheless, there are clearly some differences in consumption priorities and marketplace behaviors that demand marketers' attention.[21] One reason is the vast market potential of this group: If African-Americans were a separate nation, their buying power would rank 12th among Western countries.[22] Because of the growing economic power of this segment, African-American consumers often represent a fresh opportunity for marketing in otherwise saturated markets. The following are some facts pointing to important usage differences in some product categories.[23]

- African-Americans account for only 2 percent of all spending on trucks and vans, while they account for almost a quarter of all spending on mass transit. This difference reflects the concentration of African-Americans in urban areas.
- African-Americans purchase 10 percent of televisions, radios, and sound equipment.
- African-Americans buy 17 percent of all encyclopedias and reference books sold.
- African-Americans spend 28 percent more than other American consumers do on baby products.
- African-Americans buy 27 percent more cooking ingredients than average.
- African-Americans buy more than one-half of all the cognac sold in the United States.

● African-Americans comprise 19 percent of the market for toiletries and cosmetics and 34 percent of that for hair-care products. African-American women spend over $500 a year on health and beauty products, an amount three times that of white women.

Although some marketers assume that African-American consumers who have moved up the social ladder forsake their ethnic identities, this assumption does not appear to be the case. Middle-class African-Americans instead appear to span subcultures, exhibiting the attitudes of the white middle class while still holding on to their African-American heritage.[24] African-American shoppers respond well to products that appeal to their racial pride.[25] This tack was taken in an ad targeted to African-Americans by Miller beer featuring a middle-class African-American man. The copy read, "He moved up, but not out."

African-Americans and the Media

African-Americans are heavy users of media. African-American households watch an average of ten hours of television a day, a rate 39 percent higher than the average American household. This segment tends to prefer established programming and is less likely to experiment with new offerings. As a result, they are more likely to be loyal to major networks, cable networks, and superstations, such as WTBS, which attract about 10 percent of the African-American viewing audience. In addition, readership of local morning daily newspapers (as opposed to major regional papers) is 30 percent higher than it is with adults overall, and African-Americans also are more likely to read classified ads and circulars.

AFRICAN-AMERICAN REPRESENTATION IN MAINSTREAM MEDIA

Historically, African-Americans have not been well represented in mainstream advertising, but this situation is changing. African-Americans now account for about 25 percent of the people depicted in ads (a rate even greater than their actual proportion of the overall population), and commercials are increasingly likely to be racially integrated.[26] The more striking and important change, though, is the way African-American people are portrayed on television. Unlike earlier shows that presented African-Americans in stereotyped roles, such as *Sanford and Son* and *The Jeffersons,* most television roles created for African-Americans (e.g., *Family Matters* or *The Fresh Prince of Bel Air*) now tend to depict them as middle- to upper-class individuals who also happen to be black.[27]

AFRICAN-AMERICAN-ORIENTED MEDIA

Several major magazines, such as *Jet, Ebony, Essence,* and *Black Enterprise,* target this segment exclusively, and with great success. *Jet,* for example, claims to reach over 90 percent of the African-American male audience.[28] African-American media tend to depict consumers in their natural social environments and more positively than do the general media, so it is not surprising that many African-Americans gravitate to these magazines and newspapers.[29] A new generation of magazines, including such titles as *The Source, Vibe, Shade,* and *Image,* is springing up to meet the demands of this growing market.[30] In addition, other forms of media are being revamped with an African-American spin. One recent development is the introduc-

*M*ARKETING PITFALL

The R.J. Reynolds Tobacco Company ignited a lot of controversy when it announced plans to test-market a menthol cigarette, called Uptown, specifically to African-American consumers in the Philadelphia area. Although the marketing of cigarettes to minorities was not a novel tactic, it was the first time a company explicitly acknowledged the strategy. Many critics immediately attacked the proposal, arguing that the campaign would exploit poor African-Americans—especially since African-American people suffer from a higher incidence of tobacco-related diseases than any other group. The publishers of African-American-oriented newspapers and magazines were caught in the middle, since they stood to receive substantial advertising revenues from the campaign. For example, approximately 10 percent of *Jet*'s advertising revenues came from cigarette advertising. For its part, Reynolds claimed that its actions were a natural result of shrinking markets and the need to more finely target increasingly small segments.

Unlike other ethnic groups, which do not seem to display marked cigarette preferences, the tastes of African-American consumers have been easy to pinpoint. According to Reynolds, 69 percent of African-American consumers preferred menthol, more than twice the rate of smokers overall. Since after-market research indicated that African-Americans tend to open cigarette packs from the bottom, the company decided to pack Uptowns with the filters facing down. Reynolds claimed that the product was not designed specifically for African-Americans, although it acknowledged that it was likely to attract a disproportionate share of African-American smokers. Following a storm of criticism by both private health groups and government officials (including the Secretary of Health and Human Services), the company announced that it was canceling its test-marketing plans. It would not comment on the likelihood that the cigarette would ever be introduced.[31]

tion of so-called multicultural romance novels, which feature African-American heroes and heroines. While the basic elements of a romance novel remain, these books feature numerous references to African-American culture. And, the heroine is more likely to possess "curly brown locks" than "cascading blond hair."[32]

A Crest toothpaste ad done by an African-American agency had a powerful impact on target consumers. It depicts a simple act: A father lovingly showing his son how to knot a tie. The copy reads, "I'm going to be involved with my son as much as I can."[33] This idealized father/son relationship often is taken for granted by whites, but it hits home to many African-American consumers, 40 percent of whom grow up in fatherless households.[34] Advertising has in general tried to promote a positive image of African-American men by stressing family involvement.

The use of African-American celebrities and sports figures is also on the rise. The proliferation of African-American role models appears to be reducing the racial distinctions formerly made by many. However, this strategy does not guarantee success with African-American consumers. For example, while Pepsi has used singer Michael Jackson in its ad campaigns, its research showed that he did not appeal to 25- to 40-year-old African-Americans, who interpreted his plastic surgery and eccentric behavior as a desire to distance himself from his African-American roots.[35] On the other hand, an African-American version of the popular cartoon character Bart

Advertising to African-Americans often is better executed when it is sensitive to important cues and avoids symbols irrelevant to the African-American subculture. For this reason, it is not uncommon for companies to commission specialized agencies to develop separate ad campaigns specifically targeted to the African-American market. This print ad for the Chrysler Neon incorporates a standard shot of the car saying "Hi" but adds snappy visual elements intended to appeal to an African-American audience. Courtesy of Chrysler Corporation.

Simpson became extremely popular in the African-American community in the early 1990s. Bart has since been recast in the image of several African-American celebrities, including Malcolm X, Bob Marley (Rasta Bart), and Michael Jordan (Air Bart). Bart's popularity in the African-American subculture has been attributed to his status as an outsider with an attitude who battles established society.[36]

LATINOS

The Hispanic subculture, a segment that was until recently largely ignored by many marketers, is a sleeping giant. The growth and increasing affluence of this group has now made it impossible to overlook, and the Latino consumer is now diligently courted by many major corporations. As one example of this emphasis, Nike made history in 1993 by running the first Spanish-language commercial ever broadcast in prime time on a major American network. The spot, which ran during the baseball All-Star Game, featured boys in tattered clothes playing ball in the Dominican Republic, or *La Tierra de Mediocampistas* (The Land of Shortstops). This title refers to the fact that over 70 Dominicans have played for major-league ball clubs, many of whom started at the shortstop position.

This groundbreaking spot also laid bare some of the issues involved in marketing to Latinos. Many found the commercial condescending (especially the ragged look of the actors) and felt that it promoted the idea that Latinos don't really want

MARKETING OPPORTUNITY

The recent proliferation of ethnic dolls in America's toy stores reflects society's growing cultural diversity. While, in the past, non-Caucasian dolls appeared only in collections of dolls from around the world, all major manufacturers have now introduced ethnic dolls to the mass market. African-Americans spend well over $700 million a year on toys and games, so toy marketers are sitting up and taking notice. The American Girls Collection recently introduced Addy Walker, the first nonwhite doll in the series. Addy comes packaged with a set of books that describe her daily life and her (fictional) history as a slave, and details were provided by an advisory board of experts who ensured that Addy's experiences were told from an African-American perspective.

Other new entrants include Kira, the Asian fashion doll, and Emmy, the African-American baby doll. Mattel introduced a trio of dolls named Shani (which means "marvelous" in Swahili), Asha, and Nichelle that represent the range of African-American facial features and skin tones (Shani also has a boyfriend named Jamal). And, while Mattel has sold an African-American version of Barbie for over 20 years, it only recently began to promote the doll in television and print campaigns.[37]

to assimilate into mainstream Anglo culture.[38] If nothing else, though, this commercial by a large corporation highlights the indisputable fact that the Latino market is now being taken seriously by major marketers. Another example is a product—Buñuelitos—developed by General Mills specifically for the Latino market. Cereal is very popular in this segment, and the promising demographics of Latino consumers convinced the company that introducing a separate product would pay off. The company tested different flavors on Mexican-American consumers, who preferred a honey-and-cinnamon flavor. Cinnamon is a spice that is widely used in Latino cuisine, and honey is the traditional Mexican sweetener. The brand name is an adaptation of *buñuelos,* a traditional Mexican pastry served on holidays. Research persuaded the company *not* to put Spanish copy on the box, since the consumers surveyed felt that products made in the United States are of higher quality. The commercial was shot in Mexico but uses universal Spanish so as not to alienate non-Mexican Latinos. The principal character is an *abuelita* (grandma), a respected figure in Latino culture. She is shown eavesdropping as a mother gives the cereal to her children. She tries it herself and finds that it tastes like *buñuelos.*[39]

The Allure of the Latino Market

Demographically, two important characteristics of the Latino market are worth noting: First, it is a young market. The median age of Latinos is 23.6 years, compared with the U.S. average of 32. Second, the Latino family is much larger than those of the rest of the population. The average Latino household contains 3.5 people, compared to only 2.7 people for other U.S. households. These differences obviously affect the overall allocation of income to various product categories. For example, Latino households spend 15 percent to 20 percent more of their disposable income than the national average does on groceries.[40] There are now over 19 million Latino consumers in the United States, and a number of factors make this market segment extremely attractive to advertisers.

● Latinos tend to be brand loyal, especially to brands from their country of origin. In one study, about 45 percent reported that they always buy their usual brands, while only one in five said they frequently switch brands.[41]

● Latinos are highly concentrated geographically by national origin, which makes them relatively easy to reach. Over 50 percent of all Latinos live in the Los Angeles, New York, Miami, San Antonio, San Francisco, and Chicago metropolitan areas.[42]

● Education levels are increasing dramatically. In the period between 1984 and 1988, the number of Latinos with four years of college increased by 51 percent. While the absolute numbers are still low compared to the general population, the number of men in managerial and professional jobs increased by 42 percent, and the corresponding increase of 61 percent for women was even more encouraging.[43]

APPEALING TO LATINO SUBCULTURES

The behavior profile of the Latino consumer includes a need for status and a strong sense of pride. A high value is placed on self-expression and familial devotion. Some campaigns have played to Latinos' fear of rejection and apprehension about loss of control and embarrassment in social situations. Conventional wisdom is to create action-oriented advertising and to emphasize a problem-solving atmosphere. Assertive role models who are cast in nonthreatening situations appear to be effective.[44]

Procter & Gamble is the biggest advertiser in Latino media. The company spends nearly $21 million a year catering to this segment. P&G also was one of the first to establish a Latino corporate marketing structure that has Latino group brand managers. It has focused on introducing such products as diapers, cleansers, and grooming products that capitalize on the youth and large family size prevalent among Latinos.[45]

As they are with other large subcultural groups, marketers are now beginning to discover that the Latino market is not homogeneous. Subcultural identity is not as much with being Latino as it is with the particular country of origin. Mexican-Americans, who make up about 62 percent of all Latinos, are the fastest-growing subsegment; their population has grown by 40 percent since 1980. In contrast, Cuban-Americans are by far the wealthiest subsegment, but they are also the smallest Latino ethnic group and are older on average than are other Latinos.[46] Because of large cultural differences among segments, it is important to address specific wants and needs of Latino subgroups. The Winn-Dixie supermarket chain, for example, promotes holidays and dishes native to individual countries and employs the theme, "Winn-Dixie *tiene el sabor de mi pais*" (Winn-Dixie has the flavor of my country).[47]

MARKETING BLUNDERS

Many initial efforts by Americans to market to Latinos were, to say the least, counterproductive. Companies bumbled in their efforts to translate advertising adequately or to compose copy that could capture desired nuances. These mistakes do not occur so much anymore as marketers have become more sophisticated in dealing with this market and as Latinos themselves have been involved in advertising production. The following are some translation mishaps that have occurred.[48]

- The Perdue slogan, "It takes a tough man to make a tender chicken," was translated as "It takes a sexually excited man to make a chick affectionate."
- Budweiser was promoted as the "queen of beers."
- A burrito was mistakenly called a *burrada,* which means "big mistake."
- Braniff, promoting its comfortable leather seats, used the headline, *Sentado en cuero,* which was interpreted as "Sit naked."
- Coors' slogan to "get loose with Coors" appeared in Spanish as "get the runs with Coors."

Understanding Latino Identity

Native language and culture are important components of Latino identity and self-esteem (about three-quarters of Latinos still speak Spanish at home), and these consumers are very sympathetic to marketing efforts that acknowledge and emphasize the Latino cultural heritage.[49] More than 40 percent of Latino consumers say they deliberately attempt to buy products that show interest in the Latino consumer, and this number jumps to over two-thirds for Cuban-Americans.[50]

Many Latinos are avid consumers of soap operas, called *telenovelas.* Ethnic soap operas, shown on American television, are becoming big business. Univision, the biggest Spanish-language network, airs ten different ones each day. These shows are produced by Latin American networks, but some viewers have complained that they do not address such problems of Latinos as illegal immigration, getting a job, or speaking the language.[51]

Since the beginning of the 1990s, Latino radio stations have been blossoming; there are now over 390 stations in the United States. This growth is partly due to the increasing size and economic clout of the Latino consumer segment. It is also attributable to stations' efforts to attract younger listeners by playing more contemporary musical styles, called *tejano, banda, ranchera,* and *norteña.* These new formats feature bilingual disk jockeys, who are developing a patter that some have called "Spanglish." Latinos are avid radio listeners; they tune in an average of over 25 hours a week.[52] To capitalize on the growing interest in country music with a Latino flavor, several Nashville record labels have started to release albums cut by bilingual performers, such as Rick Trevino, Flaco Jimenez, and Joel Nava.[53]

THE ROLE OF THE CHURCH

While Latinos traditionally have been predominantly Catholic, millions of Latinos are leaving the Roman Catholic Church. It is estimated that about one in five Latinos now practices some form of evangelical Protestantism. This change is ascribed to two factors: First, the evangelical Protestants have adopted sophisticated marketing techniques, such as providing local clergy with profiles of Latino communities in a campaign to convert large numbers of Latino Catholics; and, second, the style of U.S. Catholicism is alien to many Latinos. Catholicism in the United States tends to be more rational and bureaucratic and is not viewed by many as being responsive to the more emotional and mystical Latino religious experience. For example, the belief in miraculous healing that is prevalent in Latin American Catholicism does not tend to be emphasized in American churches.[54]

THE ROLE OF THE FAMILY

The importance of the family to Latinos cannot be overstated. Preferences to spend time with family influence the structure of many consumption activities. As one illustration, the act of going to the movies has a different meaning for many Latinos, who tend to regard this activity as a family outing. One study found that 42 percent of Latino moviegoers attend in groups of three or more, as compared with only 28 percent of Anglo consumers.[55]

Behaviors that underscore one's ability to provide well for the family are reinforced in this subculture. Clothing one's children well is regarded in particular as a matter of pride. In contrast, convenience and a product's ability to save time is not terribly important to the Latino homemaker, who is willing to purchase labor-intensive products if it means that her family will benefit.

For this reason, a time-saving appeal short-circuited for Quaker Foods, which found that Latino women tend to cook Instant Quaker Oats on the stove, refrigerate it, and serve it later as a pudding.[56] Similarly, telephone company promotions that emphasize cheaper rates for calling family members would offend many Latino consumers, who would view deferred phone calls home just to save money as an insult![57] This orientation also explains why generic products do not tend to do well in the Latino market; these consumers value the quality promised by well-known brand names.

The pervasiveness of the family theme can be seen in many marketing contexts. When Johnson Wax decided to enter the Latino market with Future floor polish, market research revealed that Latino consumers cleaned their floors regularly but did not wax them. As a result of this finding, the company's television commercial depicted a housewife standing on her dull floor and being asked, "We know your floors are clean, but do they shine?" Traditional gender roles are then reinforced as the husband leaps into the air, shouting *resalta* (outstanding).[58]

LEVEL OF ACCULTURATION

One important way to distinguish among members of a subculture is to consider the extent to which they retain a sense of identification with their country of origin versus their host country. **Consumer acculturation** refers to the process of movement and adaptation to one country's cultural environment by a person from another country.[59]

This factor is especially important when considering the Latino market, since the degree to which these consumers are integrated into the American way of life varies widely. For instance, about 38 percent of all Latinos live in *barrios,* or predominantly Latino neighborhoods, which tend to be somewhat insulated from mainstream society.[60] Table 13–1 describes a recent attempt to segment Latino consumers in terms of their degree of acculturation.

Differences in Cultural Integration. Latino groups represent two economic extremes. On the one hand, many Cuban-American families with high educa-

TABLE 13–1 ▼ Segmenting the Hispanic-American Subculture by Degree of Acculturation

SEGMENT	SIZE	STATUS	DESCRIPTION	CHARACTERISTICS
Established adapters	17%	Upwardly mobile	Older, U.S. born; assimilated into U.S. culture	Relatively low identification with Latino culture
Young strivers	16%	Increasingly important	Younger, born in U.S.; highly motivated to succeed; adaptable to U.S. culture	Movement to reconnect with Latino roots
Hopeful loyalists	40%	Largest but shrinking	Working class; attached to traditional values	Slow to adapt to U.S. culture; Spanish is dominant language
Recent seekers	27%	Growing	Newest; very conservative with high aspirations	Strongest identification with Latino background; little use of non-Latino media

Source: Adapted from a report by Yankelovich Clancy Shulman, described in "A Subculture with Very Different Needs," *Adweek* (May 11, 1992): 44. By permission of Yankelovich Partners, Inc.

tional levels fled Castro's regime in the late 1950s and early 1960s, worked hard for many years to establish themselves, and are now firmly entrenched in the Miami political and economic establishment. Because of this affluence, businesses in South Florida now make efforts to target YUCAs (young, upwardly mobile Cuban-Americans), especially since the *majority* of consumers in Miami are now Latino![61]

On the other hand, it is estimated that anywhere from 1.8 million to 5.4 million Latino immigrants enter the country illegally each year. The majority of these people have less than a fifth-grade education and are concerned with surviving in their new country. Since they are trying to adapt to their new environment, these consumers tend to look for products they perceive to be more American, which may mean learning entirely new product categories. The implication for marketers is that these consumers must be taught about a product (e.g., air freshener, which is not common in Central America) before they can be convinced to buy one brand over another.[62]

Progressive Learning. The acculturation of Latino consumers may be understood in terms of the **progressive learning model.** This perspective assumes that people gradually learn a new culture as they increasingly come in contact with it. Thus, we would expect the consumer behavior of Latinos to be a mixture of practices taken from their original culture and those of the new culture, or *host culture.*[63]

Research has generally obtained results that support this pattern when such factors as shopping orientation, the importance placed on various product attributes, media preference, and brand loyalty were examined.[64] When the intensity of ethnic identification was taken into account, consumers who retained a strong ethnic identification differed from their more assimilated counterparts in the following ways:[65]

Who keeps Laura de Oña entertained?

Name: Laura de Oña.
Occupation: Attorney.
Age: 43.
Family: Mother of two.
Car: Mercedes Benz.
Hobbies: Playing tennis.
Last vacation spot: Hawaii
Latest book: *Atlas Shrugged.*
Radio Station: WQBA-FM, for the latest in Latin and American music.

The Super Q/FM listener profile is best represented by people like Laura de Oña. These career oriented, bilingual, educated Latins from 25 to 49 make up the majority of our listening audience. This Latin market in South Florida represents over $8.7 billion in spending power which most companies cannot ignore. You can reach this market by advertising on WQBA-FM

For information contact Veronica Serra, National Sales Manager: WQBA AM/FM (305) 441-2073.

This trade ad for WQBA-FM, a South Florida radio station, describes its Latino listeners, who fit the profile of the YUCA (Young, Upwardly Mobile Cuban-American). Courtesy of WQBA-FM Miami.

- They had a more negative attitude toward business in general (probably caused by frustration due to relatively low income levels).
- They were higher users of Spanish-language media.
- They were more brand loyal.
- They were more likely to prefer brands with prestige labels.
- They were more likely to buy brands specifically advertised to their ethnic group.

Atravesando Fronteras: CROSSING TO A NEW LIFE

For many Latinos, *atravesando fronteras* (border crossings) are a part of life. Thousands of Mexican immigrants cross back and forth between their home country and the United States every year. These journeys highlight the complex processes by which people learn the ways of another culture and develop new patterns of consumption that combine existing practices with new ones, as immigrants forge new identities for themselves in a strange, yet not so strange, land.

Leaving one's culture and family to go to a new place creates many new needs and anxieties about fitting into a new environment. Recent immigrants (both legal and illegal) encounter a strange culture and have often left family members behind. This frightening odyssey was incorporated by AT&T in its campaign to boost international calling volume. In a Spanish-language commercial called "Countryside," a young man says good-bye to his mother and promises to keep in touch. The announcer says, "The decision of leaving the family is based on a promise: Keeping it united."

A recent study of language usage among Latinos revealed an interesting finding: Although respondents preferred advertising that was in Spanish, the researchers also found that an ad done exclusively in Spanish actually created negative feelings. The researchers interpreted this finding to mean that exclusive usage of the Spanish language aroused perceivers' insecurities about fitting into mainstream Anglo culture, which "rubbed off" onto the brand being advertised.[66]

Another study, using the research technique of *ethnography* discussed in Chapter 1, probed into the ways that Mexican immigrants undergo an acculturation process as they adapt to life in the United States.[67] Interviews and observations of recent arrivals in natural settings revealed that immigrants feel a lot of ambivalence about their moves. On the one hand, they are happy about the improvements in the quality of their lives due to greater job availability, educational opportunities for their children, and so on. On the other hand, they report bittersweet feelings about leaving Mexico. They miss their friends, their holidays, their food, and the comfort that comes from living in familiar surroundings.

The nature of the transition process is affected by many factors, as shown in Figure 13–3. Individual differences, such as whether the person speaks English, influence how rocky the adjustment will be. The person's contact with **acculturation agents**—people and institutions that teach the ways of a culture—also are crucial. Some of these agents are aligned with the *culture of origin* (in this case, Mexico). These include family, friends, the church, local businesses, and Spanish-language media that keep the consumer in touch with his or her country of origin. Other agents are associated with the *culture of immigration* (in this case, America) and help the consumer to learn how to navigate in the new environment. These include public schools and English-language media.

As immigrants adapt to their new surroundings, several processes come into play. *Movement* refers to the factors motivating people to physically uproot themselves from one location and go to another. In this case, people leave Mexico due to the scarcity of jobs and the desire to provide a good education for their children. Upon arrival, immigrants encounter a need for *translation*. This means attempting to master a set of rules for operating in the new environment, whether learning how to decipher a different currency or figuring out the social meanings of unfamiliar clothing styles. This cultural learning leads to a process of *adaptation*, where new consumption patterns are formed. For example, some of the Mexican women interviewed in the study have started to wear shorts and pants since settling in the United States, although this practice is frowned upon in Mexico.

As consumers undergo acculturation, several things happen. Many immigrants undergo (at least to some extent) *assimilation*, where they adopt products that are identified with the mainstream culture. At the same time, there is an attempt at *maintenance* of practices associated with the culture of origin. Immigrants stay in touch with people in their countries; for example, many from Mexico continue to eat Spanish foods and read Spanish newspapers. Their continued identification with their culture of origin may cause *resistance*, as they resent the pressure to submerge their cultural identities and take on new roles. Finally, immigrants (voluntarily or not) tend to exhibit *segregation;* they are likely to live and shop in places that are physically separated from mainstream Anglo consumers.

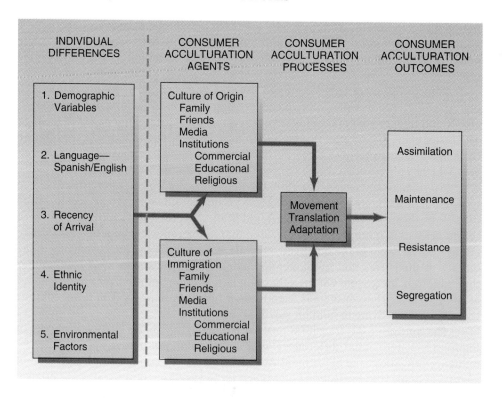

FIGURE 13–3 ▼ **A Model of Consumer Acculturation**   Source: Adapted from Lisa Peñaloza, "Atravesando Fronteras/Border Crossings: A Critical Ethnographic Exploration of the Consumer Acculturation of Mexican Immigrants," *Journal of Consumer Research* 21, 1 (June 1994): 32–54. Reprinted by permission of The University of Chicago Press.

ASIAN-AMERICANS

Although their numbers are still relatively small, Asian-Americans are the fastest-growing minority group in the United States. Marketers are just beginning to recognize their potential as a unique market segment. This subculture is attractive to

𝓜ARKETING PITFALL

While many corporations are just now waking up to the potential of the Latino market, others that sell harmful products, such as junk food, cigarettes, and alcohol, discovered this market long ago. Critics point to a high concentration of liquor stores and related advertising in Latino neighborhoods. Available evidence indicates that Mexican-born men stand a greater chance of dying of cirrhosis of the liver and that Latino men are also more likely to die of lung cancer than are Anglos. The smoking rate of fourth- and fifth-grade Latino boys is roughly five times that of Anglo boys.[68] In many cities, community action groups and others have begun programs to reverse these trends.

When immigrants make a life in a new (host) country, they rely on agents of acculturation to ease the transition. Mexican immigrants have established a network of businesses that provide them with products and services. Grocery vans run by Latinos, such as the "convenience store on wheels" shown here, supply immigrants with familiar foods. (Lisa Peñaloza, "Atravesando Fronteras/Border Crossings: A Critical Ethnographic Exploration of the Consumer Acculturation of Mexican Immigrants," Journal of Consumer Research 21, 1 [June 1994]: 32–54, Fig. 2.) Photographer Lisa Peñaloza, reprinted with permission.

marketers because Asian-Americans typically are hard working and many have above-average incomes. The average household incomes of Asian-Americans are more than $2,000 greater than those of whites and $7,000 to $9,000 higher than those of African-Americans and Latinos. These consumers also place a very high priority on education and send a large percentage of children to college. Of Asian-Americans over the age of 25, about 33 percent completed four or more years of college, twice the graduation rate of whites and more than quadruple that of African-Americans and Latinos.[69]

Segmenting Asian-Americans

Despite its potential, this group is hard to market to, because it is actually composed of subgroups that are culturally diverse and speak many different languages and dialects. The term *Asian* refers to 20 ethnic groups, with Chinese being the largest and Filipino and Japanese second and third, respectively.[70] Also, although their birth rate is increasing at almost four times the rate of most other groups, Asian-Americans still comprise only about 2 percent of the population, so mass-marketing techniques often are not viable to reach them.[71] Finally, Asian-Americans save more of their wages and borrow less, preferring to keep large balances in conservative passbook accounts rather than to invest their earnings.

On the other hand, as one Asian-American advertising executive noted, "Prosperous Asians tend to be very status-conscious and will spend their money on premium brands, such as BMW and Mercedes-Benz, and the best French cognac and Scotch whiskey."[72] This group also is a good market for technically oriented products. They spend more than average on such products as VCRs, personal computers, and compact disc players. Advertising that features Asian celebrities can be particularly effective. When Reebok used tennis star Michael Chang in one execution, shoe sales among Asian-Americans soared.[73]

Another interesting aspect is that brand loyalty—especially loyalty to Asian brands—on the whole is low. In one survey of Chinese residents of San Francisco, a

Long-distance phone companies have already recognized the value of the Asian-American market segment. They spend more than $20 million annually on advertising in Asian languages. In a TV commercial, Sprint borrows the Monkey King, an all-wise character from Chinese folklore, to make its pitch. (Christy Fisher, "Marketers Straddle Asia-America Curtain," Advertising Age *[November 7, 1994]: S–2 [2 pp.]. Copyright © 1994 by Sprint Communications Company. Reproduced with permission.*

third of the respondents could not name the brand of laundry detergent they used.[74] Finally, these consumers also tend to be fairly conservative: Citibank had to drop a New Year's ad targeted to Chinese customers after people complained about the sexual innuendo of corks popping out of champagne bottles![75]

The problems encountered by American marketers when they first tried to reach the Latino market also occurred when they targeted Asians and Asian-Americans. Some attempts to translate advertising messages and concepts into Asian media have backfired. Coca-Cola's slogan, "Coke Adds Life" was translated as "Coke brings your ancestors back from the dead" in Japanese. One company did attempt to run an ad in Chinese to wish the community a Happy New Year, but the characters were upside down.

Other advertisements have overlooked the complex differences among Asian subcultures (e.g., some advertisements targeted to Koreans have used Japanese models), and some have unknowingly been insensitive to cultural practices. KFC (Kentucky Fried Chicken), for example, ran into a problem when it described its chicken as finger-licking good to the Chinese, who don't lick their fingers in appreciation when food is good.[76] In another case, a footwear ad depicted Japanese women performing footbinding, a practice done exclusively in China.[77]

MARKETING OPPORTUNITY

Real estate marketers who do business in areas with high concentrations of Asian-American buyers are learning to adapt to some unique cultural traditions. Asians are very sensitive to the design and location of a home, especially as these aspects affect the home's *chi,* an invisible energy current that is believed to bring good or bad luck. Asian home buyers are concerned about whether prospective houses offer a good *feng shui* (translated literally as "the wind and the water"). One home developer in San Francisco sold up to 80 percent of its homes to Asian customers after making a few minor design changes, such as reducing the number of "T" intersections in the houses and adding rounded rocks to the yards because harmful *chi* is believed to travel in a straight line, while gentle *chi,* to travel on a curved path. It is not unusual for specialists to inspect a home or office to ensure that the *chi* is right before a purchase is transacted.[78]

Reaching the Asian-American Consumer

Many marketers are discouraged by the lack of media available to reach Asian-Americans.[79] Practitioners generally find that advertising in English works best for broadcast ads, while print ads are more effective when executed in Asian languages.[80] Filipinos are the only Asians who predominantly speak English among themselves; most Asians prefer media in their own languages.[81] The most frequently spoken languages among Asian-Americans are Mandarin Chinese, Korean, Japanese, and Vietnamese.[82] In an attempt to reach these groups, Pacific Bell produces its brochures in three of these languages.

As is the case with other racial and ethnic subcultures, a crop of new magazines is trying to capture younger Asian-Americans. One new offering is *A. Magazine,* which is written for and about affluent Asian-Americans aged 18 to 40.[83] Even mass-retailer Sears is getting into the act: The company recently became the first major department store to formally target the Asian-American market by hiring an advertising agency to develop messages targeted to this segment.[84] Finally, the AsiaOne radio network provides national broadcasting in seven Asian languages.[85]

One success story stands out. One of the first companies to realize the potential of the Asian-American segment was the Metropolitan Life Insurance Company. Since Asian-American consumers tend to be well educated and place a very high priority on the education and security of their children, they seemed ideal prospects for insurance products. Qualitative research showed marked differences among Asian subsegments in their attitudes toward insurance. These differences paralleled those between Cuban-Americans and Mexican-Americans, in that the degree of acculturation within subsegments affects members' understanding and interest in products and services.

In general, Asians tended to be leery of buying insurance, superstitiously equating its purchase with old age and death. The company found that Chinese consumers emphasize family members' protection and education, so they were more likely to be interested in whole-life policies. On the other hand, Vietnamese consumers, many of whom were recent immigrants, tended to be unfamiliar with the concept of insurance. Still, this group was seen as having potential, since they are very survival oriented.[86] Based on this research, the company introduced a Chinese ad campaign that stressed the role of insurance in protecting children. As a reward for its efforts, Met Life increased its premiums among Asian-Americans by 22 percent in one year.[87]

RELIGIOUS SUBCULTURES

Heritage Village, a religiously oriented entertainment center in South Carolina, illustrates the relationship between religion and consumer behavior. Attendance at this 2,300-acre complex is exceeded only by that of the Disney theme parks. It features a church, a passion play, and replicas of Old Jerusalem, along with a bustling shopping mall called Main Street USA. A central theme of the park is its idealized presentation of America's past and traditional values—the pristine vision of America desired by those who make the Heritage Village pilgrimage.[88]

The Impact of Religion on Consumption

Religion per se has not been studied extensively in marketing, possibly because it is seen as a taboo subject.[89] However, the little evidence that has been accumulated indicates that religious affiliation has the potential to be a valuable predictor of consumer behavior.[90] Religious subcultures, in particular, may exert a significant impact on such consumer variables as personality, attitudes toward sexuality; birthrates; and household formation, income, and political attitudes.

One study that examined this issue, for example, found marked differences among Catholic, Protestant, and Jewish college students in preferences for weekend entertainment activities, as well as in the criteria used in making these decisions. Price was a relatively more important criterion for Protestants, while desire for companionship was highest for Jews. Catholics were more likely to designate dancing as a favored activity than were the other two groups but much less likely to select sex.[91]

At least on paper, the United States is the most religious Western country. More than 90 percent of Americans say they believe in God, and more than 40 percent claim to have attended church services in a given week. However, recent data comparing reported attendance with actual head counts at services indicate a gap between attitudes and behavior—or, at least, reported behavior. These findings show that about half the respondents who tell pollsters that they go to church services on a regular basis are not telling the truth! Since most people believe that going to church is a socially desirable activity, they are likely to say they do it even when they don't.

A major survey on religious attitudes that included 113,000 respondents sheds some interesting light on the current state of American religions. The study reports that Roman Catholics dominate the New England area, Baptists are pervasive in the South, and Lutherans concentrate in the upper Midwest. Nonbelievers (about 8 percent of American adults) are most likely to be found in the Pacific Northwest and in the Southwestern desert. This survey also highlights the emergence of new religious affiliations. For example, it found that there are more Scientologists than Fundamentalists, and it also found sizable numbers of followers of wicca (witchcraft) and New Age faiths.[92] Some of the demographic characteristics of many different religious subcultures are summarized in Figure 13–4.

The Catholic Subculture

Approximately one-quarter of Americans are Roman Catholic.[93] The Catholic Church is characterized by a rigid organizational structure, and personal interpretations of events are minimized. Some observers have inferred that Catholic consumers as a result tend to be fatalistic and are less likely to be innovators.

Catholics have more children than either Protestants or Jews do. Sexuality is seen as instrumental, in the sense that it is performed for the purpose of procreation

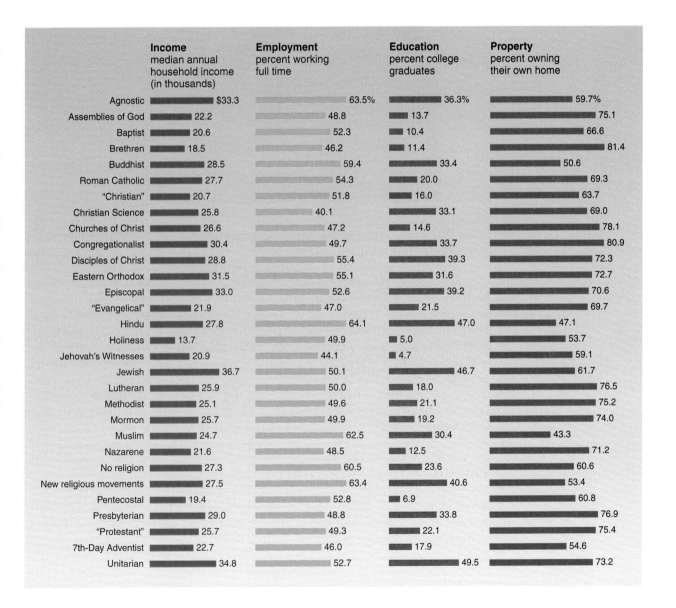

	Income median annual household income (in thousands)	Employment percent working full time	Education percent college graduates	Property percent owning their own home
Agnostic	$33.3	63.5%	36.3%	59.7%
Assemblies of God	22.2	48.8	13.7	75.1
Baptist	20.6	52.3	10.4	66.6
Brethren	18.5	46.2	11.4	81.4
Buddhist	28.5	59.4	33.4	50.6
Roman Catholic	27.7	54.3	20.0	69.3
"Christian"	20.7	51.8	16.0	63.7
Christian Science	25.8	40.1	33.1	69.0
Churches of Christ	26.6	47.2	14.6	78.1
Congregationalist	30.4	49.7	33.7	80.9
Disciples of Christ	28.8	55.4	39.3	72.3
Eastern Orthodox	31.5	55.1	31.6	72.7
Episcopal	33.0	52.6	39.2	70.6
"Evangelical"	21.9	47.0	21.5	69.7
Hindu	27.8	64.1	47.0	47.1
Holiness	13.7	49.9	5.0	53.7
Jehovah's Witnesses	20.9	44.1	4.7	59.1
Jewish	36.7	50.1	46.7	61.7
Lutheran	25.9	50.0	18.0	76.5
Methodist	25.1	49.6	21.1	75.2
Mormon	25.7	49.9	19.2	74.0
Muslim	24.7	62.5	30.4	43.3
Nazarene	21.6	48.5	12.5	71.2
No religion	27.3	60.5	23.6	60.6
New religious movements	27.5	63.4	40.6	53.4
Pentecostal	19.4	52.8	6.9	60.8
Presbyterian	29.0	48.8	33.8	76.9
"Protestant"	25.7	49.3	22.1	75.4
7th-Day Adventist	22.7	46.0	17.9	54.6
Unitarian	34.8	52.7	49.5	73.2

FIGURE 13–4 ▼ **The Demographics of Religious Subcultures** Source: "The Religious Pecking Order" by Blumrich in *Newsweek*, November 29, 1993, p. 80. Copyright © 1993 by Newsweek, Inc. All rights reserved. Reprinted by permission.

This controversial Benetton ad was rejected by some magazines because of what some perceived to be offensive religious symbolism. Photographer: O. Toscani for Benetton.

rather than recreation. There is some evidence that this attitude is changing: As far back as 1975, the idea that a husband and wife may engage in sex for pleasure alone was endorsed by 50 percent of Catholics, as compared to only 29 percent in 1965.[94]

Members of this religious group traditionally have a lower socioeconomic status than do Jews and Protestants. This deficit may stem from a variety of causes, including historical religious discrimination. Other factors include traditionalism, restricted knowledge seeking, and an emphasis on collective rather than individual initiative. As is the case with all religious subcultures, many of these dimensions are in flux, as younger Catholics search for ways to reconcile their faith with the demands of modern life. In general, more-committed Catholics tend to retain a conservative orientation, while others are more liberal. For example, in one recent survey, observant Catholics were only half as likely to favor abortion rights as were all Catholics combined.[95]

The Protestant Subculture

About 10 percent of Americans identify themselves as Protestants.[96] In contrast to that of Catholics, Protestant dogma stresses the faith of the individual. The Bible is viewed more as descriptive than as evidence of divine control. This tradition encourages the acquisition of scientific knowledge. Protestants tend to be less authoritarian and to value work and personal hardship as an avenue toward upward social mobility.

While not all Protestants are wealthy, they appear in disproportionate numbers in the upper classes. Explanations for this relative affluence include the following:[97]

● An emphasis on industriousness and hard work.
● A low fertility rate that facilitates the upward mobility of children.

Muscular Christianity

In the Mennonite Church some of our most satisfying work-outs take place not in gyms but in the yards of hurricane victims and the homes of the poor.

Satisfaction happens when you put Christian faith into action by choosing a life of giving, instead of a life of merely getting.

This Sunday, check out a church that will challenge you to sweat . . . to work out your faith in ways that make a difference.

For information on the church nearest you and a free book on putting faith in action call

800-462-

The Mennonite Churches

Our Family Can Be Your Family

Some churches are adopting modern marketing techniques to attract worshippers and increase "market share." A few are conducting market research to identify the needs of what are called "the unchurched Harry and Mary"—people who have no formal connection to religious institutions. In some cases, these churches have found that they are competing for people's increasingly scarce leisure time and are looking for ways to make their activities more attractive. This ad for the Mennonites implies that adherents can combine exercise with faith. Some church members considered the ad too sexy and thus inappropriate. What do you think? (Cyndee Miller, "Churches Turn to Research for Help in Saving New Souls," Marketing News [April 11, 1994]: 1 [3 pp.].) Courtesy of The Mennonite Media Ministries.

● A U.S. social structure in which Protestants were historically part of the *power-elite*.

Early American colonists were overwhelmingly Protestant, which allowed this group to create the foundations of the American social system and thus create barriers to entry for other groups. The Protestant establishment still dominates leadership positions in the private sector and is also overrepresented in science, education, government, and the military.[98] It is only recently that Irish Catholics have reached economic parity with Protestants, while Conservative and Reform Jews have surpassed this level.[99]

The WASP (White Anglo-Saxon Protestant) subculture may be thought of as the one ethnic group not acknowledged to be an ethnic group. After all, no one has yet used the term WASP-American! Despite this ethnic invisibility, the WASP subculture has been a dominant force in the larger picture of American culture.[100] In fact, the WASP has been a symbol of the American ideal for some time. For many immigrants, the WASP ideal still symbolizes the light at the end of the tunnel: If one desires to assimilate, to make it in America, the WASP lifestyle is the goal.

As a result of this idealized view of the WASP, the formal eating rituals devised by WASPs and propagated by such guides as *Etiquette* by Emily Post are assumed to be the "proper" way to eat and entertain. The leisure activities associated with this subculture (e.g., golfing, yachting, and squash) often are seen as socially correct.[101] Marketers have done more than their share to propagate this ideal. Idealized images of the WASP subculture are frequently employed in advertising to epitomize the good life and the amenities associated with old money (see Chapter 12). In particular, the success of influential designer Ralph Lauren hinges on his ability to create images of an idealized WASP lifestyle.

The Jewish Subculture

Jewish ethnicity exerts an exceptionally strong influence, since it incorporates both cultural and religious dimensions. American Jews tend to be of relatively high socioeconomic status, and average family size is relatively small (with the exception of some Orthodox groups). While this subculture is well represented in business and the arts, in reality less than 2 percent of the American population is Jewish.[102]

Judaism reinforces individual responsibility for actions and self-education.[103] Jewish consumers have a personality structure characterized by need for achievement, anxiousness, emotionality, and individualism.[104] One study of Jewish versus gentile consumers indeed found that the Jewish respondents were more likely to have been exposed to educational materials in childhood, to use more sources in the process of information search, to be product innovators, and to transfer more consumption information to others.[105]

The Muslim Subculture

There are between 3 million and 4 million Muslims in America. While many people equate this subculture with Arab culture, the two are not the same. The term Arab refers to an ethnic identity, while Muslim is a religious affiliation. Not all Arabs are Muslims, and not all Muslims are Arabs. In fact, one in four Muslims is black. The number of people who claim affiliation with this religious subculture is growing; it has been estimated that American Muslims could outnumber American Presbyterians by the year 2000. There are over 1,100 mosques in the United States.

Some marketers have specifically employed Jewish symbolism in their advertising campaigns. This ad for Sun Maid provides an example of this strategy. The Bank Leumi Trust Company of New York, an Israel-based bank, capitalized on its ethnic ties to try to reach Jewish and gentile customers with the following ad copy used to promote individual retirement accounts: "Some people need a little help getting to the Promised Land. If you dream of retiring to a land of milk and honey, you're going to need plenty of bread."[106] One famous campaign for a bakery company used Chinese, African-American, and other spokesmen to tell consumers, "You don't have to be Jewish to love Levy's real Jewish Rye." Courtesy of Sun-Diamond Growers of California.

Muslims tend to be conservative, and like many of the other subcultures discussed in this chapter, they value a close-knit family structure. The family is the ultimate authority, and bad acts performed by an individual are seen as a reflection on the entire family unit. At this point very little is done by major marketers to target this subculture, though this situation may change as its numbers increase.[107]

The Born-Again-Christian Subculture

Recent years have seen a dramatic increase in the number of consumers who profess to be born-again Christians, or evangelicals. A recent Gallup Poll indicates that one-third of American adults say they are born again. While this movement has affected a variety of social classes and consumer types, it is strongest among women, older adults, and Southerners. It is also a relatively downscale phenomenon: The number of adults who describe themselves as being "born again" steadily decreases as education and income levels rise.[108] The born-again movement is exerting a significant impact on American marketing, as well as on *demarketing,* which is the discouraging of demand for certain products and services. This community has been influential in altering the content of media programming and advertising that is seen to unduly emphasize sex and violence.

The evidence is unclear as to whether the consumption behavior of born-again Christians is radically different from that of other subcultures. In general, these consumers are more likely to endorse traditional sex-role orientations, to be below-average users of credit, and to place relatively low emphasis on purchasing national brands. They also are not as likely as is the general public to listen to rock and roll music (perhaps due to its perceived emphasis on sex and drugs) and prefer gospel and contemporary Christian music. And, while there are no differences in terms of

*M*ARKETING OPPORTUNITY

One of the most significant Jewish-related marketing developments is the increase in demand for kosher food. Each year, about 500 new kosher products appear on the market to satisfy this demand. This trend is being driven by two developments: the increased religious observance by young Jews and the belief among many gentiles that kosher food is of higher quality. In addition to some Jews, Seventh-Day Adventists and Muslims have very similar dietary requirements and are good customers for kosher food.[109] It is estimated that less than a third of the 6 million consumers who buy kosher products are Jewish.[110]

The potential of the kosher market has prompted some of the nation's largest manufacturers to get involved. General Foods distributed 100,000 copies of a children's activity booklet called *Brachos* (Prayers) for Breakfast. Wise Potato Chips produces kosher chips, and Eagle Snacks also makes kosher snack foods. Of the 330 products made by Pepperidge Farm, Inc., 255 are now kosher.[111] In a new twist, one small firm is even selling kosher lipstick because carmine, a commonly used red pigment, turns out to be nonkosher because it is made from the crushed exoskeletons of insects, a forbidden food to observant Jews![112]

MARKETING PITFALL

Some merchants who cater to the born-again segment have run into trouble for targeting these consumers too exclusively. A car dealer in Virginia is representative of attempts to service only true believers. He unveiled a Christian Members Buying Plan, which would allow members to purchase their cars at rock-bottom prices. In addition, he proposed to donate part of the profit from every sale to the buyer's church. The American Civil Liberties Union and other groups quickly objected to the plan, arguing that it discriminates against non-Christians. The ACLU had been involved in an earlier dispute, wherein a Florida gas station owner had posted a sign reading, "For Christians Only: 10 percent discount on labor."[113]

such activities as eating out or attending concerts, born-again Christians do attend movies less frequently than do other groups.[114]

Christian broadcast media have become a powerful cultural force for many consumers. Approximately 12 percent of all U.S. radio stations have a religious format. In fact, religious programming is now the third most popular kind in the United States. In addition, about 200 local television stations regularly feature religious programming, and television preachers have an estimated audience of over 15 million people—a number that represents almost the combined memberships of the United Methodist, Presbyterian, and Episcopal churches.[115]

Not surprisingly, some research indicates that born-again Christians subscribe to religious magazines at a much higher rate than do other Christians and that they are higher-than-average subscribers to home-oriented magazines. Also of no surprise is the finding that almost 15 percent of these consumers list a televised church service as one of their three favorite television programs.

The Christian publishing industry has also shown phenomenal growth. According to trade figures, 37 million people spend $1.4 billion annually at Christian bookstores. According to one industry official, consumers are now very selective about what they buy, so Christian merchants must adopt a commitment to excel as "God's retailer."[116] Many Christian bookstores have expanded their product mix. In addition to the traditional assortment of inspirational books and records, most carry what one official termed "holy hardware." These stores stock items ranging from "I-Am-Blessed" jogging suits to watches with pictures of the twelve apostles. Grace, the prolife doll, delivers this message when squeezed, "God knew me even before I was born. . . . I used to be a little person inside my mother's tummy. . . . My mommy thinks I'm very special. She's so happy she had me." More than 20,000 of these dolls, priced from $40 to $50, were sold in a four-month period.[117]

- Consumers identify with many groups that share common characteristics and identities. These large groups that exist within a society are *subcultures,* and membership in them often gives marketers clues about individuals' consumption decisions. A large component of a person's identity is often determined by his or her ethnic origins, racial identity, and religious background. The three largest ethnic/racial subcultures are African-Americans, Latinos, and Asian-Americans, but consumers with many diverse backgrounds are beginning to be considered by marketers, as well.

- Recently, several minority groups have caught the attention of marketers as their economic power has grown. Segmenting consumers by their *ethnicity* can be effective, but care must be taken not to rely on inaccurate (and sometimes offensive) ethnic stereotypes.

- African-Americans are a very important market segment. While, in some respects, the market expenditures of these consumers do not differ that much from those of whites, African-Americans are above-average consumers in such categories as personal-care products. In the past, African-American were either ignored or portrayed negatively in mainstream advertising, but such depictions are changing as more African-Americans actually work on the development of campaigns and as specialized African-American media increase in importance.

- Latinos and Asian-Americans are other ethnic subcultures that are beginning to be actively courted by marketers. The size of both groups is increasing rapidly and, in the coming years, will dominate some major markets. Asian-Americans on the whole are extremely well educated, and the socioeconomic status of Latinos is increasing as well.

- Key issues for reaching the Latino market are consumers' degree of *acculturation* into mainstream American society and the recognition of important cultural differences among Latino subgroups (e.g., Puerto Ricans, Cubans, Mexicans).

- Both Asian-Americans and Latinos tend to be extremely family oriented and are receptive to advertising that understands their heritage and reinforces traditional family values.

- While the impact of religious identification on consumer behavior is not clear, some differences among religious subcultures do emerge. In particular, cultural characteristics of Protestants, Catholics, and Jews result in varied preferences for leisure activities and orientations toward consumption. Some of these factors are closely related to social class. White Anglo-Saxon Protestants (WASPs), in particular, have played a dominant role in the formation of American cultural values largely due to their cultural emphasis on achievement and their early domination of the American power structure.

- The market power of the growing numbers of born-again Christians is uncertain at this point, but opportunities exist to cater to the unique needs of this segment.

Acculturation agents p. 481

Consumer acculturation p. 478

De-ethnicitization p. 468

Ethnic (or racial) subculture p. 465

Progressive learning model p. 479

Subcultures p. 463

CONSUMER BEHAVIOR CHALLENGE

1. R.J. Reynolds's controversial plan to test-market a cigarette to African-American consumers raises numerous ethical issues about segmenting subcultures. As one observer noted, "The irony is that if R.J. Reynolds made shoes or shirts and specifically marketed to African-Americans, they would probably be regarded as progressive and socially positive."[118] Does a company have the right to exploit a subculture's special characteristics, especially to increase sales of a harmful product like cigarettes? What about the argument that successful businesses design products to meet the needs and tastes of their target markets? For example, the chapter also notes that Maybelline developed a makeup line specifically for African-American women, yet this did not seem to bother anyone. What do you think?

2. The chapter notes that products can function as socialization agents for ethnic groups, citing the example of the air-freshener product category. What other examples can you find that serve this important function? What special problems do these create for marketers?

3. Describe the progressive learning model, and discuss why this phenomenon is important when marketing to subcultures.

4. Born-again-Christian groups have been instrumental in organizing boycotts of products advertised on shows they find objectionable, especially those that, they feel, undermine family values. Do consumer groups have a right or a responsibility to dictate the advertising a network should carry?

5. In a related issue, an official with a Christian organization defended the Christian Members Buying Plan described in the chapter, arguing that "We are sick and tired of Christians and Christian values being expunged from every area of public life. This isn't separation of church and state; this is a private merchant."[119] Do you agree?

6. Can you locate any current examples of marketing stimuli that depend upon an ethnic stereotype to communicate a message? How effective are these appeals?

7. To understand the power of ethnic stereotypes, conduct your own poll. For a set of ethnic groups, ask people to anonymously provide, using the technique of free association, attributes (including personality traits and products) most likely to characterize each group. How much agreement do you obtain across people? Compare the associations for an ethnic group held by actual members of that group to those of nonmembers.

8. African-American singer Gladys Knight recently took a lot of heat for agreeing to serve as a spokesperson for the Aunt Jemima brand. One commentator said, "You have a famous black singer perpetuating the stereotypes that go along with the trademark. . . ." On the other hand, the singer stated, ". . . What matters to me is what's inside the box. I'm simply saying, 'This is a good product.' "[120] Which side do you take and why?

9. Locate one or more consumers (perhaps family members) who have immigrated from their country of origin. Interview them about how they adapted to their host culture. In particular, what changes did they make in their consumption practices over time?

ABC NEWS CONNECTION

Ethnic Cosmetics: A Rainbow of Possibilities

Although several small firms have long been in the business of supplying African-American women with specialized cosmetics products, the big guys have only recently gotten into the game. Companies like Maybelline, Estée Lauder, and Revlon now realize that expanding their product lines to include virtually all of the colors of the rainbow is simply good business. Millions of women of color no longer have to make do with shades that don't precisely match their own unique skin tones. For mainstream companies that have been battling against the tide of saturated markets, profits may lie at the end of the rainbow.[121]

SIMMONS CONNECTION

Ethnic and Religious Subcultures

Maria is a good example of an American consumer who is deeply immersed in a particular ethnic subculture. Although she herself is a native-born U.S. citizen, her family and neighborhood have strong ties to their ethnic origins. And she lives in a neighborhood that has managed to preserve at least some of the elements of Latino culture. In fact, her neighborhood may be very similar to neighborhoods in foreign cities such as Buenos Aires or Mexico City.

It is often easier for consumers to maintain their ethnic heritage if they are presented with the opportunity to do so. The concentrations of ethnic groups often found in larger American cities provide a "critical mass" that can support distinctive ethnic subcultures. This critical mass can provide greater availability of community or religious groups or even the availability of specialty products such as foreign language newspapers and specialty food items. So geography may be an important variable in determining how readily an ethnic group can maintain a distinct identity.

Similarly, media vehicles of popular culture often cater to particular ethnic and/or religious subcultures and thereby provide a form of virtual community (a sense of identity with other members of the viewing/listening/reading audience).

An important aspect of one's ethnic identity is how strongly someone participates in his or her culture of origin as compared with the dominant culture in which he or she presently lives. One indicator of this is the language that is spoken at home. The Simmons datafile provides two important breakdowns for this: whether Spanish is the only language spoken at home or whether Spanish and English are both spoken.

Using the information provided in the Simmons datafile for this chapter, in what sort of community is Maria most likely to live? What can you say about the political outlook of members of this ethnic subculture?

The datafile also contains information about television program preferences. These are all taken from broadcast network stations. Are there any programs that possess distinctive appeal for Spanish-speaking Americans? What about Asian-Americans?

Hint: Since Maria is of Latino origin and reads Spanish-language newspapers, you can assume that her family speaks some amount of Spanish at home.

Maxwell House coffee, for example, found it had to take steps to counter an image problem among boomers: Its consumer research showed that coffee drinkers were perceived by many to be nervous, older, and somewhat downscale. In fact, unit sales of coffee had declined about one percent a year since 1962 as a new generation changed its drinking habits. In response, the company introduced its "Private Collection" label to appeal to more upscale baby boomers.[48]

Levi Strauss owes much of its success to baby boomers, who adopted blue jeans as a symbol of their generation. But sales of blue jeans peaked in 1981 and then fell steadily as these consumers (and their waistlines) outgrew their blue jeans. The company introduced a new line of pants that provide a looser fit, called Dockers, to win back its traditional consumers. The success of Dockers has created a new clothing category, "new casuals," as other manufacturers attempt to regear for aging boomers.[49]

As the oldest members of the baby boomer generation turn 50 in 1996, many businesses are begining to cash in on the mass onset of menopause, which on the average begins at the age of 51. It has been estimated that about 3,500 women a day go through "the change." In the past, this condition was largely ignored or hidden, but as assertive baby boomers are beginning to be affected, societal attitudes are changing. The new frankness about this condition has led to a boom in self-help books, estrogen supplements, and exercise classes.[50]

While middle-aged women experience physical changes as they undergo menopause, men are not immune. So-called "male menopause" or "midlife crisis" affects many men psychologically—and some medical evidence for physical changes in brain chemistry during this time is beginning to appear as well. As humorist Dave Barry notes, this is a humiliating time when a man wears ". . . enormous pleated pants and designer fragrances, encases his pale porky body in tank tops, and buys a boat shaped like a sexual aid. He then abandons his attractive, intelligent wife to live with a 19-year-old aerobics instructor who once spent an entire summer reading a single magazine article called 'Ten Tips for Terrific Toenails.'"

Marketers are eager to provide solutions to menopausal men's social anxieties. The Hair Club for Men has about 40,000 members who have received new heads of hair with the help of "hair-replacement engineers." Plastic surgeons also report a sharp rise in the number of men undergoing aesthetic surgery; in 1990, men had almost a third of all nose jobs and accounted for 10 percent of the liposuction procedures (where excess fat is sucked out of body parts). Still, Dave Barry feels all this activity is wasted. "Regardless of how many gallons of Oil of Olay you smear on yourself," he warns, "you're going to start aging faster than a day-old bagel on a hot dumpster."[51]

Segmenting Boomers: The "New-Collars"

Although upscale consumers exert an influence on popular culture and marketing efforts far out of proportion to the size of their segment, they by no means speak for all baby boomers. Not all boomers are affluent professionals who drive Mercedes or BMWs, wear Rolex watches, and play squash!

An important baby boomer segment that is beginning to make its presence felt has been termed **new-collar workers.** These consumers occupy a gray area between professional and blue-collar jobs. Many of them hold service jobs, such as flight attendants, dental hygienists, and computer operators, vital to the functioning of our

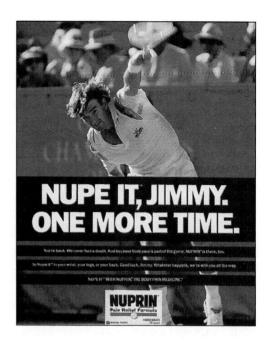

This ad for Nuprin featuring Jimmy Connors at age 39 is among the many attempting to target aging baby boomers.
Courtesy of J. Walter Thompson.

services-dominated economy. They make approximately $15,000 to $30,000 a year, so they are neither affluent nor poor, despite the fact that many are college educated.

As a group, new-collars tend to be individualistic, pragmatic, and skeptical of institutions. These traits set them apart from older generations of gray- and pink-collar service workers, who largely identified with the more traditional ideals of the working class. New-collars are a hybrid of traditional values and the liberalizing effects of their experiences growing up in the 1960s. They tend to exhibit a strong commitment to the family but are more flexible—stylistically, sexually, and so on—than were their parents. These consumers tend to read such publications as *People* magazine and *TV Guide,* and music plays an important role in their lives as a bonding experience. Rock singer Bruce Springsteen can be thought of as the "poet laureate" of the new-collar segment.[52]

MATURE CONSUMERS

The old woman sits alone in her dark apartment, while the television blares out a soap opera. Once every couple of days, she slowly and painfully opens her triple-locked door with arthritic hands and ventures out to the corner store to buy essentials like tea, milk, and cereal, always being sure to pick the least expensive brand. Most of the time she sits in her rocking chair, thinking sadly of her dead husband and the good times she used to have.

Is this the image you have of a typical elderly consumer? Until recently, many marketers did. As a result, they largely neglected the elderly in their feverish pursuit of the baby boomer market. But as our population ages and people are living longer and healthier lives, the game is rapidly changing. A lot of businesses are beginning to replace the old stereotype of the poor recluse. The newer, more accurate image is of a mature consumer who is active, is interested in what life has to offer, and is an enthusiastic customer with the means and willingness to buy many goods and services.[53]

Gray Power: Shattering Stereotypes

The elderly market consists of approximately 52 million people aged 55 and older, although for many purposes consumers are not classified as "elderly" until they reach the age of 65, when Social Security retirement benefits begin. The Bureau of Labor Statistics estimates that the mature market will grow by 62 percent between 1987 and 2015, compared to a 19 percent rate of growth for the overall United States population.[54] This increase makes the mature market the second-fastest-growing market segment in the United States, lagging only behind the baby boomers. Such dramatic growth can largely be explained by improved medical diagnoses and treatment and the resulting increase in life expectancies.

Still, outdated images of mature consumers persist. The editors of *Modern Maturity* magazine, which is sent to 23 million readers, reject about a third of the ads submitted to them because they portray older people in a negative light. On the other hand, an ad for US Air is more in keeping with the new look of the mature consumer: A fit, tanned older couple lounges by a pool, and the tagline reads, "Now is the time to have the time of your life."[55]

There is abundant evidence that the economic health of elderly consumers is good and getting better. In the period between 1979 and 1987, householders 65 and over showed an income gain of 16 percent, the largest increase of any age group. Some of the important areas that stand to benefit from the surging gray market are described in Table 14–4.

It is crucial to remember that income alone does not capture the spending power of this group. Elderly consumers are finished with many of the financial obligations that siphon off the income of younger consumers. Eighty percent of consumers past age 65 own their own homes, and 80 percent of those homes are mortgage free. In addition, child-rearing costs are over with. And, as evidenced by the popularity of the bumper sticker that proudly proclaims "We're spending our children's inheritance," many seniors now feel better about spending money on themselves rather than skimping for the sake of children and grandchildren.

TABLE 14–4 ▼ Growth Opportunities in the Gray Market

CATEGORY	TRENDS	GROWTH AREAS
Home	Emphasis on convenience and leisure time	Games, video, cooking, housekeeping aids
Health care	Need for nutritionally correct foods, health foods	Nursing homes, pharmaceuticals, exercise facilities
Travel and leisure	Leisure time, disposable income	Cruises, tourism
Education	Decline in number of college-aged students; more positive attitudes toward learning; self-help among older, better-educated consumers	Colleges, "how-to" books, and videos
Financial planning	Need for retirement planning, greater assets than in the past	Speculative investing, vacation homes
Health and fitness	Desire to recapture youth and retard aging	Cosmetic surgery, vitamins, skin treatments, bifocal contact lenses

Source: Adapted from Jeff Ostroff, "An Aging Market," *American Demographics* (May 1989): 26. Reprinted with permission, © *American Demographics*.

Key Values of the Elderly

As we age, our values and priorities change. Researchers have identified a set of key values that motivate older consumers. For marketing strategies to succeed, they should be related to one or more of these motivational factors.[56] These values can be summarized as follows:

- *Autonomy*—Mature consumers want to lead active lives and to be self-sufficient. The advertising strategy of Depends, undergarments for incontinent women made by Kimberly-Clark, is centered around a famous actress, June Allyson, who plays golf and goes to parties without worrying about her condition.

- *Connectedness*—Mature consumers value the bonds they have with friends and family. Quaker Oats successfully tapped into this desire with its ads featuring actor Wilford Brimely, who dispenses grandfatherly advice about eating right to the younger generation.

- *Altruism*—Mature consumers want to give something back to the world. Thrifty Car Rental found in a survey that over 40 percent of older consumers would select a rental-car company if it sponsored a program that gave discounts to senior-citizen centers that wanted to buy vans for their patrons. Based on this research, the company launched its highly successful program, "Give a Friend a Lift."

Several hotel chains are targeting the mature market. Choice Hotels is making adjustments to its pricing structure, room design, and promotional strategy. New rooms—all on the first floor for easier access—offer brighter lighting and larger buttons on the phones and TV remote controls. The chain offers travelers over the age of 50 a 30 percent discount on rooms. This ad for Rodeway Inn shows a similar strategy. Source: Cyndee Miller, "Seniors Lured to Hotel Rooms by Seductive Trappings," Marketing News (December 6, 1993): 9. Photo: Courtesy of Choice Hotels International.

● *Personal growth*—Mature consumers are very interested in trying new experiences and developing their potential. In some of its ads for health-care products, Prudential is featuring the late-in-life accomplishments of such people as Clara Barton, Benjamin Franklin, and Noah Webster.

Self-Concept: You're Only as Old as You Feel

Market researchers who work with the elderly often comment that people think of themselves as being 10 to 15 years younger than they actually are. In fact, research confirms the popular wisdom that age is more a state of mind than of body. A person's mental outlook and activity level has a lot more to do with his or her longevity and quality of life than does *chronological* age, or the actual number of years lived.

A better yardstick with which to categorize the elderly is **perceived age,** or how old a person feels. Perceived age can be measured on several dimensions, including "feel-age" (i.e., how old a person feels) and "look-age" (i.e., how old a person looks).[57] The older consumers get, the younger they *feel* relative to actual age. For

No. 2 in a series on how to advertise to Mature America.

Take off 15 years. At least.

They look and act years younger than their mothers and fathers did in their maturity. Proper nutrition, a zest for fitness and an active lifestyle have handed many of them a whole new lease on life. The lesson to marketers? Talk to a person, not a birth date. Enjoy their continuing youth with them. They love a pistachio ice cream cone, have a great time "umping" a Little League game. How do you cast them in advertising? Looking and acting 10 to 15 years younger than preceding generations at the same age. A just completed Yankelovich study* commissioned by Modern Maturity reveals that Americans 50 and over are as vain about the way they look, eat as much fun food, are as likely to bike or hike as people a decade younger. The magazine that understands how young they feel, that even helps them feel that way, is Modern Maturity. A circulation of 17.4 million makes Modern Maturity the second largest magazine in America, and the fastest growing of the big three. For more insights into Mature America and its magazine, call Peter Hanson at (212) 599-1880. **Modern Maturity**

The beginning of a new lifetime.

The major theme in this Modern Maturity *ad is that consumers in the senior market segment think of themselves as ten to fifteen years younger than they actually are. Courtesy of* Modern Maturity Magazine, *a publication of AARP. Copyright © Mature Americans, the Daniel Yankelovich Group, 1987.*

this reason, many marketers emphasize product benefits rather than age appropriateness in marketing campaigns, since many consumers do not relate to products targeted to their chronological age.[58]

In fact, some marketing efforts targeted to the elderly have backfired because they reminded people of their age or presented their age group in an unflattering way. One of the more famous blunders was committed by Heinz. A company analyst found that many elderly people were buying baby food because of the small portions and easy-chewing consistency, so it introduced a line of "Senior Foods" made especially for denture wearers. Needless to say, the product failed. Consumers did not want to admit that they required strained foods (even to the supermarket cashier). They preferred to purchase baby foods, which they could pretend they were buying for a grandchild.

Segmenting Seniors

The senior subculture represents an extremely large market: the number of Americans 65 and older exceeds the entire population of Canada.[59] Because this group is so large, it is helpful to think of the mature market as actually consisting of four subsegments: an "older" group (aged 55–64), an "elderly" group (aged 65–74), an "aged" group (aged 75–84), and finally a "very old" group (85 and up).[60]

The elderly market is well suited for segmentation. Older consumers are easy to identify by age and stage in the family life cycle. Most receive Social Security benefits, which allows marketers to obtain their names and addresses. In addition, many belong to organizations catering to the elderly. The American Association of Retired Persons has become a formidable lobbying force for the interests of older citizens: Its main publication, *Modern Maturity,* has the largest circulation of any American magazine!

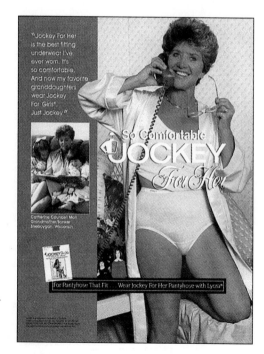

Jockey Apparel is one of many advertisers that is increasingly featuring attractive older models in its ads. JOCKEY FOR HER, SO COMFORTABLE *and* JOCKEY *figure are trademarks of and are used with permission of Jockey International, Inc.*

One productive way to segment older consumers is to classify them in terms of how they confront the advent of old age.[61] Some people become depressed, withdrawn, and apathetic as they age; some are angry and resist the thought of aging; and some appear to accept the new challenges and opportunities this period of life has to offer.

For example, one ad agency devised a segmentation scheme for American women over the age of 65 on two dimensions: self-sufficiency and perceived opinion leadership.[62] The study yielded many important differences among the groups. The self-sufficient group was found to be more independent, cosmopolitan, and outgoing. They were more likely to read books, attend concerts and sporting events, and dine out.

This finding highlights the stereotype that elderly people are set in their ways, stubborn, and resistant to change. The implication is that mature consumers are exceptionally brand loyal and unwilling to try new products or services. This belief appears to be true only to the extent that the elderly are more experienced and skeptical of product claims and puffery. They don't appear to be as fickle as younger consumers are but will try new things if given a good reason for doing so.[63]

The Elderly and the Media

A number of specialty magazines have been introduced in recent years that focus on the active lifestyles of today's elderly. These include such publications as *Modern Maturity* and *50 Plus*. Mature consumers in general devour information about the outside world. Television is a very important medium, because the elderly often rely on TV as a window onto society. The elderly watch 60 percent more television than

*M*ARKETING OPPORTUNITY

Many consumer products will encounter a more sympathetic reception from the elderly if packages are redesigned to be sensitive to physical limitations. While aesthetically appealing, packages are often awkward and difficult to manage, especially for those who are frail or arthritic. Also, many serving sizes are not geared to smaller families, widows, and other people living alone, and coupons tend to be for family-sized products rather than for single servings.

Seniors have difficulty with pull-tab cans and push-open milk cartons. Ziploc packages and clear plastic wrap also are difficult to handle. Packages need to be easier to read and should be made lighter and smaller. Finally, designers need to pay attention to contrasting colors. A slight yellowing of the lens as one ages makes it harder to see background colors on packages. Discerning between blues, greens, and violets becomes especially difficult. The closer identifying-type colors are to the package's or advertisement's background color, the less visible they are and the less attention they will command.

A few companies are beginning to confront these issues. Procter & Gamble is working on a snap-top lid for Tide detergent, and General Motors is redesigning some Oldsmobiles to include bigger buttons and clearer dashboard displays. A number of apparel manufacturers are replacing buttons with Velcro snaps.[64]

average households and prefer programs that provide news and current events as a way to keep up. They also watch more golf, baseball, and bowling on television than the average consumer. The elderly tend to listen to radio news at all times of the day and are above the norm in readership of news magazines.

In one survey, one-third of consumers over age 55 reported that they deliberately did *not* buy a product because of the way an elderly person was stereotyped in the product's advertising.[65] Most contemporary advertising underrepresents the elderly, a situation that will have to change as the population ages. For example, more than one-third of Americans over the age of 50 are regular consumers of soft drinks, yet few older consumers are ever seen in soft drink advertising.

Some marketers, however, are beginning to glamorize older people, including DeBeers diamonds, Clairol hair-coloring products, and American Express. This strategy appears to be sound: In a Gallup Poll, 77 percent of respondents reported that they react positively to advertising featuring older people, and 63 percent believe that advertisers are overly obsessed with youth.[66] A longitudinal (i.e., historical) analysis indicated that the portrayal of the elderly in magazine advertising is in fact increasing and that the people in these ads tend to have prestigious positions.[67]

In general, the elderly have been shown to respond positively to ads that provide an abundance of information. Unlike other age groups, these consumers usually are not amused, or persuaded, by imagery-oriented advertising. A more successful strategy involves the construction of advertising that depicts the aged as well-integrated, contributing members of society, with emphasis on them expanding their horizons rather than clinging precariously to life.

Some basic guidelines have been suggested for effective advertising to the elderly. These include the following:[68]

- Keep language simple.
- Use clear, bright pictures.
- Use action to attract attention.
- Speak clearly, and keep the word count low.
- Use a single sales message, and emphasize brand extensions to tap consumers' familiarity.
- Avoid extraneous stimuli (i.e., excessive pictures and graphics that detract from the message).

● People have many things in common with others merely because they are about the same age. Consumers who grew up at the same time share many cultural memories and belong to the same *age cohort*.

● Consumers often feel positively about products they used when they were younger, so they may be receptive to marketers' *nostalgia* appeals that remind them of these experiences.

● Five important age cohorts are children, teens, baby busters, baby boomers, and mature consumers. *Teenagers* are making a transition from childhood to adulthood, and their self-concepts tend to be unstable. They are receptive to products that help them to be accepted and enable them to assert their independence. Because many teens earn money but have few financial obligations, they are a particularly important segment for many nonessential or expressive products, ranging from chewing gum to clothing fashions and music. Because of changes in family structure, many teens also are taking more responsibility for their families' day-to-day shopping and routine purchase decisions.

● Baby busters, or members of generation X, are widely assumed to be cynical, pessimistic about their futures, and skeptical of advertising claims. However, these stereotypes appear to apply to only a fraction of consumers in this age cohort. Marketing messages targeted to this group should be authentic and noncondescending to be effective.

● College students are an important market, but they are hard to reach via conventional media. In many cases, they are living alone for the first time, so they are making important decisions about setting up households. Many marketers appeal to this group by staging events or other elaborate promotions.

● *Baby boomers* are the most powerful age segment because of the segment's size and economic clout. As this group has aged, its interests have changed and marketing priorities have changed as well. The needs and desires of baby boomers affect demands for housing, child care, automobiles, and clothing. Only a small proportion of boomers are as affluent and materialistic as all are assumed to be. Other emerging subsegments, such as *new-collar workers,* are probably more representative of future directions this age subculture will take.

● As the population ages, the needs of mature consumers will also become increasingly influential. Many marketers traditionally ignored the elderly because of the stereotype that they are too inactive and spend too little. This stereotype is no longer accurate. Most of the elderly are healthy, vigorous, and interested in new products and experiences—and they have the income to purchase them. Marketing appeals to this age subculture should focus on consumers' self-concepts and perceived ages, which tend to be more youthful than their chronological ages. Marketers should also emphasize concrete benefits of products, since this group tends to be skeptical of vague, image-related promotions. Personalized service is of particular importance to this segment.

CHAPTER SUMMARY

KEY TERMS

Age cohort p. 502	Event marketing p. 518	Perceived age p. 525
Baby boomers p. 502	New-collar workers p. 521	Tweens p. 509
Baby busters p. 502		Wall media p. 518

CONSUMER BEHAVIOR CHALLENGE

1. What are some possible marketing opportunities present at reunions? What effects might attending such an event have on a consumer's self-esteem, body image, affect, and so on?

2. When is nostalgia an effective way to appeal to consumers? Can this technique backfire? Find ads that use a nostalgia appeal, and critique their likely effectiveness.

3. Why have baby boomers had such an important impact on consumer culture in the second half of this century?

4. Baby busters are widely assumed to be cynical and lazy. Do you agree? What role has the media played in forming this stereotype?

5. What are some of the marketing ramifications of the growth of the new-collar segment?

6. Is it practical to assume that people age 55 and older constitute one large consumer market? What are some approaches to further segmenting this age subculture?

7. Find good and bad examples of advertising targeted to elderly consumers. To what degree does advertising stereotype the elderly? What elements of ads or other promotions appear to determine their effectiveness in reaching and persuading this group?

ABC NEWS CONNECTION

Twentysomething

Grunge Kids. Slackers. Generation X. Twentysomethings. Media pundits and marketers have been hard at work trying to stick labels on a new generation of consumers in their twenties. Many of these descriptions have hung on despite being contradicted by consumption data showing that this group is not necessarily as different as thirty- or fortysomethings would like to believe.

For example, although some critics claim that twentysomethings soak up all of their ideas from watching MTV all day long, in reality this age group watches "only" an average of three hours of TV per day. That may sound like a lot, but it's no more time than the previous generation put in front of the boob tube. And, rather than cackling to "Beavis and Butthead," the top-watched shows are the same network offerings favored by all ages, including "Home

Improvement," "Seinfeld," and "Coach."

Twentysomethings do confront a changed economic and social reality. They are less confident about the stability of jobs, earnings, and relationships. They sometimes are accused of being crybabies about their job prospects, yet it is true that over a ten-year period median weekly earnings for this age group have fallen. And, reported rates of sexual activity are more comparable to people in their 50s than to those in their 30s.[1] If marketers have learned anything about this age group, it is that twentysomethings resist being pegged as a monolithic, apathetic target market that is just waiting to have "hip" products pushed down its throat. This segment provides a more realistic portrayal of the many diverse consumers who happen to be in their twenties.

[1] Nicholas Zill and John Robinson, "The Generation X Difference," *American Demographics* (April 1995): 24 (6 pp.).

NOTES

1. Riccardo A. Davis, "Norelco Ads Speak to Young, Old Shavers," *Advertising Age* (November 29, 1993): 37.

2. Neil Howe and William Strauss, "The New Generation Gap," *Atlantic Monthly* (December 1992): 67; Natalie Perkins, "Zeroing in on Consumer Values: Cohort Analysis Reveals Some Key Differences Among the Generations," *Advertising Age* (March 22, 1993): 23.

3. Bickley Townsend, "Ou sont les reiges d'antan? (Where are the snows of yesteryear?)" *American Demographics* (October 1988): 2.

4. Cf. Morris B. Holbrook, "Nostalgia and Consumption Preferences: Some Emerging Patterns of Consumer Tastes," *Journal of Consumer Research* 20 (September 1993): 245–56; Morris B. Holbrook, "Nostalgia Proneness and Consumer Tastes," in John A. Howard, *Buyer Behavior in Marketing Strategy,* 2d ed. (Englewood Cliffs, NJ: Prentice Hall, 1994): 348–64; Morris B. Holbrook and Robert M. Schindler, "Age, Sex, and Attitude Toward the Past as Predictors of Consumers' Aesthetic Tastes for Cultural Products," *Journal of Marketing Research* 31 (August 1994): 412–22.

5. "Chuckles' Rebirth," *American Demographics* (May 1987): 23.

6. Jeffrey P. Rosenfeld, "Reliving It Up," *American Demographics* (June 1987): 48.

7. Kevin Goldman, "New Campaigns Tip the Hat to Nostalgia," *Wall Street Journal* (August 9, 1994): B4; Raymond Serafin, "Mustang Love: Ford Revs Up Romantic Heritage to Sell New Model of Sports Cars," *Advertising Age* (October 4, 1993): 4.

8. Melissa Turner, "Kids' Marketing Clout Man-Sized," *Atlanta Journal* (February 18, 1988): E10.

9. Russell W. Belk, Kenneth D. Bahn, and Robert N. Mayer, "Developmental Recognition of Consumption Symbolism," *Journal of Consumer Research* 9 (June 1982): 417.

10. Robert N. Mayer and Russell W. Belk, "Fashion and Impression Formation Among Children," in *The Psychology of Fashion,* ed. Michael R. Solomon (Lexington, MA: Lexington Books, 1985): 293–308.

11. Jennifer Lawrence, "Gender-Specific Works for Diapers—Almost Too Well," *Advertising Age* (February 8, 1993): S–10 (2 pp.); Kelly Shermach, "'Reassure Parents the Product's Good for Baby,'" *Marketing News* (October 10, 1994): 1 (2 pp.).

12. Michael Meyer and Dody Tsiantar, "Ninja Turtles, Eat Our Dust," *Newsweek* (August 8, 1994): 34–35.

13. James U. McNeal, *Kids as Customers: A Handbook of Marketing to Children* (New York: Lexington, 1992).

14. Patricia Sellers, "The ABCs of Marketing to Kids," *Fortune* (May 8, 1989): 114; Turner, "Kids Marketing Clout Man-Sized."

15. Brad Edmondson, "Snakes, Snails, and Puppy Dogs' Tails," *American Demographics* (October 1987): 18.

16. Quoted in Linda Wells, "Babes in Makeup Land," *New York Times Magazine* (August 13, 1989): 46.

17. Ellen Graham, "Children's Hour: As Kids Gain Power of Purse, Marketing Takes Aim at Them," *Wall Street Journal* (January 19, 1988): 1.

18. Joe Agnew, "Children Come of Age as Consumers," *Marketing News* (December 4, 1987): 8.

19. Alice Cueno, "Targeting Tweens: Madison Avenue's Call of the Child," *U.S. News & World Report* (March 20, 1989): 84; Carol Hall, "Tween Power," *Marketing and Media Decisions* 22 (October 1987): 56–62; Kit Mill, "Pre-Teen Buying Power," *Marketing and Media Decisions* (April 1989): 96–98.

20. Laura Zinn, "Teens: Here Comes the Biggest Wave Yet," *Business Week* (April 11, 1994): 76 (8 pp.).

21. Junu Bryan Kim, "For Savvy Teens: Real Life, Real Solutions," *Advertising Age* (August 23, 1993): S–1 (3 pp.).

22. Selina S. Guber, "The Teenage Mind," *American Demographics* (August 1987): 42.

23. Cyndee Miller, "Phat is Where It's At for Today's Teen Market," *Marketing News* (August 15, 1994): 6 (2 pp.); Zinn, "Teens: Here Comes the Biggest Wave Yet."

24. Quoted in Cyndee Miller, "Phat is Where It's At for Today's Teen Market."

25. Ellen Goodman, "The Selling of Teenage Anxiety," *Washington Post* (November 24, 1979).

26. John Greenwald, "Will Teens Buy It?" *Time* (May 30, 1994): 50–2; Laurie M. Grossman, "Coke Hopes 'OK,' New Drink, Will be the Toast of Teens," *Wall Street Journal* (April 21, 1994): B7.

27. Ellen R. Foxman, Patriya S. Tansuhaj, and Karin M. Ekstrom, "Family Members' Perceptions of Adolescents' Influence in Family Decision Making," *Journal of Consumer Research* 15 (March 1989): 482–91.

28. Andrew Malcolm, "Teen-Age Shoppers: Desperately Seeking Spinach," *New York Times* (November 29, 1987): 10.

29. Malcolm, "Teen-Age Shoppers."

30. John Blades, "Tracking Skippies: TRU Researches Habits of Elusive Teens," *Asbury Park Press* (March 2, 1991): C1.

31. Malcolm, "Teen-Age Shoppers."

32. Rose A. Horowitz, "California Beach Culture Rides Wave of Popularity in Japan," *Journal of Commerce* (August 3, 1989): 17; Elaine Lafferty, "American Casual Seizes Japan; Teenagers Go for N.F.L. Hats, Batman and the California Look," *Time* (November 13, 1989): 106.

33. Blayne Cutler, "Move Over, Miso," *American Demographics* (May 1988): 56.

34. Karen Lowry Miller, "You Just Can't Talk to These Kids," *Business Week* (April 19, 1993): 104 (2 pp.).

35. Quoted in Jennifer Cody, "Here's a New Way to Rationalize Not Cleaning Out Your Closets," *Wall Street Journal* (June 14, 1994): B1.

36. Cf. Paul Herbig, William Koehler, and Ken Day, "Marketing to the Baby Bust Generation," *Journal of Consumer Marketing* 10, 1 (1993): 4–9.

37. Laura Zinn, "Move Over, Boomers," *Business Week* (December 14, 1992) 7.

38. Douglas Lavin, "Chrysler Directs Neon Campaign at Generation X," *Wall Street Journal* (August 27, 1993): B1 (2 pp.); Cyndee Miller, "Xers Know They're a Target Market, and They Hate That," *Marketing News* (December 6, 1993): 2; Raymond Serafin and Cleveland Horton, "X Marks the Spot for Car Marketing," *Advertising Age* (August 9, 1993): 8; Jennifer Steinhauer, "How Do You Turn on the Twentysomething Market?" *New York Times* (April 17, 1994): F5.

39. Scott Donaton, "The Media Wakes Up to Generation X," *Advertising Age* (February 1, 1993): 16 (2 pp.); Laura E. Keeton, "New Magazines Aim to Reach (and Rechristen) Generation X," *Wall Street Journal* (October 17, 1994): B1 (2 pp.); Cyndee Miller, "X Marks the Lucrative Spot, But Some Advertisers Can't Hit Target," *Marketing News* (August 2, 1993): 1 (2 pp.); Todd Pruzan, "Advertisers Wary of Generation X Titles," *Advertising Age* (October 24, 1994): S–22 (2 pp.).

40. *The Mademoiselle Report: Redefining a Generation* (New York: Mademoiselle, 1994).

41. Quoted in Daniel Shannon, "In a Class By Itself," *Promo: The International Magazine for Promotion Marketing* (July 1994): 51 (6 pp.).

42. Beth Bogart, "Word of Mouth Travels Fastest," *Advertising Age* (February 6, 1989): S–6; Janice Steinberg, "Media 101," *Advertising Age* (February 6, 1989): S–4.

43. Shannon, "In a Class By Itself."

44. Stuart Elliott, "Beyond Beer and Sun Oil: The Beach-Blanket Bazaar," *New York Times* (March 18, 1992): D17; Judith Waldrop, *The Seasons of Business: The Marketer's Guide to Consumer Behavior* (New York: American Demographics, Inc., 1992).

45. Peter Francese, "A Symphony of Demographic Change," *Advertising Age* (November 9, 1988): 130.

46. Fabian Linden, "Middle-Aged Muscle," *American Demographics* (October 1987): 4.

47. Paulette Thomas, "Peddling Youth Gets Some New Wrinkles," *Wall Street Journal* (October 24, 1994): B1 (2 pp.).

48. Amy Dunkin, "Maxwell House Serves Up a Yuppie Brew," *Business Week* (March 2, 1987): 62.

49. Andrew Pollack, "Jeans Fade but Levi Strauss Glows," *New York Times* (June 26, 1989): D1.

50. Patricia Braus, "Facing Menopause," *American Demographics* (March 1993): 44 (5 pp.).

51. Quoted in Blayne Cutler, "Marketing to Menopausal Men," *American Demographics* (March 1993): 49.

52. Kenneth I. Walsh and Sharon F. Golden, "The New-Collar Class," *U.S. News & World Report* (September 15, 1985): 59.

53. Cf. George P. Moschis, "Gerontographics: A Scientific Approach to Analyzing and Targeting the Mature Market," *Journal of Consumer Marketing* 10, 3 (1993): 45–53; George P. Moschis, "Consumer Behavior in Later Life: Multidisciplinary Contributions and Implications for Research," *Journal of the Academy of Marketing Science* 22, 3 (1994): 195–204.

54. William Lazer and Eric H. Shaw, "How Older Americans Spend Their Money," *American Demographics* (September 1987): 36; see also Charles D. Schewe and Anne L. Balazs, "Role Transitions in Older Adults: A Marketing Opportunity," *Psychology & Marketing* 9 (March/April 1992): 85–99.

55. Kevin Goldman, "Seniors Get Little Respect on Madison Avenue," *Wall Street Journal* (September 20, 1993): B4.

56. David B. Wolfe, "Targeting the Mature Mind," *American Demographics* (March 1994): 32–36.

57. Benny Barak and Leon G. Schiffman, "Cognitive Age: A Nonchronological Age Variable," in *Advances in Consumer Research* 8, ed. Kent B. Monroe (Provo, UT: Association for Consumer Research, 1981): 602–06.

58. David B. Wolfe, "An Ageless Market," *American Demographics* (July 1987): 27–55.

59. Lenore Skenazy, "These Days, It's Hip to be Old," *Advertising Age* (February 15, 1988).

60. Lazer and Shaw, "How Older Americans Spend Their Money."

61. Ellen Day, Brian Davis, Rhonda Dove, and Warren A. French, "Reaching the Senior Citizen Market(s)," *Journal of Advertising Research* (December/January 1987/88): 23–30; Warren A. French and Richard Fox, "Segmenting the Senior Citizen Market," *Journal of Consumer Marketing* 2 (1985): 61–74; Jeffrey G. Towle and Claude R. Martin, Jr., "The Elderly Consumer: One Segment or Many?" in *Advances in Consumer Research* 3, ed. Beverlee B. Anderson (Provo, UT: Association for Consumer Research, 1976): 463.

62. Day, Davis, Dove, and French, "Reaching the Senior Citizen Market(s)."

63. Many studies have examined elderly consumers' shopping patterns and product choices; see J. Barry Mason and William O. Bearden, "Profiling the Shopping Behavior of Elderly Consumers," *The Gerontologist* 18, 5 (1978): 454–61; James R. Lumpkin and Barnett A. Greenberg, "Apparel-Shopping Patterns

of the Elderly Consumer," *Journal of Retailing* 58 (winter 1982): 68–89; Mary C. LaForge, "Learned Helplessness as an Explanation of Elderly Consumer Complaint Behavior," *Journal of Business Ethics* 8 (May 1989): 359–66; Betsy D. Gelb, "Exploring the Gray Market Segment," *MSU Business Topics* 26 (spring 1978): 41–46; Elaine Sherman, "The Senior Market: Opportunities Abound," *Direct Marketing* 50 (June 1987): 82; Valarie A. Zeithaml and Mary C. Gilly, "Characteristics Affecting the Acceptance of Retailing Technologies: A Comparison of Elderly and Nonelderly Consumers," *Journal of Retailing* 83 (spring 1987): 49–68; Mary C. Gilly and Valarie A. Zeithaml, "The Elderly Consumer and Adoption of Technologies," *Journal of Consumer Research* 12 (December 1985): 353–7.

64. "Gray Expectations: A New Force in Design," *Business Week* (April 11, 1988): 108; Mary Bender, "Packaging for the Older Consumer," (speech delivered at the Annual Winter Conference of the Gerontology Institute of New Jersey, Princeton, NJ, March 6, 1987).

65. Melinda Beck, "Going for the Gold," *Newsweek* (April 23, 1990): 74.

66. J. Ward, "Marketers Slow to Catch Age Wave," *Advertising Age* (May 22, 1989): S–1.

67. Anthony C. Ursic, Michael L. Ursic, and Virginia L. Ursic, "A Longitudinal Study of the Use of the Elderly in Magazine Advertising," *Journal of Consumer Research* 13 (June 1986): 131–3.

68. Ward, "Marketers Slow to Catch Age Wave."

V

CONSUMERS
AND CULTURE

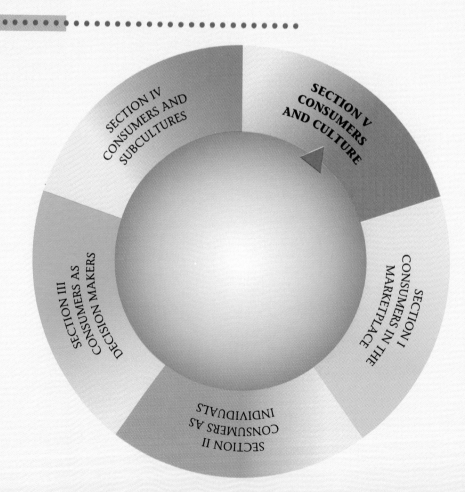

SECTION IV
CONSUMERS AND
SUBCULTURES

SECTION V
CONSUMERS
AND CULTURE

SECTION I
CONSUMERS IN THE
MARKETPLACE

SECTION III
CONSUMERS AS
DECISION MAKERS

SECTION II
CONSUMERS AS
INDIVIDUALS

The final section of this book considers consumers as members of a broad cultural system. Chapter 15 looks at some of the basic building blocks of culture and the impact these have on consumer behavior. Chapter 16 focuses on the importance of understanding consumers' lifestyles and also on how these lifestyles among consumers around the world are studied. Chapter 17 concludes with a focus on how some of the important, emerging developments in our culture affect our lives as consumers. This chapter also takes a look at some harmful aspects of consumer behavior: this "dark side" of consumer behavior includes such issues as addiction, vandalism, and shoplifting. Finally, the chapter comes full circle as it further considers a central issue first raised in Chapter 1, that is, how marketers contribute to everyday consumer culture and how they even have an impact on our perceptions of what is "real" in important ways.

As Amanda is browsing through the racks at her local Limited store in Wichita, Kansas, her friend Alexandra yells to her from the accessories section, "Amanda, check this out! This chain is just what you need to go with your new outfit!" Alex is right. The oversized bright gold chain would go perfectly with her new gold baseball cap, and besides it looks just like the ones she has seen worn on MTV rap videos.

As Amanda takes the chain to the cash register, she's looking forward to wearing it to school the next day. All of her girlfriends in junior high compete with each other to dress just like the singers in Salt 'n Pepa and other groups. Her friends just won't believe their eyes when they see her tomorrow. Maybe some of the younger kids in her school might even think she was fresh off the mean streets of New York City! Even though she has never been east of the Mississippi, Amanda just knows she would fit right in with all of the Bronx "sisters" she reads about in her magazines. . . .

Cultural Influences on Consumer Behavior

CULTURE AND CONSUMPTION

People often buy products because of what they mean, rather than for what they do. Consumption choices simply cannot be understood without considering the cultural context in which they are made: Culture is the "lens" through which people view products.

Amanda's purchase of a gold chain reflects her desire to associate (with help from the media and marketers) with glamor, adventure, and trendiness. As a privileged member of "white-bread" society, her display of this chain has a very different meaning in her suburban world than it would to street kids in New York City or Los Angeles. It might even be interpreted by these "cutting-edge" types as a sign that this item is no longer in fashion, and it is time to move on to something else (which has in fact happened).

Indeed, it is quite common for mainstream culture to modify symbols identified with "cutting-edge" subcultures and present these to a larger audience. As this occurs, these cultural products undergo a process of **cooptation,** where their original meanings are transformed and often trivialized by outsiders. In this case, rap music was to a large extent divorced from its original connection with the struggles of young African-Americans and is now used as an entertainment format for other fans.[1]

Amanda lives in a white middle-class area in the Midwest, but she is able to "connect" symbolically with millions of other young consumers by wearing styles

These Absolut ads featuring popular artists help to blur the boundaries between marketing activities and popular culture. Absolut Vodka logo and bottle design are trademarks owned by V&S VIN & SPIRIT AB. Imported by Carillon Importers, Ltd., Teaneck, N.J.

TABLE 15–5 ▼ Cultural Formulae in Public Art Forms

ART FORM/ GENRE	CLASSIC WESTERN	SCIENCE FICTION	HARD-BOILED DETECTIVE	FAMILY SITCOM
Time	1800s	Future	Present	Anytime
Location	Edge of civilization	Space	City	Suburbs
Protagonist	Cowboy (lone individual)	Astronaut	Detective	Father (figure)
Heroine	Schoolmarm	Spacegal	Damsel in distress	Mother (figure)
Villain	Outlaws, killers	Aliens	Killer	Boss, neighbor
Secondary characters	Townfolk, Indians	Technicians in spacecraft	Cops, underworld	Kids, dogs
Plot	Restore law and order	Repel aliens	Find killer	Solve problem
Theme	Justice	Triumph of humanity	Pursuit and discovery	Chaos and confusion
Costume	Cowboy hat, boots, etc.	High-tech uniforms	Raincoat	Regular clothes
Locomotion	Horse	Spaceship	Beat-up car	Station wagon
Weaponry	Sixgun, rifle	Rayguns	Pistol, fists	Insults

Source: Arthur A. Berger, *Signs in Contemporary Culture: An Introduction to Semiotics* (New York: Longman, 1984): 86. Copyright ©1984. Reissued 1989 by Sheffield Publishing Company, Salem, Wisconsin. Reprinted with permission of the publisher.

This House & Garden *ad illustrates the life cycle of an Emerson radio to show how ideas about a mass-produced cultural product can change over time and create a classic and valuable collector's item. Reprinted by permission of* HG *Magazine, Copyright © 1989 Conde Nast Publications, Inc.*

a **cultural formula,** where certain roles and props often occur consistently.[62] Romance novels are an extreme case of a cultural formula. Computer programs even allow users to "write" their own romances by systematically varying certain set elements of the story.

Creators of aesthetic products are increasingly adapting conventional marketing methods to fine tune their mass-market offerings. Market research is used, for example, to test audience reactions to movie concepts. Although testing cannot account for such intangibles as acting quality or cinematography, it can determine if the basic themes of the movie strike a responsive chord in the target audience. This type of research is most appropriate for blockbuster movies, which usually follow one of the formulae described earlier.

Even the content of movies is sometimes influenced by consumer research. Typically, free invitations to prescreenings are handed out in malls and movie theaters. Attendees are asked a few questions about the movie and then some are selected to participate in focus groups. Although group members' reactions usually result in only minor editing changes, occasionally more drastic effects result. When initial reaction to the ending of *Fatal Attraction* was negative, Paramount Pictures spent an additional $1.3 million to shoot a new one.[63]

THE FASHION SYSTEM

The **fashion system** consists of all those people and organizations involved in creating symbolic meanings and transferring these meanings to cultural goods. Although people tend to equate fashion with clothing, it is important to keep in mind that fashion processes affect *all* types of cultural phenomena, including music, art, architecture, and even science (i.e., certain research topics and scientists are "hot" at any point in time). Even business practices are subject to the fashion process; they evolve and change depending on which management techniques, such as total quality management or just-in-time inventory control, are "in vogue."

Fashion can be thought of as a *code,* or language, that helps us to decipher these meanings.[64] Unlike a language, however, fashion is *context-dependent.* The same item can be interpreted differently by different consumers and in different situations.[65] The meaning of many products is *undercoded*—that is, there is no one precise meaning, but rather plenty of room for interpretation among perceivers.

At the outset, it may be helpful to distinguish among some confusing terms. **Fashion** is the process of social diffusion by which a new style is adopted by some group(s) of consumers. In contrast, *a fashion* (or style) refers to a particular combination of attributes. And, to be *in fashion* means that this combination is currently positively evaluated by some reference group. Thus, the term *Danish Modern* refers to particular characteristics of furniture design (i.e., a fashion in interior design); it does not necessarily imply that Danish Modern is a fashion that is currently desired by consumers.[66]

Cultural Categories

The meaning that does get imparted to products reflects underlying **cultural categories,** which correspond to the basic ways we characterize the world.[67] Our culture

This House & Garden *ad demonstrates how different products represent the same cultural categories over time. Reprinted by permission of HG Magazine. Copyright © 1989 Conde Nast Publications, Inc.*

makes distinctions between different times, between leisure and work, between genders, and so on. The fashion system provides us with products that signify these categories. For example, the apparel industry gives us clothing to denote certain times (e.g., evening wear, resort wear), it differentiates between leisure clothes and work clothes, and it promotes masculine and feminine styles.

These cultural categories affect many different products and styles. As a result, it is common to find that dominant aspects of a culture at any point in time tend to be reflected in the design and marketing of very different products. This concept is a bit hard to grasp, since on the surface a clothing style, say, has little in common with a piece of furniture or with a car. However, an overriding concern with a value such as achievement or environmentalism can determine the types of products likely to be accepted by consumers at any point in time. These underlying or latent themes then surface in various aspects of design. A few examples of this interdependence demonstrate how a dominant fashion *motif* reverberates across industries.

● Costumes worn by political figures or movie and rock stars can affect the fortunes of the apparel and accessory industries. A movie appearance by actor Clark Gable without a T-shirt (unusual at that time) dealt a severe setback to the men's apparel industry, while Jackie Kennedy's famous pillbox hat prompted a rush for hats by women in the 1960s. Other cross-category effects include the craze for ripped sweatshirts instigated by the movie *Flashdance,* a boost for cowboy boots from the movie *Urban Cowboy,* and singer Madonna's legitimation of lingerie as an acceptable outerwear clothing style.

● The Louvre in Paris was recently remodeled to include a controversial glass pyramid at the entrance designed by the architect I. M. Pei. Shortly thereafter, several designers unveiled pyramid-shaped clothing at Paris fashion shows.[68]

● In the 1950s and 1960s, much of America was preoccupied with science and technology. This concern with "space-age" mastery was fueled by the Russians' launching of the Sputnik satellite, which prompted fears that America was

A cultural emphasis on science in the late 1950s affected product designs, as seen in the design of automobiles with large tail fins (to resemble rockets). R. Gates/Frederic Lewis.

falling behind in the technology race. The theme of technical mastery of nature and of futuristic design became a *motif* that cropped up in many aspects of American popular culture—from car designs with prominent tail fins to high-tech kitchen styles.

Collective Selection

Fashions tend to "sweep" the country; it seems that all of a sudden "everyone" is doing the same thing or wearing the same styles. Some sociologists view fashion as a form of *collective behavior,* or a wave of social conformity. How do so many people "get tuned-in" to the same phenomenon at once, as happened with hip-hop styles?

Remember that creative subsystems within a culture production system attempt to anticipate the tastes of the buying public. Despite their unique talents, members of this subsystem are also members of mass culture. Like the fashion magazine editors discussed earlier, cultural gatekeepers are drawing from a common set of ideas and symbols and are influenced by the same cultural phenomena as the eventual consumers of their products.

The process by which certain symbolic alternatives are chosen over others has been termed **collective selection.**[69] As with the creative subsystem, members of the managerial and communications subsystems also seem to develop common frames of mind. Although products within each category must compete for acceptance in the marketplace, they can usually be characterized by their adherence to a dominant theme or *motif*—be it "The Western Look," "New Wave," "Danish Modern," or "Nouvelle Cuisine."

Behavioral Science Perspectives on Fashion

Fashion is a very complex process that operates on many levels. At one extreme, it is a macro, societal phenomenon affecting many people simultaneously. At the other, it exerts a very personal effect on individual behavior. A consumer's purchase decisions are often motivated by his or her desire to be in fashion. Fashion products are also aesthetic objects, and their origins are rooted in art and history. Thus, there are many perspectives on the origin and diffusion of fashion. Although these cannot be described in detail here, some major approaches can be briefly summarized.[70]

PSYCHOLOGICAL MODELS OF FASHION

Many psychological factors help to explain why people are motivated to be in fashion. These include conformity, variety seeking, personal creativity, and sexual attraction. For example, many consumers seem to have a "need for uniqueness." These consumers want to be different, but not too different.[71] For this reason, people often conform to the basic outlines of a fashion but try to improvise and make a personal statement within these guidelines.

One of the earliest theories of fashion proposed that "shifting **erogenous zones**" (sexually arousing areas of the body) accounted for fashion changes. Different parts of the female body are the focus of sexual interest, and clothing styles change to highlight or hide these parts. For example, people in the Victorian era found shoulders exciting, a "well-turned ankle" was important in the beginning of this century, and the back was the center of attention in the 1930s. Some contemporary fashions suggest that the midriff is now an erogenous zone. (Note that, until very recently, the study of fashion focused almost exclusively on its impact on women. Hopefully, this concentration will broaden as scholars and practitioners begin to appreciate that men are affected by many of the same fashion influences.)

While these shifts may be due to boredom, some have speculated that there are deeper reasons for changes in focus; body areas symbolically reflect social values. In medieval times, for example, a rounded belly was desirable. This preference was most likely a reflection of the high mortality rate when virtually constant pregnancy was necessary to stabilize population growth. Interest in the female leg in the 1920s and 1930s coincided with women's new mobility and independence, while the exposure of breasts in the 1970s signaled a renewed interest in breast feeding.[72] Breasts were de-emphasized in the 1980s as women concentrated on careers, but a larger bust size is now more popular as women try to combine professional activity with child rearing.

ECONOMIC MODELS OF FASHION

Economists approach fashion in terms of the model of supply and demand. Items that are in limited supply have high value, while those readily available are less desirable. Rare items command respect and prestige.

Veblen's notion of conspicuous consumption proposed that the wealthy consume to display their prosperity, for example by wearing expensive (and at times impractical) clothing. As noted in Chapter 12, this approach is somewhat outdated, since upscale consumers often engage in *parody display,* in which they deliberately adopt formerly low-status or inexpensive products, such as jeeps or jeans. Other factors also influence the demand curve for fashion-related products. These include a *prestige-exclusivity effect,* wherein high prices still create high demand, and a *snob effect,* in which lower prices actually reduce demand ("only a lowlife would pay such a cheap price for that!").[73]

This ad for Maidenform illustrates that fashions have accentuated different parts of the female anatomy throughout history. Copyright © 1990 by Maidenform, Inc.

SOCIOLOGICAL MODELS OF FASHION

The collective selection model discussed previously is an example of a sociological approach to fashion. In addition, much attention has been focused on the relationship between product adoption and class structure.

The **trickle-down theory,** first proposed in 1904 by Georg Simmel, has been one of the most influential approaches to understanding fashion. It states that there are two conflicting forces that drive fashion change. First, subordinate groups try to adopt the status symbols of the groups above them as they attempt to climb up the ladder of social mobility. Dominant styles thus originate with the upper classes and *trickle-down* to those below. However, this is where the second force kicks in: Those people in the superordinate groups are constantly looking below them on the ladder to ensure that they are not imitated. They respond to the attempts of lower classes to "impersonate" them by adopting even *newer* fashions. These two processes create a self-perpetuating cycle of change—the machine that drives fashion.[74]

The trickle-down theory was quite useful for understanding the process of fashion changes when applied to a society with a stable class structure that permitted the easy identification of lower- versus upper-class consumers. This task is not so easy in modern times. In contemporary Western society, then, this approach must be modified to account for new developments in mass culture.[75]

- A perspective based on class structure cannot account for the wide range of styles that are simultaneously made available in our society. Modern consumers have a much greater degree of individualized choice than they did in the past because of advances in technology and distribution. Just as an adolescent like Amanda is almost instantly aware of the latest style trends by watching MTV, *elite fashion* has been largely replaced by *mass fashion,* since media exposure permits many groups to become aware of a style at the same time.

- Consumers tend to be more influenced by opinion leaders who are similar to them. As a result, each social group has its own fashion innovators who determine fashion trends. It is often more accurate to speak of a *trickle-across effect,* where fashions diffuse horizontally among members of the same social group.[76]

- Finally, current fashions often originate with the lower classes and *trickle-up.* Grassroots innovators typically are people who lack prestige in the dominant culture (like urban youth). Since they are less concerned with maintaining the status quo, they are more free to innovate and take risks.[77]

Cycles of Fashion Adoption

In the early 1980s, Cabbage Patch dolls were all the rage among American children. Faced with a limited supply of the product, some retailers reported near-riots among adults as they tried desperately to buy the dolls for their children. A Milwaukee disc jockey jokingly announced that people should bring catcher's mitts to a local stadium because 2,000 dolls were going to be dropped from an airplane. Listeners were instructed to hold up their American Express cards so their numbers could be aerially photographed. More than two dozen anxious parents apparently didn't get the joke; they showed up in subzero weather, mitts in hand.[78]

Although the Cabbage Patch craze lasted for a couple of seasons, it eventually died out and consumers moved on to other things, such as Teenage Mutant Ninja Turtles, which grossed more than $600 million in 1989.[79] The Mighty Morphin Power Rangers, in turn, replaced the Turtles. What will be next?

Although the longevity of a particular style can range from a month to a century, fashions tend to flow in a predictable sequence. The **fashion life cycle** is quite similar to the more familiar product life cycle. An item or idea progresses through basic stages from birth to death, as shown in Figure 15–4.

UP THE CHARTS WITH A BULLET: STAGES OF ACCEPTANCE

Chapter 10 described the *diffusion of innovations*, in which products are adopted by groups of consumers over time. This diffusion process is intimately related to the popularity of fashion-related items. To illustrate how this process works, consider how the **fashion acceptance cycle** works in the popular music business. In the *introduction stage*, a song is listened to by a small number of music innovators. It may be played in clubs or on "cutting-edge" college radio stations, which is exactly how "grunge rock" groups like Nirvana got their start. During the *acceptance stage*, the song enjoys increased social visibility and acceptance by large segments of the population. A record may get wide airplay on Top 40 stations, steadily rising up the charts "like a bullet."

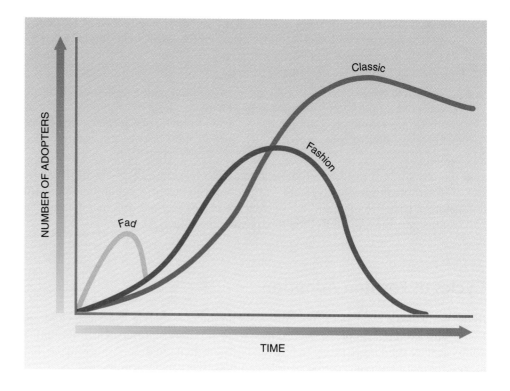

FIGURE 15–4 ▼ Comparison of the Acceptance Cycles of Fads, Fashions, and Classics. Source: Reprinted with the permission of Macmillan College Publishing Company from *The Social Psychology of Clothing* by Susan Kaiser. Copyright © 1985 by Macmillan College Publishing Company, Inc.

In the *regression stage,* the item reaches a state of social saturation as it becomes overused, and eventually it sinks into decline and obsolescence as new songs rise to take its place. A hit record may be played once an hour on a Top 40 station for several weeks. At some point, though, people tend to get sick of it and focus their attention on newer releases. The former hit record eventually winds up in the discount rack at the local record store.

Figure 15–5 illustrates that fashions are characterized by slow acceptance at the beginning, which (if the fashion is to "make it") rapidly accelerates and then tapers off. Different classes of fashion can be identified by considering the relative length of the fashion acceptance cycle. While many fashions exhibit a moderate cycle, taking several years to work their way through the stages of acceptance and decline, others are extremely long-lived or short-lived.

EXTREMES OF FASHION ADOPTION

A **classic** is a fashion with an extremely long acceptance cycle. It is in a sense "antifashion," since it guarantees stability and low risk to the purchaser for a long period of time. Keds sneakers, introduced in 1917, have been successful because they appeal to those who are turned off by the high-fashion, trendy appeal of L.A. Gear, Reebok, and others. When consumers in focus groups were asked to project what kind of building Keds would be, a common response was a country house with a

This Jim Beam ad illustrates the cyclical nature of fashion. *Courtesy of Jim Beam Brand, Inc.*

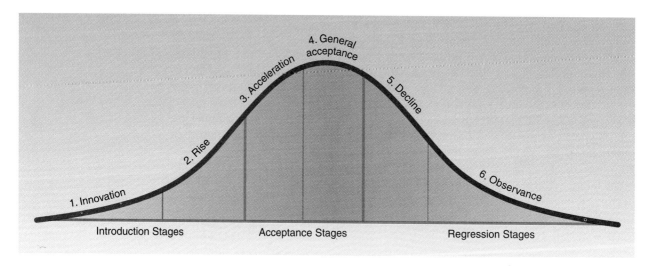

FIGURE 15–5 ▼ **A Normal Fashion Cycle**   Source: Reprinted with the permission of Macmillan College Publishing Company from *The Social Psychology of Clothing* by Susan Kaiser. Copyright ©1985 by Macmillan College Publishing Company, Inc.

white picket fence. In other words, the shoes are seen as a stable, classic product. In contrast, Nikes were often described as steel-and-glass skyscrapers, reflecting their more modernistic image.[80]

A **fad** is a very short-lived fashion. Fads are usually adopted by relatively few people. Adopters may all belong to a common subculture, and the fad "trickles across" members but rarely breaks out of that specific group. Some successful fad products include hula hoops, snap bracelets, and "pet rocks." Streaking was a fad that hit college campuses in the mid-1970s. This term referred to students running naked through classrooms, cafeterias, and dorms. Although the practice quickly spread across many campuses, it was primarily restricted to college settings. Streaking highlights several of the following important characteristics of fads.[81]

- The fad is nonutilitarian—that is, it does not perform any meaningful function.
- The fad is often adopted on impulse; people do not undergo stages of rational decision making before joining in.
- The fad diffuses rapidly, gains quick acceptance, and is short-lived.

BIRDS OF A FEATHER: CLUSTERING CONSUMERS

The search for new ways to segment markets more precisely, coupled with the increasing sophistication of data collection and analysis techniques, has enabled such companies as Western Union to incorporate geographic variables into its marketing strategies.[43] A statistical technique called *cluster analysis* allows marketers to identify groups of people who share important characteristics, even though they may live in different parts of the country.

Geodemography is based on the assumption that "birds of a feather flock together"—that is, people who have similar needs and tastes also tend to live near one another, so it should be possible to locate pockets of like-minded people who can then be reached more economically by direct mail and other methods. For example, a marketer who wants to reach white, single consumers who are college educated and tend to be fiscally conservative may find that it is more efficient to mail catalogs to zip codes 20770 (Greenbelt, Maryland) and 90277 (Redondo Beach, California) than to adjoining areas in either Maryland or California where there are fewer consumers who exhibit these characteristics.

Geographic information increasingly is being combined with other data to paint an even more complete picture of the American consumer. Several marketing research ventures now employ **single-source data,** in which information about a person's actual purchasing history is combined with geodemographic data, and this method allows marketers to learn even more about the types of marketing strategies that motivate some people—but not others—to respond.

Their idea of precise geocoding.

Ours.

Matchmaker/2000® for Windows™ is the only geocoding system that matches street address ranges to latitude and longitude coordinates. So you end up with a more precise and useful picture of where your customers and prospects are located. Matchmaker/2000 offers nationwide street coverage.

with more than 12 million address ranges. Other programs offer only half as many. Matchmaker/2000 is continuously updated. So your data is always current. And you'll achieve the highest match percentage available in the industry today. Matchmaker/2000 is an invaluable tool for market penetration studies. Point and cluster evaluations. Sales effectiveness analyses.

Scheduling and routing. And custom zone creation. You'll work smarter. And faster. The program is offered with a range of expandable and upgradable database options to meet your specific budget and application. Contact Geographic Data Technology, Inc., 13 Dartmouth College Highway, Lyme, NH 03768-9713. Or call 1-800-331-7881, x1101.

GEOGRAPHIC DATA TECHNOLOGY, INC.

1-800-331-7881 x1101

Reprinted from **American Demographics** magazine.

Modern geodemographic techniques allow companies to go well beyond broad regional differences. Many now segment markets down to the neighborhood block. The provision of this type of analysis to marketers has become a profitable niche for several market research companies. Reprinted with permission from Geographic Data Technology, Inc., Lebanon, NH.

This comprehensive strategy was first implemented in the BehaviorScan project, a project begun in 1980 by Information Resources, Inc. The system combined UPC scanners, household panels, and television to track purchases. This type of total approach allows marketers to test the impact of changes in advertising, pricing, shelf placement, and promotions on consumer behavior patterns. Similar systems are now available or under development by other organizations, such as Nielsen and SAMI/Burke.[44]

APPLICATIONS OF GEODEMOGRAPHY

Marketers have been successful at adapting sophisticated analytical techniques originally developed for other applications, such as the military and oil and gas exploration. For example, these techniques, which can now employ data at the neighborhood or even household level, are being used in a variety of ways:

● A bank examined its penetration of accounts by customer zip codes.

● A utility company compared demographic data with billing patterns to fine-tune energy conservation campaigns.

● A chain of ice cream stores helped franchisees develop sales promotion programs for local markets by providing them with demographic profiles of actual users and information about the sales potential of untapped customer groups.

ClusterPlus. One commercial system is ClusterPlus, distributed by Donnelly Marketing. This system assigns each of the country's census block groups into 1 of 47 clusters. The groupings range in affluence from the "established wealthy" (e.g., a grouping containing Greenwich, Connecticut) to "lowest-income, black, female-headed families" (e.g., a cluster that includes the Watts section of Los Angeles).

One manufacturer of baking goods used the ClusterPlus system to target consumers who bake from scratch by combining demographic information with Simmons consumption data (much like the information found in the Simmons Connection box in this book). The top-ranking clusters for this activity were in older, rural, blue-collar areas in the South and Midwest. Commercials for this segment were placed on popular shows that are widely watched in these areas, such as *Rescue: 911, America's Funniest Home Videos,* and *Major Dad.*[45]

PRIZM: The "Real" Beverly Hills 90210. Another clustering technique is the PRIZM (Potential Rating Index by Zip Market) system developed by Claritas, Inc. This system classifies every U.S. zip code into one of 62 categories, ranging from the most-affluent "Blue Blood Estates" to the least well-off "Public Assistance."[46] A resident of southern California might be classified as "Money & Brains" if he or she lives in Encino (zip code 91316), while someone living in Sherman Oaks (zip code 91423) would be a "Young Influential."[47] The system was recently updated from its original set of 40 clusters to reflect the growing ethnic and economic diversity of the United States; some new clusters include "American Dreams," "Kids & Cul-de-Sacs," and "Young Literati."[48]

Residents of different clusters display marked differences in their consumption of products from annuities to zip-lock bags. These groupings are also ranked in terms of income, home value, and occupation (i.e., a rough index of social class) on a zip quality (ZQ) scale. Table 16–4 provides an idea of how dramatically different the consumption patterns of two clusters can be. This table compares consumption data for "Furs & Station Wagons," the third-highest ranking cluster, with "Tobacco Roads," the third-lowest.

The PRIZM system is used to guide media buying and for direct mail targeting. Both *Time* and *Newsweek* have sorted their mailing lists by cluster, sending special editions with ads for luxury products to residents of "Money & Brains" and "Blue Blood Estates." Colgate-Palmolive sent samples of a new detergent developed for young families to the "Blue-Collar Nursery," a cluster which is largely occupied by new families. When Time Inc. Ventures launched *VIBE,* its urban-culture magazine, it needed to convince advertisers that the new magazine was not read solely by inner-city kids. A PRIZM analysis showed that *VIBE* also appealed to "Young Influentials" and even middle-aged members of "Money & Brains". This evidence led to advertising buys for liquor and electronics marketers.[49]

While some products may be purchased at an equivalent rate by consumers in two very different clusters, these similarities end when other purchases are taken into account. These differences highlight the importance of going beyond simple product-category purchase data and demographics to really understand a market (remember the earlier discussion of product complementarity). For example, high-quality binoculars are bought by people in the "Urban Gold Coast," "Money & Brains," and "Blue Blood Estates" but also by consumers in the "Grain Belt," in "New Homesteaders," and in "Agri-Business." The difference is that the former groups use the binoculars to watch birds and other wildlife, while the latter use them to help line up the animals in their gun sights. And, while the bird-watchers do a lot of foreign travel, listen to classical music, and host cocktail parties, the bird hunters travel by bus, like country music, and belong to veterans clubs.

TABLE 16–4 ▼ A Comparison of Two PRIZM Clusters

FURS & STATION WAGONS (ZQ3)		TOBACCO ROADS (ZQ38)	
New money, parents in 40s and 50s		Racially mixed farm towns in the South	
Newly built subdivisions with tennis courts, swimming pools, gardens		Small downtowns with thrift shops, diners, and laundromats; shanty-type homes without indoor plumbing	
Sample neighborhoods		*Sample neighborhoods*	
Plano, TX (75075)		Belzoni, MI (39038)	
Dunwoody, GA (30338)		Warrenton, NC (27589)	
Needham, MA (02192)		Gates, VA (27937)	
High Usage	*Low Usage*	*High Usage*	*Low Usage*
Country clubs	Motorcycles	Travel by bus	Knitting
Wine by the case	Laxatives	Asthma relief remedies	Live theater
Lawn furniture	Nonfilter cigarettes	Malt liquors	Smoke detectors
Gourmet magazine	Chewing tobacco	*Grit* magazine	*Ms.* magazine
BMW 5 Series	*Hunting* magazine	Pregnancy tests	Ferraris
Rye bread	Chevrolet Chevettes	Pontiac Bonnevilles	Whole-wheat bread
Natural cold cereal	Canned stews	Shortening	Mexican foods

Source: "A Comparison of Two Prizm Clusters" from *The Clustering of America* by Michael J. Weiss. Copyright © 1988 by Michael J. Weiss. Reprinted by permission of HarperCollins Publishers, Inc.

Note: Usage rates as indexed to average consumption across all 40 clusters.

GLOBAL MARKETING AND CULTURE

Learning about the practices of other cultures is more than just interesting; it is an essential task for any company in the 1990s that wishes to expand its horizons and become part of the global marketplace. In this section, we'll consider some of the issues confronting marketers who seek to understand the cultural dynamics of other countries. We'll also consider the consequences of the Americanization of global culture, as U.S. marketers (and, to some extent, those in Europe) continue to export Western popular culture to a globe full of increasingly affluent consumers, many of whom are eagerly waiting to replace their traditional products and practices with the likes of McDonald's, Levi's, and MTV.

Think Globally, Act Locally

As corporations increasingly find themselves competing in many markets around the world, the debate has intensified regarding the necessity of developing separate marketing plans for each culture. A lively debate has ensued regarding the need to "fit in" to the local culture. Let's briefly consider each viewpoint.

ADOPTING A STANDARDIZED STRATEGY

Proponents of a standardized marketing strategy argue that many cultures, especially those of relatively industrialized countries, have become so homogenized that the same approach will work throughout the world. By developing one approach for multiple markets, a company can benefit from economies of scale, since it does not have to incur the substantial time and expense of developing a separate strategy for each culture.[50] This viewpoint represents an **etic perspective,** which focuses upon commonalities across cultures. An etic approach to a culture is objective and analytical; it reflects impressions of a culture as viewed by outsiders.

ADOPTING A LOCALIZED STRATEGY

On the other hand, many marketers endorse an **emic perspective,** which focuses on variations within a culture. They feel that each culture is unique, with its own value system, conventions, and regulations. This perspective argues that each country has a **national character,** a distinctive set of behavior and personality characteristics.[51] An effective strategy must be tailored to the sensibilities and needs of each specific culture. An emic approach to a culture is subjective and experiential; it attempts to explain a culture as it is experienced by insiders. Which perspective is correct? Perhaps it will be helpful to consider some of the ways that cultures vary.

Taste and Stylistic Preferences.   Given the sizable variations in tastes within the United States alone, it is hardly surprising that people around the world have developed their own unique preferences. Unlike Americans, for example, Europeans favor dark chocolate over milk chocolate, which they regard as suitable only for children. Sara Lee sells its pound cake with chocolate chips in the United States, with raisins in Australia, and with coconut in Hong Kong. Whisky is considered a "classy" drink in France and Italy but not in England. Crocodile bags are popular in Asia and Europe but not in the United States. Americans' favorite tie colors are red and blue, while the Japanese prefer olive, brown, and bronze.[52]

MULTICULTURAL DIMENSIONS

The etic approach has been chosen by many companies who have adopted a standardized strategy for marketing products in Europe. Although the unification of the European Economic Community has not happened as smoothly as many predicted, the prospect of many separate economies eventually being massed into one market of 325 million consumers has led many companies to begin to standardize their prices, brand names, and advertising.[53]

Many companies are responding to this dramatic change by consolidating the different brands sold in individual countries into common *Eurobrands*. In the United Kingdom and France, for example, the Marathon candy bar sold by Mars, Inc., is becoming the Snickers bar (a somewhat risky move, considering that the British refer to women's underwear as "knickers").[54]

Wella, the hair-care company, is aggressively developing a European strategy. In the next five years, 80 percent of its product line will be either introduced or relaunched as pan-European brands. Other companies that have "gone global" include Merrill Lynch, Xerox, and Chase Manhattan Bank. After testing four campaigns in seven countries, Seagram's Chivas Regal scotch chose a series of 24 ads, each featuring a Chivas crest and the theme line, "There will always be a Chivas Regal."[55]

Advertising Preferences and Regulations.   Consumers in different countries are accustomed to different forms of advertising. In general, ads that focus on such universal values as love of family travel fairly well, while those with a specific focus on lifestyles do not.

In some cases, advertising content is regulated by the local government. For example, pricing in Germany is controlled, and special sales can be held only for a particular reason, such as going out of business or the end of the season. Advertising

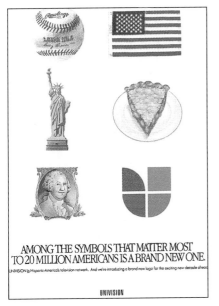

Univision, a Latino television network, attempts to associate its logo with some well-known symbols of America. Copyright by Univision, Inc. Created by Alan Stess & Associates.

also focuses more on the provision of factual information rather than on the aggressive hard sell. Indeed, it is illegal to mention the names of competitors.[56] A similar emphasis on facts can be found in Spain and Denmark. In contrast, the British and the Japanese regard advertising as a form of entertainment. Compared to the United States, British television commercials contain less information,[57] and Japanese advertising is more likely to feature emotional appeals.[58] As in Germany, comparative advertising is rare in Japan, but for a different reason: The Japanese consider this practice impolite. They instead value commercial messages that contain a lot of references to nature and sensory experiences.

Superstitions and Cultural Sensitivities.   Marketers must be aware of a culture's norms regarding such sensitive topics as taboos and sexuality. Opals signify bad luck to the British, while hunting-dog or pig emblems are offensive to Muslims. The Japanese are superstitious about the number four. Shi, the word for four, is also the word for death. For this reason, Tiffany sells glassware and china in sets of five in Japan.

The consequences of ignoring these issues became evident during the 1994 World Cup soccer matches, when both McDonald's and Coca-Cola made the mistake of reprinting the Saudi Arabian flag, which includes sacred words from the Koran, on disposable packaging used in promotions. Despite their delight at having a Saudi team in contention for the Cup, Muslims around the world protested this borrowing of sacred imagery, and both companies had to scramble to rectify the situation.[59]

Modesty.   Cultures vary sharply in the degree to which references to sex and bodily functions are permitted. Many American consumers pride themselves on their sophistication. However, some would blush at much European advertising, in which sexuality is more explicit. This dimension is particularly interesting in Japan, which is a culture of contradictions. On the one hand, the Japanese are publicly shy and polite. On the other hand, sexuality plays a significant role in the society. *Manga,* the extremely popular Japanese comic books that comprise a billion-dollar industry, stress themes of sex and violence. Nudity is quite commonplace in Japanese advertising and in the general media.[60] Bare-breasted women are routinely featured in newspapers and on television.

The Japanese are also quite cavalier about bodily functions, largely due to the lack of privacy in their society. They often rely on earthy humor to sell products. One advertisement for a hemorrhoid preparation depicts a man sitting on the toilet, whining about his pain. Another spot featured a famous Japanese actress dressed as a tampon. The Fuji Latex Company, a large condom manufacturer, built a tower at its factory shaped like its product.[61]

In contrast, a recent controversy in India illustrates problems that can arise in a more conservative culture. The government-run television network rejected a spot for KamaSutra condoms that showed a couple sitting on a bed playing chess. As the woman sweeps the pieces off the board, she mouths the word "check" while he mouths the word "mate." The tagline reads, "For the pleasure of making love."[62]

Does Global Marketing Work?

So, after briefly considering some of the many differences one encounters across cultures, do you think global marketing works? Perhaps the more appropriate question is, "*When* does it work?"

Although the argument for a homogeneous world culture is appealing in principle, in practice it has met with mixed results. One reason for the failure of global marketing is that consumers in different countries have different conventions and customs, so they simply do not use products the same way. Kellogg, for example, discovered that in Brazil big breakfasts are not traditional, and cereal is more commonly eaten as a dry snack.

In fact, significant cultural differences can even show up within the *same* country. Advertisers in Canada, for example, know that when they target consumers in French-speaking Quebec, their messages must be much different than they are when talking to their fellow countrymen who live in English Canada. Ads in Montreal tend to be a lot racier than those in Toronto, reflecting differences in attitudes toward sexuality between consumers with French versus British roots.[63]

Some large corporations, such as Coca-Cola, have been successful in crafting a single, international image. Still, even Coca-Cola must make minor modifications to the way it presents itself in each culture. Although Coke commercials are largely standardized, local agencies are permitted to edit them to highlight close-ups of local faces.[64]

As the world's borders shrink due to advances in communications, many companies continue to develop global advertising campaigns. In some cases they are encountering obstacles to acceptance, especially in less-developed countries or in those areas, such as eastern Europe, that are only beginning to embrace Western-style materialism as a way of life.[65]

To maximize the chances of success for these multicultural efforts, marketers must locate consumers in different countries who nonetheless share a common worldview. This is more likely to be the case among people whose frames of reference are relatively more international or cosmopolitan and/or who receive much of their information about the world from sources that incorporate a worldwide perspective.

Who is likely to fall into this category? Two consumer segments are particularly good candidates: 1) affluent people who are "global citizens" and who are exposed to ideas from around the world through their travels, business contacts, and media experiences and, as a result, share common tastes; and (2) young people whose tastes in music and fashion are strongly influenced by MTV and other media that broadcast many of the same images to multiple countries. For example, viewers of MTV Europe in Rome or Zurich can check out the same "buzz clips" as their counterparts in London or Luxembourg.[66] Benetton, the Italian clothing manufacturer, has been at the forefront in creating vivid (and often controversial) messages about AIDS, racial equality, warfare, and so on, that transcend national boundaries.[67]

The Coca-Cola Invasion: Exporting Western Lifestyles

In Chapter 15, we saw how a dominant culture often *co-opts* symbols from subcultures within the larger society and modifies their meanings to be consistent with mainstream beliefs and practices. A similar "borrowing" process occurs between entire cultures, particularly by non-Western groups that are captivated by the allure of Western materialism:[68]

- In Peru, Indian boys can be found carrying rocks painted to look like transistor radios.
- In highland Papua New Guinea, tribesmen put Chivas Regal wrappers on their drums and wear Pentel pens instead of nosebones.

*M*ARKETING *PITFALL*

The language barrier is one problem confronting marketers who wish to break into foreign markets. Chapter 14 noted some gaffes made by U.S. marketers when advertising to ethnic groups in their own country. Imagine how these mistakes are compounded outside of the United States! One technique that is used to avoid this problem is **back-translation**, where a translated ad is retranslated into the original language by a different interpreter to catch errors. Some specific translation obstacles that have been encountered around the world include the following:[69]

- Fresca (a soft drink) is Mexican slang for lesbian.
- When spelled phonetically, Esso means stalled car in Japan.
- Ford had several problems in Spanish markets. The company discovered that a truck model it called Fiera means ugly old woman in Spanish. Its Caliente model, sold in Mexico, is slang for a streetwalker. In Brazil, Pinto is a slang term meaning small male appendage.
- When Rolls-Royce introduced its Silver Mist model in Germany, it found that the word mist is translated as excrement. Similarly, Sunbeam's curling iron, called the Mist-Stick, translated as manure wand. To add insult to injury, Vicks is German slang for sexual intercourse, so that company's name had to be changed to Wicks in this market.

- Bana tribesmen in the remote highlands of Kako, Ethiopia, pay to watch "Pluto the Circus Dog" on a Viewmaster.
- When a Swazi princess marries a Zulu king, she wears red touraco wing feathers around her forehead and a cape of windowbird feathers and oxtails. He is wrapped in a leopard skin. All is recorded on a Kodak movie camera while the band plays, "The Sound of Music."
- In addition to traditional gifts of cloth, food, and cosmetics, Nigerian Hausa brides receive cheap quartz watches although they cannot tell time.

"I'D LIKE TO BUY THE WORLD A COKE. . . ."

As indicated by these examples, many formerly isolated cultures now incorporate Western objects into their traditional practices. In the process, the meanings of these objects are transformed and adapted to local tastes (at times in seemingly bizarre ways). Sometimes the process enriches local cultures; sometimes it produces painful stresses and strains the local fabric.

The West (and especially the United States) is a *net exporter* of popular culture. Western symbols in the form of images, words, and products have diffused throughout the world. This influence is eagerly sought by many consumers, who have learned to equate Western lifestyles in general and the English language in particular with modernization and sophistication. As a result, people around the world are being exposed to a blizzard of American products that their producers are attempting to make part of local lifestyles.

Levi's jeans, for example, are a status symbol among upwardly mobile Asian and European consumers, who snap them up even though they retail at over $80 in many countries. The company is beginning to sell the jeans in India, Hungary, Poland, Korea, and Turkey.[70] The American appeal is so strong that some non-U.S. companies go out of their way to create an American image. A British ad for Blistex lip cream, for example, includes a fictional woman named "Miss Idaho Lovely Lips," who claims Blistex is "America's best-selling lip cream."[71] Recent attempts by American marketers to "invade" other countries include the following:

- Kellogg Co. is trying to carve out a market for breakfast cereal in India, even though currently only about 3 percent of Indian households eat such products. Most middle-class Indians eat traditional hot breakfasts that include such dishes as *chapatis* (unleavened bread) and *dosas* (fried pancakes), but the company is confident that it can entice them to make the switch to Corn Flakes, Froot Loops, and other American delicacies.[72]

- The British are avid tea drinkers, but how will they react to American-style iced tea? U.S. companies, such as Snapple, are hoping they can convince the British that iced tea is more than hot tea that's gotten cold. These firms may have a way to go, based on the reactions of one British construction worker who tried a canned iced tea for the first time and said, "It was bloody awful."[73]

- Pizza Hut is invading, of all places, Italy. The country that invented pizza will be exposed to the American mass-produced version, quite a different dish than the local pizza, which is often served on porcelain dishes and eaten with a knife and fork. On the other hand, one of Pizza Hut's top performing restaurants is now located in Paris, a center of fine cuisine, so only time will tell if Italians will embrace pizza "American-style."[74]

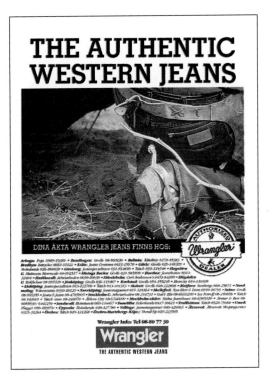

As this Swedish ad for Wrangler jeans shows, products associated with the "authentic" American West are in demand around the world. *Courtesy of Wrangler Europe.*

THE UNITED STATES INVADES ASIA

Although a third of the world's countries have a per capita gross national product of less than $500, people around the world now have access to Western media, where they can watch reruns of shows like *Lifestyles of the Rich and Famous* and *Dallas,* idealized tributes to the opulence of Western lifestyles. To illustrate the impact of this imagery around the world, we will compare its impact in two very different Asian countries.

China: Big and Poor.   Consider how the material expectations of consumers in the People's Republic of China have escalated. Twenty years ago, the Chinese strove to attain what they called the "three bigs"—bikes, sewing machines, and wristwatches. This wish list was later modified to become the "new big six," adding refrigerators, washing machines, and televisions. At last count, the ideal is now the "eight new things." The list now includes *color* televisions, cameras, and video recorders.[75] Chinese women are starting to demand Western cosmetics costing up to a quarter of their salaries and ignoring domestically produced competitors. As one Chinese executive noted, "Some women even buy a cosmetic just because it has foreign words on the package."[76]

Japan: Small and Rich.   In contrast to people in China, the Japanese have already become accustomed to a bounty of consumer goods. Still, the Japanese also are particularly enthusiastic borrowers of Western culture. American music and movies are especially popular, perhaps because they are the best way to experience U.S. lifestyles and popular culture.

The Japanese often use Western words as a shorthand for anything new and exciting, even if they do not understand their meaning. The resulting phenomenon is known as "Japlish," where new Western-sounding words are merged with Japanese. Cars are given names like Fairlady, Gloria, and Bongo Wagon. Consumers buy *deodoranto* (deodorant) and *appuru pai* (apple pie). Ads urge shoppers to *stoppu rukku* (stop and look), and products are claimed to be *yuniku* (unique).[77] Coca-Cola cans say, "I feel Coke & sound special," and a company called Cream Soda sells products with the slogan, "Too old to die, too young to happy."[78] Other Japanese products with English names include Mouth Pet (breath freshener), Pocari Sweat (refreshment water), Armpit (electric razor), Brown Gross Foam (hair-coloring mousse), Virgin Pink Special (skin cream), Cow Brand (beauty soap), and Mymorning Water (canned water).[79]

CREEPING AMERICANISM: A NEGATIVE BACKLASH

Despite the proliferation of Western culture around the world, there are signs that this invasion is slowing. Japanese consumers, for example, are beginning to show signs of waning interest in foreign products as the health of their country's economy declines. Some of the latest "hot" products in Japan now include green tea and *yukata,* traditional printed cotton robes donned after the evening bath.[80]

Some critics in other countries deplore the creeping Americanization of their cultures. Debates continue in many countries on the imposition of quotas that limit American television programming.[81] The conflict created by the exporting of American culture was brought to a head in recent trade negotiations on the General Agreement on Tariffs and Trade (GATT), which were deadlocked over the export of American movies to Europe (the United States share of the European cinema mar-

Mainland China is one of the newest markets to be opened up to American business and culture. Chinese television now carries commercials for the likes of Coca-Cola, Tang, and Contac cold capsules. Procter & Gamble manufactures goods like Pantene shampoo and Oil of Ulan locally (known as Oil of Olay in the United States). McDonald's recently opened a restaurant in Beijing that is the largest of its outlets in the world (and the only one with a Communist Party secretary). It has more than 700 seats and nearly 1,000 employees, a few of whom are shown in the photo here. Many competed for these highly valued positions that are perceived to offer prestige and upward mobility. Nicholas D. Kristof, "'Billions Served' (and That Was Without China)," New York Times (April 24, 1992): A4; James Sterngold,"The Awakening Chinese Consumer," New York Times (October 11, 1992): F1. Photo courtesy of © Kees/Sygma.

ket is about 75 percent). As one French official put it, "French films are the cinema of creation. American films are products of marketing."[82]

Even America's neighbors in Canada have gotten into the act: Reacting to the growing popularity of country music, the Canadian government recently decided to prohibit Nashville-based Country Music Television, a network which had been available to Canadian viewers for over a decade, from broadcasting in the country. Instead, it will be replaced by the Country Network, based in Canada. The new service is aiming for content that is 30 percent Canadian.[83] The French have been the most outspoken opponents of creeping Americanization. They have even tried to ban the use of such "Franglais" terms as *le drugstore, le fast food,* and even *le marketing,* though this effort was recently ruled unconstitutional.[84] The French debate over cul-

This movie poster promotes the Tom Cruise film Far and Away *to the Japanese, who are huge fans of American popular culture. © Jeffrey Aaronson/Aspen Network.*

The Consumer Behavior Odyssey, described in Chapter 1, attempted to explore consumers' relationships with products in natural settings. As a sequel, researchers embarked on The Odyssey Downunder, *an exploration of the impact of modern material culture on Aborigines in Australia. Aborigines have relatively limited economic options, and traditional customs are threatened by Western lifestyles. The researchers found the Aborigines they studied were undergoing a process of selective adaptation, where elements of modern consumer culture are incorporated with traditional emphases on sharing possessions and attachment to the land. This photo depicts an Aboriginal husband and wife (with a friend), who are showing off the fish they caught using the community's forty-foot fiberglass inboard motor boat. Fishing is a traditional activity now aided by new technology even though residents also continue to use older techniques, such as building rock fish traps and spear fishing. (Ronald Groves and Russell W. Belk, "The Odyssey Downunder: A Qualitative Study of Aboriginal Consumers," Special Session presented at the Association for Consumer Research, Boston 1994; Russell W. Belk, Ronald Groves, and Per Østergaard, "Aboriginal Consumer Culture," Unpublished manuscript, The University of Utah, 1994.) Photo courtesy of Russell Belk and Ronald Groves.*

tural contamination was brought to a head by the 1992 opening of Euro Disney in a Paris suburb. In addition to the usual attractions, hotels with names like Hotel New York, Newport Bay Club, and Hotel Cheyenne attempt to recreate portions of America. In addition to encountering serious financial problems, some Europeans have been less than enthusiastic about the cultural messages being sent by the Disney organization. One French critic described the theme park as "a horror made of cardboard, plastic, and appalling colors—a construction of hardened chewing gum and idiotic folklore taken straight out of comic books written for obese Americans."[85]

MARKETING PITFALL

Cigarettes are among the most successful of Western exports. Asian consumers alone spend $90 billion a year on cigarettes, and U.S. tobacco manufacturers continue to push relentlessly into these markets. Cigarette advertising, often depicting glamorous Western models and settings, is found just about everywhere—on billboards, buses, storefronts, and clothing—and many major sports and cultural events are sponsored by tobacco companies. Some companies even hand out cigarettes and gifts in amusement areas, often to preteens.

A few countries have taken steps to counteract this form of westernization. Singapore bans all promotions that mention products' names. Hong Kong has prohibited cigarette ads from appearing on radio and TV. Japan and South Korea do not allow ads to appear in women's magazines. Industry executives argue that they are simply competing in markets that do little to discourage smoking (e.g., Japan issues the health warning, "Please don't smoke too much"), often against heavily subsidized local brands with names like Long Life (a cigarette made in Taiwan). The warnings and restrictions are likely to increase, however; smoking-related deaths have now overtaken communicable diseases for the "honor" of being Asia's number one killer.[86]

- A consumer's *lifestyle* refers to the ways he or she chooses to spend time and money and how his or her values and tastes are reflected by consumption choices. Lifestyle research is useful to track societal consumption preferences and also to position specific products and services to different segments.

- Marketers segment by lifestyle differences, often by grouping consumers in terms of their *AIOs* (activities, interests, and opinions).

- *Psychographic techniques* attempt to classify consumers in terms of psychological, subjective variables in addition to observable characteristics (demographics). A variety of systems, such as VALS, have been developed to identify consumer "types" and to differentiate them in terms of their brand or product preferences, media usage, leisure time activities, and attitudes toward such broad issues as politics and religion.

- Interrelated sets of products and activities are associated with social roles to form *consumption constellations*. People often purchase products or services because they are associated with constellations that, in turn, are linked to lifestyles they find desirable.

- Place of residence often is a significant determinant of lifestyle. Many marketers recognize regional differences in product preferences and develop different versions of their products for different markets. A set of techniques called geodemography is used to analyze consumption patterns employing geographical and demographic data and to identify clusters of consumers who exhibit similar psychographic characteristics.

- Because a consumer's culture exerts such a big influence on his or her lifestyle choices, marketers must learn as much as possible about differences in cultural norms and preferences when marketing in more than one country. One important issue is the extent to which marketing strategies must be tailored to each culture versus the extent to which they can be standardized across cultures. Followers of an etic perspective believe that the same universal messages will be appreciated by people in many cultures. Believers in an emic perspective argue that individual cultures are too unique to permit such standardization; marketers must instead adapt their approaches to be consistent with local values and practices. Attempts at global marketing have met with mixed success. In many cases this approach is more likely to work if the messages appeal to basic values and/or if the target markets consist of consumers who are more internationally rather than locally oriented.

- The United States is a net exporter of popular culture. Consumers around the world have eagerly adopted American products, especially entertainment vehicles and items that are linked symbolically to a uniquely American lifestyle (e.g., Marlboro cigarettes and Levi's jeans). Despite the continuing Americanization of world culture, some consumers are alarmed by this influence and are instead emphasizing a return to local products and customs.

KEY TERMS

AIOs p. 585

Back-translation p. 604

Consumption constellations p. 582

Emic perspective p. 600

Etic perspective p. 600

Geodemography p. 596

Lifestyle p. 578

Materialism p. 578

National character p. 600

Nine Nations of North America p. 595

Product complementarity p. 582

Psychographics p. 583

Single-source data p. 597

20/80 rule p. 585

Values and Lifestyles (VALS) p. 588

CONSUMER BEHAVIOR CHALLENGE

1. Compare and contrast the concepts of lifestyle and social class.

2. In what situations is demographic information likely to be more useful than psychographic data, and vice-versa?

3. Alcohol drinkers vary sharply in terms of the number of drinks they consume, from those who occasionally have one at a cocktail party to regular imbibers. Explain how the 20/80 rule applies to this product category.

4. Describe the underlying principles used to construct the VALS system. What are some positive and negative aspects of this approach to lifestyle segmentation?

5. Compile a set of recent ads that attempt to link consumption of a product with a specific lifestyle. How is this goal usually accomplished?

6. The chapter mentions that psychographic analyses can be used to market politicians. Conduct research on the marketing strategies used in a recent, major election. How were voters segmented in terms of values? Can you find evidence that communications strategies were guided by this information?

7. Construct separate advertising executions for a cosmetics product targeted to the "belonger," "achiever," "experiential," and "socially conscious" VALS types. How would the basic appeal differ for each group?

8. Using media targeted to the group, construct a consumption constellation for the social role of college students. What set of products, activities, and interests tends to appear in advertisements depicting "typical" college students? How realistic is this constellation?

9. The principle of market segmentation implies that a group of people sharing some set of characteristics will be singled out as the focus of a marketing strategy. Critics of targeted marketing argue that this is discriminatory and unfair, especially if such a strategy encourages a group of people to buy a product that may be injurious to them or that they cannot afford. On the other hand, the Association of National Advertisers argues that banning targeted marketing constitutes censorship and is a violation of the First Amendment. Is segmentation an ethical marketing practice? Give the reasons for your answer.

10. Administer the Materialism Scale in Table 16–1 to a sample of business majors and another group of liberal arts majors. What predictions might you make